for the Jewish Heart

RABBI BINYOMIN PRUZANSKY

FIRST EDITION
First Impression … August 2006
Second Impression … October 2006

Published and Distributed by
MESORAH PUBLICATIONS, LTD.
4401 Second Avenue / Brooklyn, N.Y 11232

Distributed in Europe by
LEHMANNS
Unit E, Viking Business Park
Rolling Mill Road
Jarow, Tyne & Wear, NE32 3DP
England

Distributed in Australia and New Zealand by
GOLDS WORLDS OF JUDAICA
3-13 William Street
Balaclava, Melbourne 3183
Victoria, Australia

Distributed in Israel by
SIFRIATI / A. GITLER — BOOKS
6 Hayarkon Street
Bnei Brak 51127

Distributed in South Africa by
KOLLEL BOOKSHOP
Ivy Common
105 William Road
Norwood 2192, Johannesburg, South Africa

ARTSCROLL SERIES®
STORIES FOR THE JEWISH HEART
© *Copyright 2006, by* MESORAH PUBLICATIONS, Ltd.
4401 Second Avenue / Brooklyn, N.Y. 11232 / (718) 921-9000 / www.artscroll.com

*To contact the author with comments or stories, he can be reached via e-mail
at bpruz@yeshivanet.com*

ISBN:
1-4226-0132-3 (hard cover)
1-4226-0133-1 (paperback)

Typography by CompuScribe at ArtScroll Studios, Ltd.

Printed in the United States of America by Noble Book Press Corp.
Bound by Sefercraft, Quality Bookbinders, Ltd., Brooklyn N.Y. 11232

הרב דוד קוויאט

ר"מ בישיבת מיר
ורב דאגודת ישראל סניף חפץ חיים

<u>מכתב ברכה</u>

לכבוד תלמידי היקר הרב הרב בנימין יהודה פרוזאנסקי שליט"א

ראיתי העלים מספרך אשר כתבת שעומד להוציא לאור אי"ה
והוא מלא וגדוש עם סיפורים חשובים שמביא חיזוק להקוראים
בהם, וזה נחוץ בדור הזה לחזק איך להחיות עם אמונה וישרות
ומידות טובות.
ולכן אברכהו שימשיך להצליח בכל חפציו, והקב"ה יברכו להגדיל
תורה ויאדיר

ממני המברכו בכל הלב

דוד קוויאט

Rabbi Reuven Feinstein
131 Bloomingdale Road
Staten Island, New York 10309
718-317-0819

שלום ראובן פיינשטיין
ראש הישיבה
ישיבה ד׳סטעטן איילענד
718-356-2101

Rabbi Binyomin Pruzansky נ״י sent me a selection of stories he intends to print through ArtScroll. Rabbi Pruzansky feels that these stories will help the reader grow from the experiences of the individuals involved in the stories.

He has broken down the material into seven categories each an important subject in itself, in order to help the reader focus on the lesson. It should be the will of ה׳ that the purpose of the author be accomplished, so that the אמונה and ביטחון of the individual reader be strengthened, so that תורה will ultimately spread.

May the author and his family be blessed with all that is good and that he shall continue to influence people to good until the coming of the Redeemer.

Rabbi Pinchas Breuer
Rav OF Agudas Yisroel
"Bais Binyomin" Flatbush

הרב פנחס ברייער
רב דק"ק אגודת ישראל
"בית בנימין" פלטבוש

בס"ד

ה' מנחם אב תשס"ו לפ"ק

Reb Binyomin Pruzansky שליט"א, יושב על התורה ועבודה
in the עיר התורה of Lakewood, has presented us with
a collection of stories capturing the essence of Jewish
day to day life, in terms of השגחה פרטית and how every
little effort on behalf of a fellow Jew, can make all the
difference, and even change someone's life. It adds special
fragrance when its compiled by a בן תורה who is deeply
stooped in אמונת חכמים. His style of writing touches the
heart and will surely give חיזוק to its readers.

With much appreciation,

Rabbi Pinchas Breuer

1167 E. 29 Street Brooklyn N.Y. 11210

Table of Contents

The Power of Prayer

Miraculous Events

Not by Chance

Loving-kindness

To Sanctify His Name

A World of Torah and Mitzvos

Making a Difference

Glossary

Dedication

When friends ask what motivated me to write a book of inspirational stories, they get an answer that is itself a story. It is a story of a *talmid* and his Rebbe, a story of happiness, sorrow and growth.

When I came back to America in 1999 after learning for two years in Eretz Yisrael, I was not just looking for another yeshivah. I was looking for a Rebbe — someone who would guide me, advise me and help me to continue growing in *avodas Hashem*. It was not as simple a quest as I thought it would be; where does one turn to find a Rebbe?

In the midst of this quandary, I got a phone call from a friend who was learning in Yeshivah Torah Vodaath. He had the perfect *chavrusa* for me, he reported. I simply had to try learning with him. The man's name was Dovid Rothstein, my friend said, and he described him as "amazing." There was just one fact I needed to know, though. He was an older man.

"Older? What do you mean?" I asked.

My friend explained that Reb Dovid was a retired lawyer from Boston who had recently come back to Torah Vodaath to learn full time. But despite his unusual background, he said, "You'll love learning with him."

I agreed to try it for a day.

I came to the yeshivah and spent a day learning with Reb Dovid, and it went very well. I decided to join Torah Vodaath so that I could learn with him.

In Reb Dovid, I found a very rare individual — someone who had a clear Torah outlook in life and a broad understanding of the world. He brought fresh insight to every topic. Soon, the word was out that, sitting in the back of the *beis medrash*, there was a wise man who could advise people on *shidduchim*, learning, business — everything.

People approached him constantly for advice, and he would tell them exactly what he thought, whether they wanted to hear the truth or not. Reb Dovid attended Rabbi Reisman's *shiur* every day and took meticulous notes, even though he was more then 30 years older then the average *talmid* in the *shiur*. It didn't matter to him, as long as this *shiur* was where he felt he would learn best.

When I arrived late, he would urge me to come earlier. He imbued me with an understanding of the importance of being a Torah Jew. Sometimes, I found it hard to believe that the words I was hearing were issuing from a Harvard Law School graduate, rather than from a seasoned Torah scholar. One of the points he impressed upon me was the care that must be taken to check the kashrus when dining out in a restaurant or buying take-out food, or even when eating at a *chasunah*.

Gradually, I realized that I had found my Rebbe in the most unlikely of individuals. Who would have thought that my Rebbe would be a lawyer? Yet I came to realize that Reb Dovid had always been a yeshivah *bachur*; he just happened to practice law on the side. He and his wife had left their comfortable home in Boston and moved into a small apartment in Flatbush in order to be near the yeshivah. That was what mattered most to them.

After learning with Reb Dovid in Torah Vodaath for six months, I decided that it would be best for me to return to Eretz Yisrael to learn at the Mir Yeshivah. Every so often, during that wonderfully productive year, I would call Reb Dovid in Brooklyn to give him a progress report.

One night, in the middle of night *seder*, a friend ran over to me and handed me his cell phone to take an important call.

"Binyomin? It's Chaim Dov," said the serious voice on the other end. "Did you hear the news about Dovid Rothstein?"

"No! What happened?"

"I'm sorry to tell you this, but he had a massive heart attack."

"What? What are you talking about, how is he ...."

"He didn't make it, Binyomin. I'm sorry. The *levayah* is tomorrow."

In a state of shock, I thanked my friend for the information and hung up. I left the *beis medrash* and stepped out into the cool night in a daze, unable to contain my tears. My heart was broken. My Rebbe was gone.

I remember walking the streets around the Mir, picturing Reb Dovid in my mind's eye and feeling the piercing pain of loss over and over again. I wandered the streets for hours, trying to accept this Divine decree. Finally, I returned to the Mir *beis medrash*. It was 2:30 a.m. and the room was empty. I walked up to the *chazzan's* lectern and lay my head down on it, weeping uncontrollably as I stood before the *aron kodesh*.

All at once, I was overcome with a flash of clarity that I had never before experienced. I understood that Hashem is the Master of the Universe, and man is His servant, sent to the earth for a particular, unique mission. When that mission is completed, each of us is summoned back to Hashem. I realized man's only purpose in life is to serve Hashem.

Then and there, I made a decision, a firm commitment to an ideal I had long considered, but never enunciated. I lifted my head from the lectern and looked at the *aron kodesh*. "Hashem, I am going to devote my life to serving You," I said. "I am going to devote myself to learning, teaching and spreading Your Torah, but I can only do it if You will help me along the way, guiding my footsteps through life." I had always wanted to state out loud that this was my mission in life, but I never had the inner strength to put it into words. This was something Reb Dovid had always urged me to do. He inspired me to grow in Torah, and his influence is still with me today.

A few years ago I had a brainstorm. I realized how much Reb Dovid, someone who wasn't a well-known Torah figure or Rebbe, had inspired me and many others. I felt that there should be a book about such people — not the world-famous people, but rather, the seemingly regular people who live inspiring lives. This book would tell stories anyone could relate to, about people everyone could emulate.

About a year ago, I finally turned that thought into action. What evolved was a collection of inspiring stories about all types of people. Some are well-known *gedolim*, and others are people who live around the corner. But each of them has a story that should be told.

I dedicate this book to you, Reb Dovid, and to all those like you who have a major impact on many lives, people whose deeds could fill many books. They are the fathers and mothers, the teachers and brothers, the seemingly simple people in our lives who have inspired us to reach for the stars. They should know that they have inspired us, and that we are forever indebted to them.

Author's Preface

t is with the deepest gratitude to the *Ribbono Shel Olam* that
I present this book of inspirational stories. The stories in this
book have certainly had a major impact on my personal life
and have inspired me to reach for greater heights. It is my
fervent hope that they will inspire my readers in a similar way.

This is actually my second attempt in producing a work that
will benefit the Torah world. My first attempt was a *mussar sefer*. I
wanted to write something that would help people to grow closer
to Hashem. I believed that if I could produce a good *sefer* on
self-improvement, this would surely fulfill my goal. I gathered a
substantial amount of material from the classic *mussar sefarim* and
began to write.

During the summer, as a rebbi in a summer camp, I saw a great
opportunity to test my *mussar* lessons before a live audience. I
soon realized that the students were absorbing very little. The deep
thoughts of *Chazal*, served up without embellishment, did not
captivate or excite them. I then decided to work with a different
approach, to convey my message by means of a story. I quickly
understood the power of a story as my students began listening to
every word and comprehending the message as well.

When I began working on this book, I realized that this project
would accomplish the goal of my *mussar sefer*. The stories are in

fact a living *mussar sefer*; the lessons are brought to life in terms that can be grasped and used to help us elevate ourselves. It is the greatest *mussar sefer* I could have ever hoped to produce, and I pray that it makes a *Kiddush Hashem*.

The Gemara in *Sotah* (40a) relates that R' Abahu and R' Chiya bar Abba came to a certain town. Each one went to give a lecture. R' Chiya bar Abba was speaking on halachic topics and R' Abahu was speaking on *aggadatta* stories of the Talmud. Everyone in town went to the lecture given by R' Abahu, and no one attended R' Chiya bar Abba's lecture on halachah. R' Chiya bar Abba was deeply disturbed that no one wanted to attend his halachic lecture, and in an effort to appease him, R' Abahu told the following parable to those attending his lecture:

"What happened today is similar to a case where two merchants entered a town. One was selling fine gems and pearls and the other was selling pins and needles and other household items. The people in the town flocked to the one selling the household items since his wares were very inexpensive."

R' Abahu intended to demonstrate that, while R' Chiya bar Abba's halachic lecture was certainly the more superior of the two, R' Abahu's simpler topic, woven from stories and parables, drew the townspeople to him.

The *Eitz Yosef* comments on this Gemara, "Don't think that R' Abahu meant to say that a lecture on law was indeed greater then a lecture on the stories of the Talmud, because in truth the stories of the Talmud are greater, for it is through them that one comes to recognize the Creator of the world."

You may wonder how the telling of stories causes a person to recognize that Hashem runs the world.

It is because when you hear stories about people who had a *tefillah* answered or an amazing event of Divine Providence that affected their lives, you become a witness to their moment of recognition that Hashem truly supervises every event that unfolds and constantly watches over us. As you follow the series of events that leads them to this conclusion, you, too, will come to your own conclusions. You will be able to see that Hashem is with you as well, and will recognize that Hashem indeed runs the world. You, too, will realize that Hashem wants what is best for you, and that even through the most difficult challenges, He is constantly showering you with His kindness.

Acknowledgments

would like to take this opportunity to thank the *Ribbono Shel Olam* for giving me the *zechus* to write this book. I experienced a tremendous amount of *siyata dishmaya* throughout this entire project; for this and for everything Hashem has done for me and my family, I am eternally grateful.

It has been the greatest privilege and honor to have spent my summers in close proximity with one of the elder *talmidei chachamim* of America, my rebbi, **Harav Dovid Kviat.** He is well known in the yeshivah world for his *sefarim Succos David* on *Shas* and *Chumash*. The countless hours that he has granted me of his precious time to discuss Torah and *hashkafah* topics has made an enormous impact on my life. He has taught me what it means to be a true *ben Torah*. There are no words to express my feelings of *hakaras hatov* and admiration for him. May Hashem bless him with *arichas yamim veshanim* and good health.

My years spent learning in Eretz Yisrael in Yeshivas Lev Avrohom led by **R' Yechezkel Weinfeld,** was instrumental in making me what I am today. Thank you is not enough.

My Rav, **Rabbi Gavriel Finkel,** has always given me of his time and advice over the last few years. He has been very encouraging in this project and others. Thank you for believing in me.

My dear cousin, **Rabbi Ari Pruzansky**, has been a tremendous source of *chizzuk* for me over the years. He has constantly encouraged me and has always been there for me. **R' Binyomin Balser**, my cousin and *chavrusa*, has always pushed me to strive to do my best.

It is a great *zechus* for me to be a part of *kollel* **Beth Medrash Govoha** in Lakewood where I have grown in Torah and *avodah* over the last five years. I feel honored to be a part of this great Torah community.

My dear parents, **Reb Yosef and Marsha Pruzansky**, have always been inspiring role models. Our house was always based on Torah and *chesed*. The numerous Shabbos guests who graced our table over the years taught me what it means to be a giver not a taker. My father has always done whatever he could to make other people happy and content; watching him in action countless times has always made me proud to be his son. My mother's ability to see the good in everyone and to assist others in the fine details of their lives is a shining example to our entire family of how far one must go in thinking of others.

My in-laws, **Rabbi Shmuel Gedaliah and Raizel Pollak**, have treated me as a true son. Their house is one of Torah and *kedushah*. My father-in-law as rebbi and *baal tefillah* in the Mirrer Yeshivah and a close *talmid* of R' Pam has taught me by example what it means to be a servant of Hashem. He has instilled in me and our entire family that our sole purpose in life is to become closer to Hashem. Thank you for all the *chizzuk*.

The editor of this book was **Mrs. Chana Nestlebaum.** She has taken her amazing talents and has used it to serve and honor Hashem. She has the unique ability to make a story come to life with her brilliant approach to the written word. With this book she has proven once again why she is known as one of the best in Jewish literature today. Thank you for making my dream a reality. May Hashem bless the Nestlebaum family with happiness and health and may she continue to succeed in making a tremendous *Kiddush Hashem*.

It is a great honor to have my book published by ArtScroll. I thank **Rabbi Meir Zlotowitz** and **Rabbi Nosson Scherman** for having confidence in my work from Day 1, and for their assistance throughout the project. I also appreciate the thought they put into creating a beautiful title for the book.

Thank you, **Rabbi Avrohom Biderman,** for your warm assistance throughout the project. Thank you, **Mrs. Judi Dick,** for your insightful comments and editing. **Eli Kroen** has produced a magnificent cover for the book; thank you. I thank the entire ArtScroll staff for everything they have done to produce a great work.

This book would not have been possible without the help of the many people who were kind enough to share a piece of their history with me. They shared my goal of inspiring people and therefore took the time to contribute their story. I thank all of you, those whom I will mention and those who wanted to retain their privacy yet shared their inspiration with the world.

The following have contributed stories to the book: **Reb Eli Mintz, Rabbi Yerucham Pitter, Rabbi Shlomo Gissinger, Rabbi Yakov Haber, Rabbi Moshe Yanofsky, Rabbi Pinchas Breuer, Rabbi Zev Leff, Rabbi Avrohom Gurwitz, Rabbi Avrohom Chaim Feuer, Rabbi Zalman Feuer, Rabbi Chesky Tauber, Rabbi Naftoli Cukier, Rabbi Dovid Orlofsky, Rabbi Dovid Moskowitz, Rabbi Yechiel Perr, Rabbi Avrohom Perr, Rabbi Sholom Borinstein, Rabbi Alexander Stern, Rabbi Yisroel Brog, Reb Ariel Moyal, Rabbi Avrohom Alter, Rabbi Chaim Leib Pam.**

Special thanks goes to **Rabbi Avrohom Kleinkaufman** and **Rabbi Avrohom Braun** for all the time and effort that they put into this project.

Special thanks to my siblings for their encouragement and support: **Avi** and **Rivky Pruzansky, Michoel** and **Raizy Pruzansky, Shea** and **Baila Caller,** and **Shulamis Pruzansky.**

Thank you, **Shmuel and Shaindy Grama, Avrohom** and **Bruchy Pollak, Eli** and **Ettie Liberman,** and the entire Pollak family.

My wife **Rochie** has helped me reach new heights in life. She has given me the time and support that I needed to develop in Torah while I learn in *kollel*. She has always stood behind me in my quest to become a true *ben Torah*, and has helped me immensely in this book. May Hashem continue to shower his kindness upon our family, and may our children continue to grow in Torah and *yiras Shamayim*.

Binyomin Pruzansky
Lakewood, N.J

Introduction: Stories of Our Lives

E very day as we live our lives, we are writing a story. Some chapters are exciting, filled with monumental changes or nerve-wracking challenges. Many chapters are more subtle. A word said. A favor granted or refused. A choice, a chance meeting, a prayer. From the view of Heaven, none of these chapters lack import. Each has repercussions that may echo into the decades, or even centuries, to come. Each has a ripple effect that changes the lives of those around us. Each pulls upon a string that connects us to the spiritual world.

The stories we present here run the gamut from high drama to gentle tale, but each — like life itself — carries with it a profound message. Some illustrate the power of prayer, some reveal the levels of greatness a person can reach, and all unveil the constant Divine Providence that is there for anyone with eyes to see. These are stories that belong to *Klal Yisrael*, for they reflect our lives and our striving, through the events of our daily lives, to find meaning and closeness to Hashem.

But a storybook is not a textbook. A story succeeds in illuminating the workings of Heaven only when it vividly and engagingly depicts life, people and places as we know them here in our world. These stories are written for the reader, filled with rich, visual images and real people with real personalities. Some names and locations have been changed for purposes of privacy, but the essential facts of each story have been garnered from those who have experienced or witnessed them firsthand. Altogether, these stories form a colorful patchwork of lives lived by ordinary and extraordinary Jews, each doing his or her best to serve Hashem.

The Power
of Prayer

The Soul's Prayer

or Jews in the Ukrainian city of Lvov (Lemberg), 1989 was the year of miracles. It was that year, in the wake of the Soviet Union's demise, that the city's main shul was returned to the long-oppressed Jewish community. Even after decades of Communist rule aimed at eradicating religious faith, Lvov contained a large population of Jews who, despite their complete lack of knowledge of their heritage, managed to cling tenuously to their Jewish identity. Therefore, even with fear of the authorities still quivering in their hearts, throngs of Lvov's Jews poured into the restored synagogue on the first night of Rosh Hashanah in that year of miracles. With a mixture of caution and pride, they crossed the once-forbidden doorway with their children in tow, gazing around the room with the wondering eyes of strangers. The vast majority of people sitting there had no idea what to expect, nor what would be expected of them as they prepared to pray for the first time in their lives.

The *chazzan* who was to preside over this monumental occasion was Reb Eli Mintz of Monsey, New York. From the moment he had heard about the reopening of the shul for Rosh Hashanah, he was driven by an urge to be a part of it. With no idea of what he would encounter, he offered to lead the prayers for the desperately starved *neshamos* of the former Soviet Union.

Reb Eli was well aware of the historic impact of this particular Rosh Hashanah service, in this particular spot in the world at this singular point in time. It was an opportunity that had to be maximized — one single shot that had to hit its target, for there would never be another first time. The spiritual insurance he needed, Reb Eli determined, could best be obtained through Rabbi Shlomo Halberstam, the Bobover Rebbe. Who would better understand the tragic history that saturated the air of Lvov than the Rebbe, whose own father, the *Kedushas Tzion*, was murdered along with his family in that very city?

Reb Eli succeeded in obtaining an appointment with the Rebbe. There, he told of the precious opportunity that had been placed in his hands. How could he make sure that his *tefillos* penetrated the hearts of these bereft Jews? How could he help them connect to the Father Whose very existence had been invalidated by everyone and everything they had known for the past 70 years? The Rebbe, too, was awed by the gravity of Reb Eli's mission. The advice he provided translated into an experience that moved Heaven and earth.

As Reb Eli stood before the curious, cautious congregation on that Rosh Hashanah, he understood that few, if any, of the people there would have had the opportunity to learn how to pray. Teaching Hebrew had been forbidden for decades, as had been Torah learning and prayer services. Only those old enough to remember life before the Communists, or those brave enough to have practiced their Judaism in secret, would have even the most rudimentary tools for approaching the Rosh Hashanah prayers. What, then, could the *chazzan* say that would allow their hearts and souls to open to Hashem? Reb Eli told a story. He spoke in Yiddish, with a community leader, Reb Melech Shochet, standing at his side translating into Russian:

"*Shalom aleichem*, my dear brothers and sisters. We know that Hashem listens to our prayers. He understands every language, and He even understands our sighs and groans. Listen, my friends, to a story. There was a time when the Jews of Berditchev were having great difficulties. There were pogroms, exorbitant taxes and many dangers facing their community. On the morning prior to Yom Kippur, the holy Reb Levi Yitzchak of Berditchev spoke to his congregants. He urged them, in view of the dangerous and difficult times they were facing, to prepare for *Kol Nidrei* that night by coming to shul and praying from the deepest recesses of their hearts for Hashem to abolish the troubles that had been decreed for their community.

"That night, every soul in Berditchev poured into the shul. The room resounded with their wrenching prayers. Among the crowd sat an uneducated wagon driver whose heart cried out as did the others, but whose lips were incapable of articulating even the simplest words of prayer. He had never learned, and that night, he cried with frustration at his inability to express the longings of his soul. Finally, unable to contain himself any longer, he turned to Hashem and pleaded, 'Master of the Universe, You know that I do not know how to *daven*. All I know is the *alef-beis*, which my father taught me as a child. Please, Hashem, take the letters of the *alef-beis* that I will say to You now, and turn them into the right words.' He then began reciting out loud 'Alef ... Beis ... Gimmel ...' Many of those around him wondered what he was doing, reciting a school-boy's *alef-beis* at such an urgent time. But when the congregation had finished its prayers, the Berditchever Rebbe addressed them joyfully, informing them that in the merit of the wagon driver's *alef-beis*, the decree had been canceled."

By the time Reb Eli finished this story, every eye in the shul was turned to him. He raised his voice and pleaded, "My dear brothers and sisters, many of you who came today do not know how to *daven* and it's not your fault. Please just do as much as you can. Say *Shema Yisrael*, say *Ani Ma'amin*, say whatever prayer you know and if you don't know anything at all then simply say the *alef-beis*! Yes, you can even say the *alef-beis*!"

Next to Reb Eli stood a frail old Jew dressed in a well-worn woolen suit. His weathered face had betrayed no emotion as he listened to the impassioned speech, but now, there were tears running down his drawn, nut-brown cheeks. In Yiddish, he suddenly cried out to Reb Eli, "I want to say the *alef-beis*! I want to say it too! But I don't even know how to do that."

With this old man's pained proclamation, Reb Eli suddenly understood the depth of spiritual deprivation endured by the people seated before him. "My dear, fellow Jews," he announced. "Let us say the *alef-beis* together. Repeat after me, Alef! ..."

The hundreds of Jewish souls gathered together in the shul that night cried out in one thunderous voice, "*Alef!*" And then *beis*, and then *gimmel* and *daled*, all the way to *yud*. Each new letter fanned the roaring flames of their suddenly ignited souls, the sound carrying them higher and higher. Reb Eli knew there was yet more within them, still greater depths to be plumbed, and so when they came to *yud*, he urged them on, "Again, let's say it louder!" By this time, the emotion in the room was a riptide that left no one standing where he or she had started. People sobbed with emotion, crying like children whose only desire was to be once again held in their Father's embrace. To anyone who witnessed this scene, there was no doubt that these letters ascended straight to Heaven, to be arranged into the most exquisite prayer the Jewish people could offer.

"Now," said Reb Eli, "I am going to *daven* in the customary way." He began the evening services.

Nearly twenty years have elapsed since the doors of the shul first reopened to the Jews of Lvov, and yet, the impact of that first Rosh Hashanah remains. To this day, Rosh Hashanah services begin with the unique custom of reciting the *alef-beis*, reminding the educated and the ignorant alike that prayer, at its essence, is the "service of the heart."

Every Jewish soul yearns to connect to Hashem, but the pathway sometimes appears to be blocked. At our times of deepest need, we over-

*come the obstructions and simply cry out from the depths of our hearts,
using whatever words — or even letters — we can. And it is these prayers
that are our most eloquent and that are most beloved by Hashem.*

Hear My Cry

The terrible news bypassed Mrs. Farber's brain and
struck a direct blow to her heart. She felt a heavy, hor-
rible churning inside that surprised her in its intensity.
It had been three years since she had seen Sarah, three
years since the vivacious young teacher had resigned her position to move with her new husband to the East Coast. Mrs.
Farber recalled the almost maternal pleasure she had taken
in watching this graceful young woman go about her day as a
teacher in her school for Russian girls. As a seasoned principal, she quickly recognized the quality of heart that aroused
the students' admiration. Their eyes followed every move Sarah
made. They thrived in her classroom, knowing instinctively
that they, in turn, were admired and loved by their teacher.

Perhaps it was because Mrs. Farber felt this motherly warmth
toward Sarah that she also felt a pang as the months, and then
years flew by and Sarah was still without a child. *Such a loving,
patient girl*, Mrs. Farber thought. *Surely there must be a child waiting
in her future.*

But today, news of Sarah had come, and it was unbearably sad.
Finally, a child was on its way, but routine blood tests revealed

that Sarah had been stricken with leukemia. The longed-for dream would have to be terminated so that lifesaving treatments could begin.

How can a woman so young and sweet bear such a decree? Mrs. Farber wondered. She envisioned Sarah's slim, energetic form heading down the corridor toward her classroom, flanked by her happily chattering students. The Sarah she remembered was young and invincible, on her way to a new life as a married woman. But today, Sarah was back in her parents' home, weak and frightened. Mrs. Farber longed to have the opportunity to hold her hand, speak words of encouragement to her and somehow help her face the challenge life had handed her.

A few days later, Mrs. Farber made plans to visit Sarah in the hospital. It took some doing, but she was finally able to delegate the seemingly infinite list of tasks involved in keeping the school running smoothly. Now she would have the necessary time to travel to the hospital and stay for awhile by Sarah's side. She drove to the hospital filled with a sense of urgency, her heart reaching out ahead of her, straining toward Sarah. When at last she arrived at the patient's room, she discovered an empty bed.

"She was feeling a little stronger today," the nurse informed Mrs. Farber. "She took a walk with her husband. She only left a short while ago, so they might not be back for some time."

A little stronger, Mrs. Farber thought to herself. *Baruch Hashem!* She wouldn't think of interfering in any way with the limited time Sarah could spend with her husband, so she turned around and headed home.

A few days later, Mrs. Farber renewed her determination to see Sarah, and started out again. This time, she arrived to find her former star teacher fast asleep. She spent a few moments studying Sarah's pale, yet still beautiful face. Sarah breathed softly, creating an almost imperceptible rising and falling of the thin blanket that lay across her. *How tenuous is our hold on life*, thought Mrs. Farber. She sat by the peacefully sleeping patient and begged Hashem to heal this precious young woman. She waited a few moments more and then headed home.

Around Succos time, with nothing more to be done for Sarah at the hospital, she was discharged to her parents' home. At last Mrs. Farber thought of something concrete she could do to be of some small assistance. She took out her large stockpot and began peeling and slicing a heap of flavorful vegetables. She would make her special soup. It was delicious, healthy and hearty. Perhaps it would make Yom Tov preparations a little easier on Sarah's family, and give them all a little comfort and strength. She left it simmering for an entire day, until the aroma and flavors had reached their peak. Then, she sent it to the family with her best wishes.

Succos went by with a flurry of guests and Chol HaMoed trips, restoring a greater measure of joy to Mrs. Farber's life. The day after Yom Tov, however, she heard that Sarah had taken a serious turn for the worse. Mrs. Farber felt a stab of terrible guilt. Whatever she had tried to do, it was not nearly enough. *What will I say to her when I stand before her* aron *(coffin)?* she thought. *I'm sorry? I tried? There wasn't enough time to be there with you?* She had planned to make sure Sarah knew how much she admired her and how much she noticed all the extra touches she had put into her job — simple things like adding *nekudos* (vowels) to song lyrics for the girls who had difficulty reading. No one asked her to do these things. She did them because it meant so much to her that the girls could participate fully, with understanding and enthusiasm for what they were doing. *I would have told her, "These are the things I noticed, Sarah, and I want you to know how much they counted,"* Mrs. Farber thought. *Now I might never have the chance.*

She envisioned herself standing mute before Sarah's *aron*, choked with tears of loss and, more painful still, tears of regret. She felt that she was teetering on the verge of hysteria, and so she forced her mind to be still. She slid her *siddur* from the bookshelf and retreated to the spot in the corner of the dining room that was her place for prayer. The low, slanted rays of sunlight cast an orange tinge on the wall in front of her. She began Minchah, trying to apply her full focus to each word as it came before her, so that her mind would not wander into emotionally charged territory. Then she came to the words *refa'einu Hashem*. "Heal us, Hashem. Heal Sarah! Let me do something to help her!"

With these words cascading from her lips, an unbearable grief ripped through her. Tears rushed to her eyes, and then, something let go inside her — some control that had kept this heartbreak at a distance that made it manageable. It was as if the emergency brake had been released on her emotions, and she was now rolling wildly downhill. She heard the sound of her own wrenching sobs. They were not the quiet, teary-eyed sounds of a grown woman who has seen life and has gained a mature perspective. They were the raw, choking cries of a child who wanted something with all her heart. She wanted to see her Sarah, to hold her hand and somehow make things better. As her body shuddered with grief, she found herself gasping for air, frightened that she might simply pass out on the spot.

Mrs. Farber gathered whatever strength was left within her and quickly concluded *Shemoneh Esrei*. The house was now dark, and the family would soon be coming home for dinner. She flicked on the light in the kitchen and went directly to the freezer, where she found a container filled with the leftover vegetable soup from Succos. *A little hot soup*, she thought. *That will calm me down and soothe my throat.*

She poured the soup into a pot on the stove and turned on the flame. Soon, its comforting aroma was drifting into the air. She began pouring it into her favorite ceramic soup mug, but stopped short at the shrill chirping of the phone.

"Mrs. Farber, this is Sarah's mother," said the shy voice on the other end. "I know this is a bit of an imposition, but what wouldn't a mother do for her child? I'm calling because Sarah isn't able to eat anything solid now, and she just asked me if you might have any leftovers from the soup you sent us for Succos."

"I would love to bring you some of my soup," Mrs. Farber replied. "I'll be over in a few minutes."

There was no doubt in Mrs. Farber's mind that this call was an answer to her prayer — the most fervent, emotional prayer she had ever uttered. It was as if the soup were bubbling on the stove, just waiting for its purpose to be revealed. She took the soup and set out for Sarah's house. *It's amazing,* she thought. *I've been frustrated for weeks trying to see her, and here, after one tefillah that came from so deep in my heart, Hashem gives me an immediate answer. I'm finally going to Sarah.*

When Mrs. Farber entered the house, she found Sarah sitting at the kitchen table. Sarah smiled broadly and invited her guest to sit down. They spent a happy hour together reminiscing about school and catching up on the girls' progress. But for Mrs. Farber, the most important subject was Sarah herself, and all that she had done for her students. "You have a unique talent for teaching," she said. "You can't imagine how much you've given the girls who were lucky enough to have you as their teacher."

It was not long after that visit that Sarah's health deteriorated, and she was readmitted to the hospital. One day, Sarah's mother called Mrs. Farber and shared with her the sad news that the end appeared near. "You can come and be with her if you would like," the mother suggested.

Mrs. Farber dropped everything and got to the hospital as quickly as possible. She took a seat by Sarah's side and gently held her hand, hoping to transfer some of her own warmth and life-spirit into Sarah. Whether or not Sarah could hear her, Mrs. Farber spoke softly into her ear, hoping that somehow, her words would penetrate and provide her with courage for her journey to the Next World. "You lived a wonderful life," Mrs. Farber told her. "You gave so much to *Klal Yisrael* and so much to the world." As Mrs. Farber held onto Sarah's hand, the words of *Shema Yisrael* were recited, and Sarah's beautiful *neshamah* departed.

"Goodbye, Sarah. I'll miss you forever," Mrs. Farber whispered.

Weeks later, Mrs. Farber told her daughters the story of her tear-drenched prayer and the answer she received. No, Sarah was not healed. That was not Hashem's plan. But with just one afternoon spent together over a bowl of hot soup, Mrs. Farber's burning desire to comfort and strengthen Sarah had been answered instantly and fully.

The gates of Heaven are never closed to tears. When we pour out our hearts to Hashem from the deepest depths of our being, we are always answered.

Storming the Heavens

ometimes you finish *davening* and you wonder, *What did I just do?* You know you said the right words and answered "amen" in the right places. But somehow, you know that if you could dig a little deeper, you'd find something more. Much more.

It was with this idea in mind that I stood in the midst of the crowded *beis medrash* one day, scanning the faces of the people learning there. One of them, I had decided, was going to be my *chavrusa*, my partner in learning the laws of *tefillah*. It had to be someone serious, someone whose learning style fit well with my own, and of course, someone who, like me, wanted to upgrade his lines of communication with Hashem.

My eyes landed upon Eli Safdeye, who sat alone laboring over a Gemara. I knew Eli fairly well, as he had sat next to me for much of the year. We had spoken from time to time and I could tell from those conversations and from observing him that he was serious about his learning. Perhaps he would agree to be my partner in this venture.

When I approached Eli with the proposal, he was enthusiastic.

"In fact," he said, "I really want to learn more about *tefillah* because I run a *minyan*."

Eli's *minyan* was part of Beit David, a large Sefardic shul in Flatbush. The shul had recently established a separate Shabbos *minyan* for boys 8 to 21, along with an afternoon class for teenagers. The shul had been seeking someone to run the *minyan*, and Eli's name had been suggested.

"I decided that this was really something that I wanted to be a part of, because Sefardim have a special feeling towards *tefillah*," Eli explained. "They're very spiritually connected to prayer. I realized that if I could help reach into these boys' *neshamos* to help ignite their *tefillos*, it would be an awesome experience."

Eli took the job, which entailed leading the *minyan*, delivering a *d'var Torah* and teaching the afternoon class. Motivated by his desire to inspire the boys and keep them coming to the afternoon class, rather than choosing from other, more social activities, Eli searched for the precise topic that would engage their hearts.

"I chose the topic of *tefillah*," Eli explained. "I felt that the biggest impact I could make on them was to get them to understand every word in *Shemoneh Esrei*.

"We had a group of about 20 boys, and I knew that the way I introduced the class was going to make or break it for them. I had to give them a good reason to listen to what I was teaching. So I told them, 'Guys, if you want to be guaranteed a good *parnasah*, if you want an insurance policy against illness, if you'd like to have your name written down in *Shamayim* for happiness for the rest of your lives, then listen to me, because I have the secret potion for you. It's the power of *tefillah*.'

"We began learning each week, and my *minyan* became an instant success. The guys were very excited to come. They asked questions and they grew. And as the year progressed, I noticed that our *Motzaei Shabbos* Maariv was getting longer and longer. They were slowing down and concentrating because it was becoming more meaningful to them. This is what my *minyan* is all about."

When Eli finished describing his *minyan*, I knew Hashem had sent me the perfect *chavrusa* for this subject. We studied the laws of *tefillah* each day and covered many laws of *Shemoneh Esrei*. Eli was finding that the learning gave him new material to impart to his boys each Shabbos. We moved along at a steady pace for about six weeks, and it seemed likely that we would be able to complete all the laws of *Shemoneh Esrei* before the summer break.

Instead, one day at the end of our learning, Eli somberly informed me that he would no longer be able to learn with me.

"Are you kidding? Why not? I thought we were doing really well!" I replied. I was disappointed and surprised. If he hadn't been happy with the arrangement, he surely hadn't indicated it to me up until that moment.

It was then that Eli revealed an episode from his past, and a frightening new episode upon which his future would rest.

"A few years ago, when I was learning in Eretz Yisrael, I found a strange lump on my neck. I went to the doctor and found out that it was exactly what I had feared — cancer. I came back to New York for treatments and went through the whole thing — the nausea, the hair falling out. I wouldn't leave my house for months. But finally, when it was all over, the doctors said they had gotten rid of it and my chances of a normal, healthy life were good.

"But you know, all these predictions are just predictions, and this one was wrong. It's back, and I have to undergo chemo again. I'm sorry, Binyomin, but it takes everything out of me. I won't be able to go on learning."

I didn't know what to say. Part of me expected him to suddenly crack a smile and tell me it was all a bad joke. How could everything change so radically? How could someone so young, someone whose life revolved around the normal, everyday ups and downs, suddenly be plunged into a life-and-death situation? Nothing had changed, and yet for Eli, everything had changed. It was inconceivable.

Eli continued talking to me, revealing more of the tragedy this diagnosis had set in motion: "A few months ago, I was dating a girl and things were going well. After we went out a few times, I told her about my medical history. I explained to her how the doctors said the chances of recurrence were very slim. She thought about it for a week and ended up breaking it off. At the time I was devastated. But you know, now that this happened, I'm glad she did it. Imagine if we were married now and the cancer came back. How would she feel? How would I face myself?

"Now my *rebbeiim* told me that when I'm able to go out again, I have to tell the girl about my medical history before we even meet. What do you think my chances are of ever finding a *shidduch*? Who would want to become involved in such a situation?"

As I walked Eli out of the *beis medrash*, my mind was blank. I could think of nothing to say that could comfort him — nothing that would not sound hollow and trite. We shook hands and I simply told him, "*Refuah sheleimah*, Eli. Hashem will help. Please keep in touch."

Tears stung my eyes as I walked away and headed down the block. All around me, the street was filled with festivity. A new *sefer Torah* was being dedicated, and throngs of people were following the procession as it surged down the avenue to the sounds of joyous music. Mothers held their small children up to see this glorious sight, and yeshivah boys danced around and around the rabbi who bore the Torah under its *chuppah* (canopy). To me, it seemed like a scene beamed in from another world. Here, in my world, there should be gray skies and tearful faces; while a young man's vibrant life is hanging by a thread, can people still sing and dance?

I spoke out loud to Hashem as I walked down the street in a daze. "Please, Hashem, heal my friend. Please have mercy on Eli. You just have to save him! Don't let him die."

Eli soon discovered that he could not expect much encouragement from the doctors' prognostications. A recurrent cancer is a different situation than a first-time case, and no one was giving Eli soothing statistics to rely upon. He knew that, even with the most advanced medical treatments, *tefillah* offered the only cure. Now, he was praying for his life.

Chemo treatments began, but Eli attempted to maintain a sense of normalcy. With all his heart, he wanted to shield the boys at the *minyan* from knowledge of the situation. If only his hair would not fall out, he reasoned, they would have no reason to suspect anything and he would not have to tell them. But after two weeks of treatment, there was no hiding the truth. Eli thought hard about how to break this crushing news to the *minyan*. Surely the news would throw their budding passion for *tefillah* into doubt. They would wonder: *How could the man who taught them about the protective power of prayer be stricken with such a dire illness?* He prayed to find the words that would allow the boys to come to the right understanding.

It was a warm June afternoon when Eli's class convened to learn more from their beloved leader about the power of *tefillah*. Usually, Eli would set the table with chips, popcorn, soda and candy for the boys. But on this afternoon, the tables were bare, a notable difference that Eli hoped would signal to them that something serious was in the air. Indeed, the boys did sense the gravity of the moment. When Eli asked them to pull their chairs close to him, the atmosphere of the room was charged with a tense silence. Every eye turned to Eli.

"Listen, guys," he began, "I would love to sugarcoat what I am about to tell you, but unfortunately there is no way for me to do so. Boys, I am very sick."

He briefly recounted his first round of illness in 2001, and his doctors' hopes that they had conquered the disease. Now, he explained, the situation was more serious than before, and he would not be able to continue leading the *minyan* while he was in treatment.

"Guys, listen carefully to me. For the past year I have been handing you the tools you need to save me. Slowly but surely, I have been spoon-feeding you my cure. It's not going to be the doctors at this point, and it's not going to be the medicine. My only hope for a cure is every single *tefillah* that you say from now until I get better. Guys, I NEED YOU! I am not going to be able to go on unless Hashem allows it, and through your *tefillos* He will heal me."

For teenage boys living normal, carefree lives, Eli's message was transforming. Someone's life was in their hands. What they did, what they said when they opened their mouths to speak to Hashem, suddenly mattered more than they could ever have imagined it would. Succeed, and they would have Eli sitting there with them for years to come. Fail, and his beloved presence would be gone. This was the power of *tefillah*, and it was in their hands.

Eli's boys became fierce soldiers armed for battle. Maariv that night was their first fearless march forward in this fight for Eli's life. Their *Shema Yisrael* caused the air itself to vibrate with a sound so intense that it was physically palpable. Their *Shemoneh Esrei* was drenched with tears and emotion as the boys hammered upon the gates of Heaven with their pleas. Some, embarrassed by their own emotion, tried to hide their faces behind their *siddurim*. In the corner was Daniel, who had cynically challenged Eli with the question, "Why do Chassidim have to shake back and forth and raise their hands to the ceiling when they pray? Why can't they act normal?" He was swaying like a *lulav*, throwing his hands to the Heavens like a beggar pleading for mercy.

The fire of their *tefillah* never burned out. Every week, in Eli's absence, they divided the entire *Tehillim* to say on his behalf. Their *Shemoneh Esrei* rose up from the depths of their heart as they thought of their sorely missed friend and the battle he was fighting. They were his allies, his reinforcements, and they would not let him down.

But they were not carrying the burden alone. In Eretz Yisrael, there were boys who rose to Eli's defense as well. Many were boys from a teens-at-risk program for which Eli had served as a dorm counselor. Some of the boys brought their *tefillos* to the Kosel. One boy positioned himself in the spot that was closest to where the Holy of Holies had stood and wept to Hashem, begging for Eli's life. News of these sincere efforts came to Eli, who was heartened by the outpouring of love from all those whose lives he had touched.

Summer arrived in full force, and despite Eli's bald head and medical morass, he decided to stay engaged with the healthy, living world around him. Before his diagnosis, he had been offered a position as a head counselor in a day camp, and he decided to take the job.

Diving into his job with all his energy, Eli devoted himself to giving his campers the most memorable summer of their lives. Understanding that his appearance might worry the children, he visited each bunk and explained that he had to take a medicine that made his hair fall out. He reassured them that he would get better, and the campers said *Tehillim* each day to assure that he would. From that point, all that the campers noticed was the fun and enthusiasm Eli brought with him each day.

One hot August morning, Eli came to camp with a heart full of trepidation. Right after Shacharis, he would have to leave for the hospital, where he would undergo a CT scan that would show conclusively whether the disease had retreated in the face of two months of aggressive treatment. It was his own personal Judgment Day, at the end of which he would have a clearer vision — for better or worse — of what the future would bring.

When Shacharis was finished, Eli, still in *tefillin*, stood before the campers and spoke.

"Boys, today I am going off to do something that is very, very important to my getting better. I know you're too young to understand the whole thing, but you can understand one thing. That is that I need Hashem's help, and I need all of you to help me say *Tehillim* with all your might."

For a moment, Eli allowed his eyes to meet the gazes of the youngsters who sat in front of him. Their puzzled, sad faces cut through his last reserve of emotional control, and his heart overflowed its well-fortified banks. For the first time since his ordeal began, he began to cry in public. His lips quivering and body shaking with sobs, he let go a flood of tears that carried with them all the fear and pain he held inside.

He turned his back toward the campers and turned his eyes toward Heaven. Screaming with all the strength that remained to him, he called out King David's words of unwavering faith: "*Shir la'ma'alos. Esa einai el heharim, mei'ayin yavo ezri!*" (I turn my eyes to the mountains. From where will my help come?)

From behind Eli, 125 young, impassioned voices repeated the phrase with all their might. Line by line, the camp followed Eli through the verses that reiterate Hashem's watchful, loving care forever. As Eli left camp to learn his fate, his fear had been replaced by rock-solid faith in the power of his campers' prayer. The CT scan confirmed his faith, providing a picture of a disease that was finally on the run, although not yet conquered.

I hadn't seen Eli during the summer, but I had heard that after camp was over, he had been staying close to home. It was Elul, and I was learning for the month in a small *beis medrash* with a few *kollel* men. We needed some manpower, and I thought that perhaps Eli could use something to occupy his mind and his time. I called Eli and invited him to join us.

"Binyomin, thanks for thinking of me," he replied. "It's just what I need. I'm going to try to make it, and I'll bring along Moshe Gobioff to learn with me."

The next day, I sat near the door so I could greet Eli as soon as he arrived. After a short while, I heard his familiar voice in the entrance hall. Running out to the hall to meet him, I pasted a broad smile on my face. Eli reached out for my hand and offered a hearty "*Sholom aleichem*," sounding like his old self. But his face told a different story, a wrenching tale of incredible suffering. I walked with him and Moshe into the *beis medrash*, uninvited tears blurring my vision.

During the next two weeks, I was privileged to witness the awesome sight of Eli pressing forward, throwing himself into his learning despite the pain, worry and fatigue that were his constant companions. It was this vision that stayed before my eyes even in the midst of my son's *upsherin* during that period. My only message to my guests was gratitude — thanking Hashem for every bit of good, for every moment of life. I told them about Eli, his struggles, his defeats and his victories. My voice, cracking with emotion, seemed to penetrate the guests' hearts. But most of all, it was my own heart that opened, as never before, to a full appreciation of Hashem's goodness.

Weeks later, Yom Kippur arrived. Seeking a complete, undiluted intensity in the *davening*, I chose to *daven* in yeshivah. There, I knew, the *tefillos* would be as pure as I could find anywhere in this world. I took my seat in the front of the shul and looked around at those preparing, as I was, to engage in the day's all-consuming prayers. Behind me, to my surprise, I saw Eli. He was wrapped in his *tallis*, his face set in an expression of steel-like determination. Periodically throughout the *davening*, I would catch sight of him again, absorbing a few stray sparks of the high-voltage electricity his *tefillos* were clearly generating. Each glance at him energized my own pleas on his behalf. *Hashem! Please give him life!* I begged.

On top of the precariousness of Eli's overall situation was a specific trial he knew he would be facing after Yom Kippur. He was scheduled to return to the hospital. The goal was to rid his body of this dreaded disease once and for all. In essence, the medicines would bring Eli to death's door for the purpose of restoring him to life.

Perhaps it was this that Eli had in mind when the *chazzan* chanted the somber melody of *U'Nesaneh Tokef*. How could someone in Eli's position endure the prayer's words, "Who will live and who will die?" His beleaguered body shuddered with his weeping as he stood there, one among hundreds of men, none of whom knew his fate for the coming year. Finally, the davening concluded with the final statement of faith: *Hashem Hu HaElokim* — Hashem, He is G-d — and Eli shouted it to the Heavens. Pronouncing those words, Eli shed all illusions of control. He relinquished it all to Hashem and prayed only that he would merit Hashem's mercy — that the oceans of prayers from him, his family and his boys would be accepted in Heaven.

After Yom Kippur, Eli was admitted to the hospital for the planned treatments. When Simchas Torah arrived, his soul longed to dance, but his body was confined to a hospital bed, connected to a tangle of tubes. Eli looked around at the barren surroundings and imagined the scene in shul at that moment. He found himself assessing the possibility of getting up out of bed and grabbing hold of two *sefarim* that rested on a nearby table.

Without giving it much more thought, he simply rose, carefully maneuvering around the tubes, and made his way to the table where the *sefarim* waited. One, *Nesivos Shalom*, he cradled in his right hand. The other, a *Chumash Bereishis*, he held in his left hand. Raising them up above his shoulders, he began to sing, *"Toras Hashem Temimah, Toras Hashem Temimah ..."* His weak voice strengthened as he clutched the only "Torah" available to him that night and danced *hakafos* around his bed. For those few moments, he was filled with joy, alone in the company of Hashem and his precious *sefarim*.

The treatment took weeks to complete. When it was finished and Eli was released, his devastated immune system forced him to remain isolated at home, with only very limited human contact. One friend visited regularly and tried to learn with Eli a little bit. However, Eli's weakness affected his powers of concentration as well. He couldn't focus, he couldn't remember, and the situation was unbearably frustrating for him. His friend stuck with him, patiently helping Eli to salvage what he could of the joy of learning.

With much time alone to ponder his life to date, and the future that lay before him, Eli began to sink into despondency. It wasn't the suffering he had endured that weighed down his spirits. Rather, it was his assessment of the future. Even if he were to survive this disease, he feared that getting married and starting a family were out of the question. His entire image of the life he would have was shrouded in loneliness and confusion.

These saddening thoughts began to intrude upon all his waking hours. One day, as he *davened* Minchah in his room, he began to feel as if his heart would burst with grief. Upon the words *Refa'einu Hashem* — Heal us, Hashem — his emotions burst from their restraints. His face burned with torrents of tears as he mourned his lost future. Though Hashem had bestowed upon him a miraculous second lease on life, he wondered if it were indeed a blessing, for it seemed at that moment to be a life sentence for a solitary, unfulfilled existence.

Somehow, Eli pulled himself through the rest of *Shemoneh Esrei*. The release of emotion had left him feeling spent, but cleansed of the dark negativity that had taken hold. As he concluded the prayer, bowing before the One Who had helped him through his trial so far, he felt the comfort of Hashem's presence. Hashem heard his cry, Eli was certain. Hashem would help him, no matter what life would bring. There could be no doubt.

After about a month of confinement, Eli was still bald and weak, but the cancer appeared to have finally been eradicated. His doctors declared him well enough to circulate among people again, and there was one group who topped his list — his boys at the *minyan*.

The following Shabbos morning, the boys witnessed the sight they had been longing to see. There was Eli, standing at the front of the room beaming a smile that each boy felt was directed right at him.

"Guys, I'm back!" Eli told them jubilantly. "I am here because of you! It's all because of you. Do you realize what you gave me? You gave me life. Obviously, it was Hashem Who did it, but who did Hashem do it for? It was for you, with your *tefillos*, because you wanted me back to lead you further." The electric joy in the air ignited the boys' *tefillos*, and the boys learned something new that day — the incredible heights that can be reached by *davening* with *simchah*.

When the *minyan* had finished, one of the boys' fathers came to welcome Eli back, and to make him an offer.

"A noted *Mekubal* from Eretz Yisrael is arriving in two days," the man told Eli. "He will be staying at our home. Why don't you come and get a *berachah* from him? He is known as a great *tzaddik* whose words come true, and he has been able to change things that no one else could."

With Eli's health stable, his main concern at the moment was his future. Could the *Mekubal* help bring to fruition his dream of marrying and starting a family? Eli was doubtful, but accepted the invitation nonetheless. At least a *berachah* could offer a shred of hope.

Tuesday afternoon, Eli and his father took their places in a long line of people seeking the *Mekubal's berachos*. Finally, it was Eli's turn. He and his father were escorted into a private room, and there, before them, sat the great *chacham*, wrapped in a multi-colored robe that seemed transported directly from the days of

Avraham, Yitzchak and Yaakov. His face was partly obscured by a hood, known as a *jalabah*, which he lifted as Eli approached.

He studied Eli's face and forehead for a moment and then, his intense features lit up with a broad smile. "*Al tidagi, Eli,*" he said soothingly. "*Hakol yihiyeh beseder*" — Don't worry, Eli. Everything will be fine.

The *Chacham's gabbai* then informed him of Eli's work with the *minyan*, and the great strides the boys had made under Eli's tutelage. He listened intently, and once again flashed a delighted smile in Eli's direction.

"Eli," he said, "Please send me an invitation to the wedding."

Feeling energized by the warmth and optimism of the encounter, Eli left the *Chacham's* presence. He and his father talked about the prediction of a wedding, but both of them found it almost incomprehensible. "My wedding!" Eli exclaimed with a weak chuckle. He appreciated the *Chacham's* confidence, but it somehow just didn't ring true. He felt like Sarah when the angels told her that she would bear a child in her old age; surely she wanted to believe it and yet, her initial impulse was to laugh.

One month after Eli received the *Mekubal's berachah*, a close friend of his family, Mrs. Dasi Gerstein, passed away. Eli felt especially close to her, because she had been a constant source of moral support for him when he went through his first bout of illness. Her loss stuck him deeply.

Following her passing, however, a series of unusual events were set in motion. There was an older, unmarried man who had given Dasi physical therapy. Often, his conversations would revolve around the difficulty of living alone and the ever-diminishing pool of women interested in dating him. He confided that a year had gone by without one single date. Now, a week after Dasi's passing, he was suddenly in high demand.

Another of Dasi's acquaintances had poured out her worries about her 29-year-old daughter who was as yet unmarried. Two weeks after Dasi's passing, the daughter was engaged.

Dasi had apparently arrived in Heaven with an agenda to be taken care of, and she was doing it. This wonderful woman, who was no doubt now dwelling close to Hashem, was using her position to plead the cases of those whose pain she had shared.

Finally, it was Eli's turn. One day, his friend brought him news he never thought he would hear. The friend knew of a wonderful girl who was impressed with all she had heard about Eli and was willing to go out with him.

Eli and Batsheva's first date was an unqualified success, but now that there seemed to be a potential for something more, Batsheva decided to seek advice from a rav. She told him about Eli's health history. He told her she should give Eli a chance.

The couple continued dating and, in the process, each found more and more to like and admire in the other. Finally, on the fourth date, Eli could not restrain himself from asking the question that was uppermost on his mind: "Batsheva, how in the world did you agree to go out with me, knowing that I had been sick twice?"

"You know, Eli, I don't run the world," she answered. "Hashem does, and if Hashem decided that I should marry someone who would eventually get sick, then that's what will happen, even if I marry someone who has so far been completely healthy. It's all up to Hashem. If I see that you are the one for me, then that's that. Why should I worry about it? Hashem is in charge."

Batsheva's response confirmed what Eli already knew — that he had met a truly amazing woman. They were soon engaged. With Dasi shaking the Heavens from above, and his *minyan's* and his own *tefillos* storming the gates from down below, Eli's prayers had been answered, against all odds.

During Eli's engagement, he traveled to Israel. Among his top priorities was the special hand-delivery of a wedding invitation to the *Mekubal* who had given him the *berachah*. Eli arrived at the house and reintroduced himself to the *Chacham*, reminding him of how he had asked to be invited to Eli's wedding. Eli drew an invitation from his pocket and placed it before the *Chacham*, who uncovered his face and answered Eli with nothing more than a radiant smile.

A few months later, in a hall in New York, a wedding took place that seemed to draw a rushing river of *simchah* directly from Heaven's storehouse. Eli and Batsheva were married amid dancing, *berachos* and happiness that sent every heart soaring. Eli's boys danced around him in an ecstatic circle, rejoicing with their beloved leader who had taught them, with his own pain, his own suffering and his own indomitable faith, the unfathomable power of their prayers.

Today, Eli learns in *kollel*. From his unique perspective, gained in his hard climb from illness to health, he sees clearly that his simple life — a home, a wife and a day of learning — are blessings beyond measure. May the inspiration others gain from his story be an everlasting merit for Eli and his family, and may he be blessed with long life, health and happiness. Amen.

Just when you think that your situation is hopeless — that nothing can help — recognize the power of tefillah. It is, in truth, the only effective tool that exists, and there is no problem it cannot resolve.

Open My Eyes

ometimes, Debby Gross had to turn her eyes **away** from her baby. The little child's pale, pearly skin was stretched tightly across her jutting jawbones, a stark indication of the child's emaciated condition. Her eyes lacked sparkle, her lips were chalky and dry. Ahuva, Debby's first daughter after two sons, grew weaker each day. She was a baby who would not eat, and no one could determine why.

Every day, Debby fought a battle for Ahuva's life. Wrapped in soft cotton blankets, the bundled-up little girl gave at least an illusion of heft, which Debby found a little reassuring. She spent hours each day holding this little bundle, coaxing a bottle into her slack mouth, hoping that a few drops would somehow go down and be put to work building a healthy child out of this skeletal baby. Ahuva's face would scrunch uncomfortably for a moment, and out of her mouth would come what appeared to be twice as much formula as had gone in.

Cold fear gnawed constantly at Debby's consciousness. It was a fear of the unknown; her doctor could not find the problem, let alone the cure. It was a fear of the known, as well, for Debby had dealt with severe digestive problems once already, with her oldest son, Moshe. In that case, the family had consulted a kinesiologist, a specialist who used natural methods to treat the child's eating disorder. In Debby's eyes, Dr. Cooper was Moshe's savior, but the treatments he prescribed were expensive and rigorous to carry out. It was a full-time job, and Debby now had a house full of small children to care for. How could she do it all again?

As Ahuva grew weaker, the urgency began to outweigh any practical considerations. If Dr. Cooper could help Ahuva, then Debby would just have to do whatever he told her to do. Meanwhile, she continued pursuing standard treatments, visiting the pediatrician and gastroenterologist regularly. The kinesiologist recommended a complicated regime of vitamins and potions, which Debby immediately implemented. Everyone gave Debby medicines, everyone gave advice. But Ahuva was 3 months old and nothing was working.

Emotional turmoil became part of Debby's daily life. Although Debby had grown up in a religious home, at times like this, she felt cast aside by Hashem. Every day, she found some time to pray, but she came to Hashem with a stone in her heart. She felt like a royal subject coming before a king who was taxing her to death. Such a person would bow before the king and speak his praises — that was required — but inside, the person's heart would be bitter and dry. Nevertheless, she prayed. How could she fail to do so when her daughter was wasting away before her eyes?

In contrast was Debby's husband, Josh. Religious observance was something he had adopted on his own, and he had embraced it with tremendous joy. Often, when he learned something new, some way to upgrade or refine his service to Hashem, he would relate it excitedly to his wife. She found these instances amusing or irritating, dismissing them as the childish enthusiasm of a beginner. "You don't have to grab every *chumrah* (religious stringency) you come across!" she would chide him. "G-d isn't looking for you to make your life more difficult. My parents were religious Jews and they never did that."

In fact, Debby's was a close, loving family that kept Shabbos and kashrus in a community where many Jews did not. But she grew up dressing like the girls around her, without regard to the rules of modesty followed in more stringently observant families. When she married, covering her hair was not even an option in her mind. She was comfortable with the practices and outlook she had learned from her home, and had no desire to tinker with them.

That remained true even as her terrible trials with her baby unfolded. But as the situation grew increasingly alarming, she searched for a merit that would arouse Hashem's mercy. She would give up wearing pants and wear only skirts, she determined, in the hope that this would earn a reprieve for her poor, suffering child.

Months went by in a blur of feeding, rocking, holding and, inevitably, cleaning up the formula that Ahuva would eject. At 6 months old, she weighed slightly more than a newborn. She would sit in her infant seat barely moving, staring at whatever passed before her eyes. At times, Debby could not bear the stress of feeding the child, and she turned the job over to her housekeeper. The miracles Dr.

Cooper had wrought for her son Moshe were nowhere in evidence for Ahuva, but Debby continued to bring the baby to see him and to follow his guidance. Neither was the gastroenterologist able to bring about any improvement. Debby was panic stricken, like a drowning woman thrashing about for something to keep herself afloat.

At last, she heard about Dr. Newman, a different gastroenterologist who came highly recommended for his expertise in situations just like Ahuva's. With tremendous hope in her heart, Debby brought her ailing baby to this new doctor; perhaps the miracle she was waiting for was just around the corner.

"I want to test her for several diseases that might be underlying her condition," the doctor told Debby. "In the meantime, I want you to take her off the formula she is on and switch her to this one, which I think she'll tolerate better."

"But the one she's on was recommended by my kinesiologist," Debby replied. "We used it for my son, Moshe, and it worked wonders."

"Well, unfortunately, it doesn't seem to be doing the trick in this case," the doctor said. "Try the new one and see if it helps."

Debby rode home with yet another weight atop the burden she carried. Dr. Cooper was, as her husband had once pointed out, "G-d" to Debby. How could she go against his advice? Who knew her child better, after all — this new doctor, or Dr. Cooper?

The next day, she and Ahuva happened to have an appointment with Dr. Cooper. Debby was eager to discuss the formula situation with him, certain that he would quickly dismiss the new doctor's suggestion with some reassuring bit of information unknown to the mainstream medical world.

"Let me do a quick test here and see if the formula is good for the baby," Dr. Cooper suggested upon hearing about the gastroenterologist's advice.

The test was done.

"Well," Dr. Cooper stated blandly, "I think he was right. This formula is not good for your child. You should switch it."

Debby looked at him with disbelieving eyes. Her mind poured forth silent indignation: *"Well, he was right?" That's it? Doesn't he realize I've been feeding her this stuff for the past three months?* Debby said to herself. Where was the doctor's guilt? A little regret at least? He was no more concerned than he would have been had he looked out the window and noted that the weather had changed: "Well, look at that. It appears it really is going to rain today." Meanwhile, her daughter was failing to thrive.

The appointment wound to its conclusion, with Debby struggling to keep her incredulity in check. As she tenderly placed Ahuva in her stroller, a different emotion flooded her heart. She looked at this little child Hashem had given her, studying the hollow-eyed, bony features that spoke of Ahuva's tenuous grasp on life. Doctor Cooper could not save this child. He had not saved Moshe either. Only Hashem could save her. Only He could save anyone. The doctors could do nothing more than that which they were empowered by Heaven to do. In Debby's eyes, the rest of the world suddenly fell away. There was only her broken mother's heart, her sick child and her Father in Heaven. Nothing else mattered.

As soon as Debby arrived home, she called her husband.

"... When Dr. Cooper said it really was the wrong formula. I couldn't believe it! I couldn't believe he had made such a big mistake and acted like it was no big deal. But then I realized, Josh, it was a message. None of it is in Dr. Cooper's control, or anyone's control. It's all from Hashem. There I was, looking at Dr. Cooper like he's G-d, but he isn't. Only G-d is G-d, and He is the only one Who can help us."

"Maybe that's all Hashem wants from us, Debby," her husband said soothingly. "Maybe that's what we had to realize, that we have to really put all our hope in Him. Now don't worry anymore. When you call on Hashem, He helps you."

That Thursday, Debby was casually roaming the aisles of the small grocery store near the vacation colony where she and her family were staying for the summer.

As she poked through a pile of melons, her cell phone rang.

"This is Betty from Dr. Newman's office," said a flat-toned voice on the other end. Those words alone were enough to flood Debby's mind with a sense of alarm. Ahuva had undergone the tests Dr. Newman had ordered, and this, no doubt, was the report. *Please, Hashem,* thought Debby. *Let it all be O.K.*"

"Mrs. Gross," Betty said, "the tests came back borderline."

"Borderline? What does that mean?" Debby asked.

"Well, there are some indications of disease, but it's not conclusive. We would like you to come back in on Monday for some follow-up tests. The doctor also requested that you bring in your son Moshe for some tests as well, because this type of disease sometimes takes a few years to show up. We want to make sure he is all right."

"My son?" Debby repeated, her voice laced with panic.

"Yes," said Betty. "Your son. The doctor would like to see him."

"But my son is ... he's been ..." She realized there was nothing more to add. "I will see you Monday."

The rest of the afternoon dissolved into a surreal dream. Debby saw herself, as if from a window, paying the cashier, loading her bundles into the car, pulling out into the road and driving toward home. She had felt so sure the test results would be negative. This just could not be her life; Debby Gross could not be the mother of a child afflicted with this devastating disease. Tears formed in her eyes, and the sensation of them overflowing onto her cheek seemed to unlock a deep reserve of grief. The tears signaled to her inner self, *Yes, you are sad. You are terribly sad,* and then, her tears would not stop.

The practical part of her brain noted a red light up ahead. She stopped the car and it seemed as though time had stopped as well. She visualized the adorable little newborn Ahuva, her first daughter, whom she had held so joyously in her arms less than a year ago. Deep in thought, tears streaming freely down her face, she turned her head in bewilderment toward the policeman who was now tapping on her car window.

"Lady, are you all right? You gotta get moving here. The light's changed."

She nodded and hit the gas pedal, mindlessly steering the car toward home.

That Friday night, as the Grosses sat at their Shabbos table in their country house, a heavy rain began pounding against the roof. There would be no walk in the soft summer air that night. Lightning cracked the sky open, illuminating the dining room with its harsh, bluish light. The storm must have been close by, for the thunder came in crackling claps almost simultaneously with the lightning. A mighty wind combed through the trees, creating a spooky howling sound and sending the weaker branches crashing to the ground. It was a cacophony of frightening, sudden noises and unidentifiable clangs and booms.

"Must be some branches falling on the cars," Josh surmised.

"M-m-m," Debby responded. Nature was playing a soundtrack for her heart's ruminations.

"Josh, do you mind if I go up to bed now? I'm just completely exhausted."

"Go, Debby. I'll clean up in here and put the boys to bed."

The most prized feature in the Grosses' bedroom was the large picture window. On sunny days, it framed a masterful landscape of the lush trees, quiet pathways and distant hills visible from that vantage point. Tonight, it framed a stormy show of Divine power. The power was too great; it looked like dangerous chaos to her, and yet it could not be so. Hashem was in control of it all.

I need to speak with a rabbi, Debby thought to herself. *I need someone who can give me some insight and tell me what it all means. What am I supposed to be doing? How am I supposed to know?*

It wasn't the first time this idea had occurred to Debby. She and Josh had discussed it several times before. What prevented them from taking action was their inability to decide on whom they should consult. Debby felt strongly that they could only benefit from speaking to someone who was firmly connected to the spiritual realms, someone with an extra depth of perception and sensitivity. As she watched the storm rage and thought about her situation, she suddenly remembered a conversation she had had during the previous week with her friend Bella Fine.

"You have to hear this story," Bella had told her. "It's really amazing."

The story was a brief but powerful one. Bella's husband Aaron had been learning Gemara in a shul with his *chavrusa*. The rabbi of the shul, Rabbi Ehrenfeld, walked up behind the seat in which Aaron was sitting and said, "I hear the voice of Aaron Fine here. Who are you?"

Aaron, who had never met the rabbi before, was startled. "Reb Aaron Fine was my grandfather," he told the rabbi. "I was named after him. I believe my father told me that he used to pray in this shul. Is that correct?"

"Yes, that is correct," said Rabbi Ehrenfeld. "Your grandfather was a great man. It's good to meet you. Have a good Shabbos."

From Aaron's voice alone, the rabbi had recognized him as Reb Aaron Fine's grandson. More remarkable still, the Gemara the partners had been learning was one that stated that in order to learn Torah successfully, a person must rely upon the merits of his forefathers. Somehow, the rabbi had perceived the merit of Aaron's grandfather in him.

As Debby recounted the details of the story to herself, she realized that Rabbi Ehrenfeld was the rabbi she needed to see. Another fact pointed her further in his direction; he was spending the summer in a vacation home down the block from her own. It seemed that Hashem had not even attempted to hide His hand in arranging this life raft for her.

Shabbos morning Debby woke up early, feeling more energized than she had felt for months.

"Josh, I need to speak to the rabbi," she told her husband. "I just can't function anymore. I'm not sleeping. I'm barely eating.

I have no patience for the children. I want to go speak to Rabbi Ehrenfeld. I think he's someone who can give us some direction. I hope."

After lunch, the couple headed toward Rabbi Ehrenfeld's house. It was a hot sunny afternoon, but the shade of the tall oak trees and a fresh post-rainstorm breeze made the walk pleasant.

As they neared their destination, Debby began to hesitate. "Maybe this isn't a good time," she said. "We're going to have to tell him our whole story, and I know I'm going to be crying. Maybe this isn't an appropriate thing for Shabbos."

"Let's not stop now," said Josh. "It's taken us this long to go to choose someone. If we turn around, we might lose our momentum, and we can't afford that. We need help. Don't worry, you'll be all right."

They continued toward the rabbi's house, but when they got there, they discovered that he was resting. Debby was relieved. They would come back after Shabbos.

This time, there was no hesitation. Josh called Rabbi Ehrenfeld right after *Havdalah*, and he invited the couple to come right over.

As soon as Debby met the rabbi, she knew she had found the right man. His eyes were as pure and clear as a child's; they could see everything. As she spoke, telling of all she and Ahuva had been through together in the first months of the child's difficult life, she could feel the rabbi's concern. He listened with complete focus, asking a few questions to clarify the facts. At last, Debby felt completely understood.

But Debby had not come for medical advice. She finally asked the question that had been eating away at her heart: "Why is Hashem punishing me like this? What did I do wrong?"

"Hashem is not angry with you," Rabbi Ehrenfeld said. He simply stated what he knew to be true. "On the contrary, He loves you. Sometimes He gives us very difficult tests in order to bring us closer to Him, not to push us away. That is what Hashem wants from us."

"That is what I thought, Rabbi, and that's why I don't understand what is happening now," Debby responded. "A few months ago I decided that as a merit for my daughter, I would stop wearing pants, which was a very hard thing for me to do. If I did all that for Hashem, why is He still not answering me?"

"You misunderstand how *tefillah* works," the rabbi gently explained. "We don't ask for something and receive it as if we deserve a reward. We have to come before Hashem believing that we deserve nothing, that He owes us absolutely nothing. We are beggars before Hashem, and all we can do is ask and hope that He answers us.

"But we must recognize that Hashem never abandons us. He is with us day and night. Even when your life seems dark and confusing as night, remember that Hashem is with you just as He was with you in the day, in the good times.

"Now, Mrs. Gross, I would like you to follow my instructions about how you should pray before Hashem. I want you to have the following three thoughts in mind when you pray *Shemoneh Esrei*, in the *berachah* of *Shema Koleinu* (a blessing in which one may insert personal petitions).

"First of all, say to yourself, 'Hashem, I don't know anything. I can't do anything. You know everything. You can do anything. I am only a human being.'

"Secondly, say, 'Hashem, You have the power to change any situation instantly.'

"And last of all, say, 'Please, Hashem, I want to be able to serve You better. But in order to be able serve You I need to be happy. And in order to be happy I need my daughter to be healthy.'

"These are three simple concepts with which I want you to pray before Hashem. Then I want you to make some sort of commitment toward serving Hashem."

"Commitment?" asked Debby. "Like what? What do you want me to do? I will do anything you say."

"Make a commitment that you will bring up your children in the way of Hashem and His Torah."

"O.K., I will," Debby stated.

"I want you to know that I feel that in a few days, your daughter's situation will turn around and she will get better. The tests you are worried about will turn out negative."

He walked the couple out the door. "Hashem should grant Ahuva a *refuah sheleimah*," he said.

Debby left Rabbi Ehrenfeld's house looking like the same person who had walked in, but within her, the landscape was dramatically altered. Her soul was no longer enshrouded in cold darkness, isolated from the Divine love she so dearly needed to feel. Instead, it basked in light and warmth. Hashem was drawing her near, paving the path by which she would find Him. The rabbi's simple, gentle manner illuminated this path for her.

When she arrived home, she peeked into Ahuva's crib. The child was so sick, so very sick. She had been sick for so long. Was it possible that the situation would turn around in a few days as the rabbi had predicted?

When Debby awoke on Sunday morning, she could not remain in bed for one extra moment. She dressed and headed purposefully to Ahuva's room as if she held the cure in her hand. But she didn't have the cure. She merely understood, for the first time, where the cure could be found. She would go to the Source of healing and beg. She took three steps backward, preparing to recite the *Shemoneh Esrei*, and then took three steps forward, toward her Father in Heaven, Who had been waiting for her all along. Tears began to flow instantly as she recited Hashem's praises, acknowledging His Power over everything in Creation.

At last, she reached *Shema Koleinu*. Standing beside her daughter's crib, she began steering her mind toward the thoughts Rabbi Ehrenfeld had suggested. Looking at her helpless baby, thinking about the futility of her long months of running from doctor to doctor, the first thought was not difficult to enunciate with sincere emotion. *What am I, anyway?* she said. *What do I know? What can I accomplish on my own without Hashem? Nothing!* She wept and shook with emotion, swaying back and forth, saying, as the rabbi had instructed her, *You, Hashem, can cure Ahuva. You can cure her in an instant. It's all in Your hands.* Finally, her thoughts flowed to the next statement: *I only want to serve You, but to serve You I need peace of mind. I need to be happy. Please heal my child so I can serve You with happiness!*

When all these declarations were made, Debby took a deep breath. Calmly, with full attention to the implications of what she was saying, she placed an obligation upon herself. *I commit myself to raise my children according to the ways of Hashem and His Torah.*

As Debby prayed, she felt as if she had reached the summit of a high mountain and was able to perceive the world around her with unprecedented clarity. This situation had been given to her as a way to rectify the mistakes she had made when her son Moshe had been ill. Hashem had laid out similar circumstances before her, so that she would have another chance to get it right. He had given her a chance to find Him once before, but instead, she had found only Dr. Cooper. Debby had maintained her distance from Hashem, guarding the division between her life and His will. Now, she saw that there was no such division at all. She concluded her prayers with a sense of certainty that Hashem had heard her cry, and that the tests would come back negative, beyond any doubt.

Monday morning arrived, and Debby brought Moshe and Ahuva to the doctor's office for the tests. She maintained two simultaneous dialogues, one with the doctor and one with Hashem, constantly pleading that all would be well. On Tuesday, when the results came in, Debby received a resounding answer to her prayers. All the results were negative — no borderlines, no doubts.

The same day, Ahuva was scheduled for a checkup with the gastroenterologist. Josh and Debby brought the baby in for another round of what had become a routine of disappointment. Debby placed her on the scale and the doctor began entering the weight on her chart. He stopped, pen in midair, and checked the scale again.

"I don't believe it!" the doctor exclaimed. "Look, look here! She gained seven ounces!"

He took her off the scale and placed her back on it again, just to be sure. But there was no mistaking it; Ahuva had gained.

"Well, what do you know?" the doctor said.

Debby and Josh were laughing and crying at the same time. "It's a real miracle!" Josh exulted. The doctor, now teary-eyed as well, told them to bring the baby back the following week to see if her progress continued.

When the next checkup showed that Ahuva had gained another seven ounces, Debby knew only one person with whom she wanted to share the news — Rabbi Ehrenfeld. As she reported to him on the phone about Ahuva's miraculous gains, she could practically see the delight in his eyes. "I would like to come and speak to you again," she said. He agreed.

"Here's what I don't understand," she told him at their next meeting. "My baby had been suffering for seven months, and nothing helped her. How did you know that she would be healed? How did it happen instantly?"

Rabbi Ehrenfeld had a way of answering that made miracles seem like the natural course of things, something anyone with eyes in his head could see. He claimed no great powers, no great insights. Softly, simply, he explained, "When I saw in your eyes that you had really made a commitment, I just knew that Hashem would help you."

But the simplicity of the rabbi's words in no way mitigated their power. Debby saw, for the first time, a completely undistorted view of what life is about. It was as if she had been looking through a dirty window her entire life. Now, the rabbi's words wiped it clean. Everything that happens has one purpose — to make a person purer and better, more capable of a clear connection to Hashem. There is no other goal, and the Torah is the only way to get there.

With this perspective, Debby now understood the meaning of the commitment she had made.

"I made a commitment to raise my children in the way of the Torah," she said. "What should I do to accomplish that?"

"The best place to start is with a good yeshivah for your boys," Rabbi Ehrenfeld suggested.

The oldest boy was ready to start yeshivah in the coming school year, and Debby and her husband had been debating where to send him. Debby favored a day school, much like the one she had attended as a child, which had a balance of Torah and secular studies. Her husband preferred a yeshivah that was noted for its wonderful *rebbeiim*. They had debated the subject often, and had failed to arrive at a solution. But from Debby's new perspective, the question simply disappeared. What could be more important than giving the children the best Torah foundation possible? No amount of science, math or social studies could bring them closer to Hashem.

Today, Josh and Debby are proud of their two outstanding yeshivah boys. Ahuva is a healthy toddler, bright and loveable. Debby, who has made major transformations both inside and out, no longer believes that spiritual growth is for beginners.

Every person receives many tests throughout life. Hashem gives these tests to us to draw us closer to Him, not to push us away.

Miraculous Events

Hashem's Answer

ack to yeshivah, Eli Berkoff was thinking as he rode along the green-fringed mountain roads. Although he was a friendly, outgoing person, at this moment he was glad to be sitting in the backseat, removed from the animated conversation taking place between Chaim and Shmuel in the front. The trip back from camp provided a brief time for thinking, for letting go of the relaxed mood of summer and embracing the challenges of the new year. In yeshivah, everyone knew Eli as a staunch, reliable friend, a serious student and, most notably, the "guy with the *pushka.*" Every morning at Shacharis, Eli could be seen carrying the *pushka* around the *beis medrash,* collecting a few coins or a dollar from each student. No one could say no to Eli. *Going back to yeshivah would be great,* he said to himself. There was still so much to accomplish.

His eyes scanned the passing scenery as his friend Chaim's compact four-door Oldsmobile merged neatly onto the Garden State Parkway. *Not much traffic today,* he thought gratefully. The asphalt reflected the summer sun, creating a shimmering mirage that constantly receded into the distance. But even on this sultry August day, some of the trees were already tipped with the red and orange of fall. The ride proceeded at a smooth, relaxed pace, and Chaim handled the steering wheel lightly, adjusting a little to the left, a little to the right as the road wound its way south. Suddenly, as if a phantom had grabbed the steering wheel, the car lurched sharply to the right. Chaim battled the steering wheel, yanking it with all his might back to the center, but the car had a mind of its own. Like a child's toy, it flipped on its side and began tumbling, crashing over the guardrail and launching Chaim, Eli and Shmuel into a free fall down a 100-foot cliff. Eli landed just a few feet from the car, which lay like a dead insect on its back, its wheels jutting uselessly into the air.

He didn't know how long he had been lying there before he regained consciousness. The first thing he noticed was the car. It could easily have landed on top of him, but Hashem had saved him from that crushing blow. As he looked around for his friends, however, he realized that they were trapped inside, perhaps seriously injured. Although he lay a few hundred yards away from a well-traveled highway, he felt as though he were utterly alone in a vast void — a speck of dust floating through the eternity of outer space.

Maybe I can move, he thought. *Maybe I can get out of here.* But his muscles wouldn't respond to his wish. He was in the middle of the woods with no help in sight. Then he noticed something that turned the situation from merely frightening to potentially lethal. His upper arm was deeply gashed and blood was spurting from the wound faster than he could ever have imagined blood could flow. The crimson pool beneath him was creeping quickly outward, and his life, he realized, was ebbing away with every lost drop.

He tried to scream, but he had no strength. In the midst of the thick forest underbrush, surrounded by nothing but moss-covered rocks and trees, there was no one to hear him but G-d. "*Hashem yeracheim!*" he cried. "G-d, have mercy on me. I'm completely in Your hands. Please make a miracle ... save me!"

Suddenly, out of nowhere, two men arrived at his side. They were athletic, confident-looking men who seemed completely at home in this untamed swath of roadside wilderness.

"Hi, my name is Todd, and this is my friend Brian," the taller of the two men said. "Don't worry. We're going to help you. Just so happens we're a couple of soldiers on leave from the Army, and believe me, we're trained to deal with all kinds of crazy accidents. This is nothing compared to the time we had to ...." Todd kept talking to Eli, apparently to prevent him from going into shock and sliding back into unconsciousness. Meanwhile, Brian ran to the overturned car, grabbed a jacket off the front seat and ran back to Eli, whose blood was still rushing from the wound.

"We're going to make you a tourniquet to stop the blood flow," Brian told him. He began wrapping the jacket tightly around Eli's shoulder. Todd fetched a stick and wedged it between Eli's arm and the jacket. He then twisted it to tighten the tourniquet as much as possible. The bleeding stopped.

"You're going to be all right," Todd told Eli. "An ambulance is on its way."

Eli watched helplessly as his two saviors receded back into the forest, leaving him alone once again, still desperately in need of medical attention. But before his fears could fully surface above his murky consciousness, he witnessed the magnificent sight of a crew of Hatzalah volunteers heading down the slope with a stretcher. Their faces betrayed the seriousness of the situation as they rapidly transferred him to the stretcher and edged carefully back up the slope, holding onto a rope they had rigged in advance to prevent slipping.

"This tourniquet saved your life," they told Eli as they examined Brian's and Todd's handiwork. Fortunately, this ambulance was one of the few equipped with a device called mast pants, which are pants that compress the legs and push blood back up to the heart. With the mast pants, the Hatzalah crew was able to keep Eli alive until he reached the emergency room. There, Eli found out that, of the six pints of blood contained in a healthy human body, he had lost four. His blood pressure was unobtainable.

"You were as near as you could have come to the Next World," the doctor told him.

His life had been saved, but recovery was slow. Yeshivah began that year without Eli, and his friends kept careful track of his progress. One day, a student reported to Eli's rebbi that the doctors felt they had no choice but to amputate Eli's arm. The tourniquet had cut off the blood supply so completely that the arm did not seem to be capable of recovering its full circulation.

"It's impossible," said the rebbi. "The hand that held that *pushka* every day will not be amputated."

And it was not.

Two weeks after the accident, Eli asked his mother to help him identify the men who had saved his life so that he could thank them. She contacted the state police and spoke to an officer who had been at the scene. "Sir, by any chance do you know who those kind men were who saved my son's life?" The officer replied, "What men? When we arrived, no one with the description you're givning was there." Mrs. Berkoff was confused. She decided to contact Hatzalah. Surely they would know who had helped Eli just moments before they arrived. But once again, she received a bewildered response.

As Eli and his family reviewed the frantic jumble of events surrounding the accident, they became certain that Eli's rescuers were not men at all. Would men who were kind enough and able enough to save him have left him unattended? Would two soldiers on leave have been spending their time in the empty wilderness alongside the Garden State Parkway? Would they, under natural circumstances, have arrived at just the right moment, possessing just the right rescue skills? Eli recalled the pure cry he had uttered from the depths of his soul — "*Hashem yerachaim* … have mercy on me," and he was certain that Brian and Todd were messengers of the Divine mercy for which he had pleaded. Just as Hashem had sent His messengers to our forefather, Avraham, in the form of travelers, He had sent these messengers to Eli. They had appeared, performed their mission and then disappeared from sight. No one knew who they were, and no one ever would.

"*Karov Hashem l'chol kor'av, l'chal asher yikra'uhu ba'emes*" — *Hashem is close to all who call to Him, to all who call out to Him sincerely." When a Jew calls out to his Father, he must do so with the certainty that his Father is indeed listening, and desires only good for His beloved child.*

Singing in the Rain

I heard this story from Rabbi Avrohom Chaim Feuer, shlit'a. Even though he has confirmed it, I was hesitant to print it as people may be skeptical as to its veracity. However, the lesson it imparts is simply too powerful to be left untold.

It was the Kramers' pleasant Friday-night family ritual. Mrs. Kramer would light the Shabbos candles, and then she, her husband and their 23-year-old son Eric would hop in the car and take a quick, ten-minute drive to shul. There, they would join the dozens of other Jewish families that were part of their small South African community. The services would conclude with a speech by the rabbi, followed by another quick drive home and a delectable, hot Shabbos meal.

In the Kramers' opinion, and that of the many families like them, this was just enough. They acknowledged Shabbos, attended synagogue once a week and gave as much charity as they could. You couldn't say they had abandoned their faith. In fact, they loved their faith; they just didn't let it run their lives.

It was on one of these comfortable Friday nights that Eric Kramer sat inside the modern, architecturally bold synagogue listening to the far-less modern ideas being espoused by a substitute rabbi who had stepped up to the pulpit for this one week. Something about this rabbi's demeanor caught Eric's attention, and he found himself listening with more focus than usual.

There was real passion in this rabbi's words. "*Mitzvah haba l'yadcha, al tachmitzenah,*" the rabbi exhorted. "When a mitzvah comes into your hand, don't let it become stale."

The rabbi's words kept coming, and as they entered Eric's mind, everything else began to fall away. In his imagination, he saw a mitzvah, an amorphous glowing presence hovering close to his hand. It beckoned to be swiped from the air and incorporated into Eric's being, and yet, he was afraid to touch it. This sermon, Eric was certain, had been designed for his ears alone.

Two weeks earlier, Eric had been presented with a dilemma that went directly to the heart of the rabbi's words. For many months, he had been dating Diana Burtman, a young lady from a background very similar to his own. Their relationship had been wonderful, full of fun and excitement, and heading steadily toward marriage. Then, a tragedy struck the Burtman family. Diana's brother was diagnosed with leukemia, and from that moment on, nothing else mattered.

The Burtmans flew to prestigious institutions all over the world, consulting with the top doctors in the field. None, however, could offer more than a few month's reprieve from what appeared to be inevitable doom. With medical options exhausted, Mr. Burtman at last raised his eyes Heavenward. With tears streaming down his face, he spoke out loud. "G-d, please save my son. He's my life. Please don't take him from me. I know I haven't lived in accordance with Your laws, and for that I am sorry. But listen to me please. I promise that if You will heal my son, I will lead a new life as a fully observant, *shomer Shabbos*, Orthodox Jew, and I will keep all of Your commandments. Please just send a cure for my son."

Shortly after this episode, Mr. Burtman received news of a doctor in Boston who had developed a new treatment for leukemia. The Burtmans followed the lead, and a few weeks later, their son was on the road to recovery. Now, they were ready to make good on their side of the bargain. All the members of the family committed themselves to full Torah observance, Diana included.

Two weeks prior to this Friday night, Diana informed Eric that, if he wanted to go forward with their marriage plans, he would have to become fully observant as well. "I'm sorry," she said, "but that's just the way it has to be. It won't work with one of us keeping the mitzvos and the other doing his own thing."

The conversation plunged Eric into days of introspection. What did it mean to him to be a Jew? What was so bad about being observant? On the other hand, why did he have to turn his entire life upside down? What if he didn't like it? He became obsessed with this internal argument, until suddenly, a brilliant light shone on the answer. It was in the rabbi's words. A mitzvah had come into his hand. He had to stop thinking about it and grab it before it shriveled up and blew away.

I'll do it, he vowed to himself.

When the services concluded, Eric's parents began their short walk to the car. Eric stood dumbfounded. If he had grasped the mitzvah, it was his now. He couldn't get into the car.

"I'm sorry, Dad," he told his father. "I can't drive home with you. You see, I was listening to the rabbi and I decided that this was a message for me. I've been going back and forth on what to do about Diana, and this was the answer. I have to grab the mitzvah that's in front of my hand."

"Eric, the rabbi was talking to 250 people, not just you," his father replied wryly. Surely this would pass.

"It was meant for me. Even if there were a thousand people here, this was meant for me to hear. You go ahead. I'll walk. Don't wait for me for dinner. I'll catch up when I get home."

"Listen, have you seen what's going on outside?" his father asked. "There's a hailstorm. It's not even safe. I'm sure G-d won't mind if you start being *shomer Shabbos* next week. You can't walk seven miles in this weather. You'll get pelted!"

"Don't worry," Eric said, without a trace of doubt in his voice. His parents shrugged and headed for the car, while Eric turned up his collar and prepared for the trek home.

An hour and a half later, Mr. Kramer heard a knock at his door. Hoping to see Eric safe and sound on the other side, he rushed to open it. There Eric stood, neat and dry, as though he had just stepped out of the house.

"Well, thank G-d, I see you came to your senses and got a ride," Mr. Kramer commented.

"What do you mean, Dad? I walked, just like I said I would."

"How can that be? There's not a raindrop on you. I got soaked just walking from the car to the house."

"I'm serious, Dad. I really walked home, but the strangest thing happened to me. I'll tell you, but you're not going to believe it. When I left shul, it was pouring and hailing like mad, and besides that, it was pitch black. You could barely see a foot in front of you. But as I began walking, I saw a small opening through the clouds, and the moon was shining through it, right down on me. This moonbeam made a protective shield around me, like an umbrella, that followed me all the way home. The mitzvah protected me, Dad. There's no other explanation for it."

Eric and Diana announced their engagement shortly after that miraculous Shabbos. After Eric's weeks of doubt, Hashem had pushed aside a patch of clouds and made his path extraordinarily clear. The couple married and built a home on the foundation of Torah and mitzvos.

In 1998, Rabbi Avrohom Chaim Feuer heard this story from Eric's relative. He hoped that some day he would have the opportunity to meet Eric and confirm the occurrence of this open miracle. That summer, the opportunity came with an invitation to speak in South Africa on Tishah B'Av. During his stay, he was indeed able to find Eric, who confirmed the story, still marveling at the way Hashem had led him by the hand to his new life.

Later that day, Rabbi Feuer went to Yeshivah Ohr Somayach for lunch. He spoke to a rabbi who was sitting at the table next to him, and what more riveting subject could there be than the story of Eric and the hailstorm?

When Rabbi Feuer finished the tale, the rabbi jumped up from his seat exclaiming, "I don't believe it! I was the substitute rabbi. That was my sermon. Who would have known that it would have had such an impact on someone's life?"

Chazal teach that if you make an opening in your heart for Hashem, even as narrow as the eye of a needle, Hashem will widen the opening into a large hall, and He will bring you near. Any small mitzvah that comes our way can be that tiny opening, and if we grab it, rather than pondering it and procrastinating until it becomes stale, Hashem will surely shower us with his love and bring us near.

Music for the Soul

As Sammy stepped through the cramped entryway, he could discern the silhouettes of the idols that had been reverently placed throughout the darkened room. The moment of entry had the weird thrill of a nightmare — one of those occult scenes that could stick in one's mind forever. But Sammy shook off the sense of fear as he followed behind his friends. They were walking ahead with relaxed confidence, as if they were about to claim a prize. *There's nothing to fear*, he told himself. Even Rebecca, his wife, seemed more amused and interested than frightened. Her dark Spanish eyes glanced at one idol, then another, with the serene interest of a museum goer. *It's nothing. They're nothing — just statues*, Sammy told himself.

"You light the candle for the idol, and then say these words," Michael had explained before they came here. "They believe that the idol gives you a blessing." Michael and Justin had been living in Thailand for over a year now, and they were proud of their acquired mastery of the local customs. It was a long way from San Diego, where the three boys grew up. They had met in kindergarten and stayed close throughout the years, until each went to a different college. Only Sammy was married so far. Michael and Justin were adventurers, not quite ready to settle down. Still, when the opportunity came up to visit his two friends in their Asian paradise, Sammy and Rebecca found themselves eager for a little adventure too.

This particular adventure, however, was making Sammy dizzy. *This is idol worship*, he thought to himself. *Now, I'm not the world's greatest Jew. But this is actually idol worship.* These were his thoughts as he stood before the small stone figure that smiled benignly at him — and at everything that passed before its frozen features. There stood the candle he was to light. His hand wouldn't move.

"Come on, Sammy, just do it. You'll see, it's really amazing. You get a feeling of protection the whole rest of the day, I'm telling you." Justin was urging him on as if he were a kid afraid to jump off the diving board. Rebecca watched him, smirking at his sudden, childish fear. He reached for the candle and took it in his hand. He moved it toward the small flame that would kindle it for the sake of the little stone creature before him. Suddenly, his ears were filled with a melody, emanating from the recesses of his own mind. "OY OY OY MA MA MA MA MA," the voice chanted, startling him so completely that he dropped the candle on the cold stone floor.

"Sammy, what's wrong? Are you all right?" Rebecca gasped.

"Didn't you *hear* that?" Sammy asked his wife and friends. "Didn't you hear that singing? It was so loud!" He looked around at the bewildered faces in front of him and realized that he would have to try again or forfeit his reputation as a sane individual. He retrieved the candle from the floor and slowly moved it back toward the flame. Once again, the voice rang out, the voice that only he could hear, singing, "OY OY OY MA MA MA MA MA." With not one more moment's thought, Sammy dropped the candle and fled the room, leaving Justin and Michael behind. He and Rebecca booked the next flight back to San Diego, and life returned to normal. Sammy gradually thought less frequently about the idol, the candle and the haunting melody that had stilled his hand.

Two years later, Sammy noticed an advertisement from Arachim, an outreach organization, that would be holding High Holy Days services in his area. Having attended their services once before and enjoyed the experience, he decided to spend Rosh Hashanah there this year as well. Even Rebecca, who was gentile, agreed to come along. She was, after all, a student of all kinds of cultures from Asian to African to her own South American heritage. Judaism was rich with ritual and history, and whatever small smattering of it she had gotten from Sammy and his family was always interesting.

Rosh Hashanah arrived, and Sammy and Rebecca arrived at the Arachim service. Oddly enough, the rented room where the services took place seemed far more celestial to Sammy than did the synagogue of his youth. Here, there were folding chairs and acoustic tile ceilings; there, there had been plush, upholstered pews beneath a vaulted ceiling. He recalled that the soaring stained-glass windows depicting the Twelve Tribes cast bands of tinted light upon the congregants. Most of the prayers were sung in perfect four-part harmony by a professional choir headed by a retired opera singer. And yet, Sammy's memories of that shul were not those of inspiration or spiritual ascent. They were memories of squirming, staring, dozing and chatting with Justin, whose family sat next to his.

At Arachim's services, the prayers were led by one voice, one sweet, rich voice belonging to Reb Eli Mintz. His was not a performance at all — it was a true *avodah* — a service to G-d. He undertook his responsibilities with a full heart, grateful for the chance to help the congregants convey their prayers to the Heavens and awed by the knowledge that they, and he, were praying for their lives.

Added to all those weighty thoughts was his awareness that this congregation was different; it was largely composed of people who were just beginning to taste the sweetness of an authentic Torah life. Reb Eli felt that opening these people's hearts to Hashem was yet another imperative he had to accomplish with his *tefillos.* To foster their involvement, he set up the *bimah* in the middle of the shul, where he would be surrounded by the congregation. His custom was to invite several men to stand with him and *daven* alongside him. Often, during the *tefillah*, he would grasp their hands and they would sing together the stirring melodies that had become familiar over the years.

And that is how Sammy found himself standing next to Reb Eli on this particular Rosh Hashanah. The *davening* began, and from his vantage point at the *bimah*, Sammy felt as if he were being lifted upon a great, powerful wave of sound. The wave rose and fell, sweeping Sammy along with the rhythm of the prayers. Then, a palpable hush fell over the room as Reb Eli began the first strains of the awesome *U'Nesaneh Tokef.* His voice slid solemnly into his customary tune, which he had learned from the Satmar Rebbe. "OY OY OY MA MA MA MA MA," the melody unfolded, cutting straight into Sammy's heart. Where had he heard it? Why did it shake him so? Suddenly, from his post at the *bimah*, his mind transported him directly back to the dark, frightening moment in Thailand when he had stood ready to serve an idol. This was the melody — Reb Eli's melody, which had instilled itself in the deep recesses of his soul during his last visit with Arachim — that had forced the candle from his hand.

Sammy's *davening* was transformed. His soul was rent wide open and tears cascaded from his eyes as he recited the words of *U'Nesaneh Tokef*. His voice took up the melody and returned it, filled with awe and love, to the One Who had retrieved it from his memory and played it into his ears on that fateful day in Thailand.

When the services were finished, Sammy waited nearby as dozens of people came to congratulate Reb Eli on his inspiring *davening*. At last, Sammy approached.

"Reb Eli, I want you to know that you saved me from something terrible, and I owe you a tremendous debt of gratitude," Sammy said.

By now, Mrs. Mintz had joined the two men. Sammy told the couple his story. When he finished, Mrs. Mintz looked around and ascertained that they were not being overheard. Rebecca was still chatting in the women's section, getting ready to find her husband.

"What happened was wonderful. You were saved from a terrible *aveirah*," she told Sammy. "But what about your future? That song didn't save your family life. It didn't give you a Jewish home where you can raise Jewish children. You survived the battle, but you're going to lose the war unless something changes."

She gestured toward one young woman standing near the back of the room. "Look, there are many wonderful Jewish women who would love to marry and make a Jewish home. You should have one." The Mintz family returned to their home in Monsey, and Sammy returned to his life, but nothing was the same.

The following year, when Reb Eli returned to San Diego for Rosh Hashanah, he encountered Sammy once again. His demeanor had changed. He *davened* with a quiet, burning intensity one could detect at a glance. At the end of the services, Sammy and a young woman approached Reb Eli.

"Thanks for the beautiful *davening*," he said. "It was really inspiring. And Reb Eli, I'd like you to meet my wife."

It wasn't Rebecca. It was, in fact, exactly the young woman Mrs. Mintz had pointed out the year before. And so, the song had not only saved Sammy, it had saved his future. Sammy, who is now known as Shmuel, has a new life that starts with *minyan* each morning and ends with Torah learning each evening. He has embarked on the biggest adventure of all — raising a family who will learn the Torah of their parents and bring Hashem's light into the world.

The soul is the spiritual essence of man. It is constantly yearning for holiness, but it may be suffocating beneath man's desire for the unholy pleasures of life. Sometimes it takes a spark to rekindle the fire, but sometimes all it takes is a good niggun.

A Smashing Success

Fashions changed and tastes changed, but Aaron Sorreta's wholesale apparel company stayed on top of the trends. At 29, Aaron had already been working in the industry for 16 years. His flawless instincts made his firm one of the most successful in England. But it was his hard work and desire to succeed that kept the wheels of commerce spinning.

Aaron was the dark-eyed, foreign-born hero of a true immigrant success story. He was born in India, where his parents had settled after leaving their home in Bagdad. There, his parents built a prosperous business. Aaron lived well, in a spacious, well-appointed home surrounded by plenty of love and security.

When circumstances forced his parents to leave their wealth behind and emigrate to England, he was thrust into a world he could never have imagined. Here, home was a modest apartment lacking in the gleaming accoutrements of wealth. It was a clean, adequate home, but it simply could not inspire in Aaron the sense of security he once had. For the first time, he heard the words, "we can't afford it" from his parents.

The only constant from his previous life was his family's strong tie to Jewish tradition. Each Friday night, his mother lit her Shabbos candles, and the light shone as brightly as it had upon their lovingly polished wooden table in India. Each Pesach, the family brought out a new set of dishes and pots and turned the kitchen inside-out to accommodate the Yom Tov's requirements. The plain surroundings possessed a little magic for that week.

But the tight straits of the family, especially in contrast to their comfortable lifestyle in India, imparted one overriding lesson to Aaron. Money matters. One who has it can have everything he wants and needs — at least all that money can buy. Aaron was only 13 when he began to work in his uncle's business, motivated by his desire to recoup the security and comfort of his lost childhood.

He learned the business quickly and was soon making a significant contribution to his uncle's bottom line. By the time he was 25, he was on his own, running a company that was well-respected throughout the garment industry. He had established a wide network of international suppliers, and his lines were carried by major retailers.

At that point in his life, something else began to develop as well. He had begun to take a little time from his frenetically paced workday to learn a little Torah in a local yeshiva. Gradually, his one-hour shiur turned into a few hours a day. His traditional Jewish lifestyle evolved into a committed, Torah observant life. The healthy flow of money his business churned out began to serve a new purpose. It was only a matter of time — about four years — before these changes began to exert pressure on Aaron's inner landscape. He had built a world based on one ideal — the profit motive. But now, that foundation appeared weak, shaky, perhaps even illusory. More and more clearly each day, he was able to see what really held the world together, and that was Hashem and his Torah. The goals toward which he had applied all his energy and keen intelligence for the better part of 29 years were beginning to lose meaning. He longed to spend more time learning and less time dealing.

Yet another voice spoke inside Aaron as well. He had talent as a businessman — G-d-given talent. Because of this gift, he had been able to contribute large sums of money to keep the yeshiva running. Perhaps that was his purpose in life after all. Perhaps Hashem had not put him on earth to sit and learn all day, but rather to make regular time for learning while keeping his business running strong.

These two competing visions dueled day and night in Aaron's mind. Just as it seemed that one idea had dominated and laid the other to rest, the defeated idea would rise up again to fight. He knew that he would ultimately have to make this decision alone, but how?

One day, Aaron was reciting *Shemoneh Esrei*. As the words came to his lips, he felt that each was alive, vibrant with meaning. The words in the siddur appeared aflame, flickering in front of his eyes with their intense holiness. As never before, he felt his heart had been penetrated by the words of *tefillah*. His *neshama* was communicating with its Source in a pure, crystal clear connection. *Now is the time*, he thought to himself. *Right now, I can ask Hashem to give me clarity, to tell me which way to turn.*

He reached *Sh'ma Koleinu*, a portion in the *Shemoneh Esrei* that offers a place for private supplications. The words that rose to Aaron's lips had been churning in his heart for months: *Hashem,*

I have come to a junction in my life. There is a fork in the road. On one side, I can continue running my business and set up a time to learn Torah every day, and that will enable me to continue supporting Torah learning. On the other side, I can leave my business completely and use all my time and ability to learn your Torah. Whatever you want from me, I will do. But I need a sign to tell me which way to turn. Please, Hashem send me a sign.

That Shabbos, Aaron felt more at peace than he had for months. He knew with complete certainty that Hashem had heard his petition. The decision was off his shoulders, and all he need do now was be alert, so that he would not miss the sign Hashem would send him.

As he finished his meal that Shabbos afternoon, there was a loud, urgent knock on the door. Aaron opened it to find his neighbor standing there, red-faced and stuttering with excitement.

"Did you hear? Did you hear? Did anyone call you about the accident?"

"What accident? What are you talking about?"

"Your business. Your building. There was a big accident there and the whole place is a mess. You better get down there right away!"

"I can't go right now," Aaron replied. "Whatever it is will have to wait. But thanks for letting me know."

As soon as Shabbos was over, Aaron nervously hopped into his car and sped to London's garment district, where he owned a five-story building. As he neared the area, his path was blocked by what appeared to be large convoys of army trucks, fire engines, ambulances and police cars. Soldiers and policemen filled the street. Flashers painted the night air with garish streaks of red and amber, accompanied by the ominous melody of the sirens.

Aaron pulled his car over to the side of the road and got out, making his way on foot toward his block. As he crossed the intersection, his eyes beheld a scene of complete devastation. It looked as if a guided missile had fallen from the sky and hit his building squarely on a bulls-eye. Huge chunks of his plate-glass showroom windows lay in jagged shards on the street. Wires and pipes hung from gaping holes in the outer walls. The perimeter of the building was roped off for fear that more of the building's contents, or the building itself, might at any moment crash to the sidewalk.

Aaron found a police officer who appeared to be in charge of the damage-control effort. "Officer, this is my building," he said. His voice, harsh with panic, sounded strange to his own ears. "What happened?"

"Well, I'll tell you. There was a very strange accident."

The officer proceeded to describe the series of events that led to the destruction Aaron was now viewing:

That day, a large army truck was transporting goods to the docks, where they would be shipped to troops fighting abroad. Because the garment district was closed, the truck traveled at a fast clip through the narrow streets. On the road, there lay an obstruction, a small object that the driver did not see. It was apparently at an odd angle, and when the truck hit it at a high speed, the impact caused the steering column to crack. At that point, the driver was speeding down the streets with no control of the steering wheel. The road turned, but the driver could not. His truck jumped the sidewalk and flew into the building, right through the showcase window.

At this point, an engineer joined the officer and Aaron. He explained that the truck had smashed into a major support structure of the building. The entire shop and business were destroyed, and the building would have to be torn down.

The police officer and the engineer could not have explained the smile that now spread across Aaron's face. Instead of feeling grief and loss, his heart was filled to the brim with joy. Hashem had sent him his sign. Nothing could be clearer. He was destined to spend his days in a *beis medrash*, not behind a computer screen. It was June 5, 1981, and Aaron will never forget that date.

From that turning point, Aaron became a fixture in the beis medrash day and night. He reached out to others who, like him, were beginning to see the light, and began arranging *shiurim* and events for *baalei teshuva*. Still hungry for more intense learning, he went to Israel, where he spent two years making up for lost time. Returning to England, he picked up where he had left off. Over the years, he has guided many *baalei teshuva* on their journeys back to Torah.

Today, Reb Aaron is a rebbe in a major *kiruv* yeshiva. He is doing what he was put in this world to do. Of that, there can be no doubt.

When a clear sign comes from Heaven, it helps to reaffirm our faith that Hashem is running the world. Our task is to see Hashem's messages in the small, less dramatic signs he sends us every day, and understand that there is a Creator who guides and helps us, and treats us as His beloved children.

The Real Deal

It was the screaming that attracted Mrs. Gordon's attention. As a mother of three, she had become an expert at interpreting screams, and this one meant that Jerry was fighting with his little sisters.

She dashed into the family room to intercede. It was a spacious, well-furnished room perfectly arranged for the children and their abundant toys. Like all the families in their Hollywood,

California neighborhood, the Gordons lived a comfortable, upper-class life. And like all families, rich or poor, this one had its share of sibling squabbles.

"This has to stop right now!" she said firmly. "Jerry, leave your sisters alone! If you can't play near them in peace, go find another place to play."

Suddenly, the wounded wails of the 8-year-old twin girls came to a halt. They tried not to look too smug as they quickly glanced at each other, exchanging nearly imperceptible looks of triumph.

Jerry felt the anger of unjust blame welling up inside him. His sisters knew just how to provoke him, just how to drive him crazy until all he could do was blow up at them.

"It's not my fault, Mom!" he shouted in frustration. His sweet face was now a portrait of anger, his eyebrows pressed down low and his lower lip jutting out in a classic pout. He was trying not to cry, but there seemed no other way to release the fury inside.

"Jerry, I know it takes two to fight. But someone has to be more mature, and that is you, because you are 10 and they are 8," his mother said more calmly, now that the decibel level had returned to normal.

"That's just not fair! That means that no matter what happens, it's my fault. It's not fair! Not fair!" With tears streaming down his hot red cheeks, he stomped up the stairs to his room and threw himself on his bed. He cried bitterly into his pillow until finally, somehow, he was done. Now Jerry just lay there, staring up at the blue sky framed by his window, thinking.

There has to be some way out of this, he told himself. *If only I had someone on my side, it would be different. If I had a brother, it would be two against two, and at least we'd have a chance.*

A brother. The idea gave Jerry's heart a surge of hope, and his eyes welled up again, this time with longing. He sat up straight on his bed, squeezed his eyes shut and did the only thing he could to set the "brother solution" in motion.

"G-d, I know You can hear me. My name is Jerry Gordon, and my whole life is ruined because I have so much trouble with my sisters. I know that if You would give me a brother, everything would be better. I promise that if You grant me my wish, I will try my best to be a good Jew."

The term "good Jew" was not one that Jerry could clearly define. His parents took him to shul on Rosh Hashanah and Yom Kippur, and his mother lit candles on Friday night, but aside from that, he had no idea what being a good Jew entailed. It seemed to him, however, that this promise would be something G-d would consider worthwhile.

With his burden now cast upon Hashem's shoulders, Jerry felt lighter. He got ready for bed and then, clean and calm, he began to drift off to sleep. But a new thought arose to trouble him. Even if his mother were to have another baby, and even if that baby were to be a boy, how would he know that it was his answer from G-d? He sat back up and added a postscript to his previous prayer.

"Please, G-d, I need you to give me a sign. If my baby brother is born on my birthday, then I'll know that he is a gift from You to me."

By the next morning, Jerry had all but forgotten his conversation with G-d the night before. For the next few months, life went on as usual, with the twins being adorably annoying and Jerry trying hard to keep his cool.

One day, the family was traveling together on a train. His mother and father, who always seemed so happy together, looked especially pleased and content, as if this day were a special celebration. He saw his father whisper into his mother's ear, and then, Mrs. Gordon nodded.

"Children," she announced. "I have good news to tell you. We're going to have a new baby in the family."

The girls were giddy with excitement, clapping each other's hands and hugging. Jerry just sat still for a few minutes, wearing an expression of stunned awe. A great smile spread across his face as he told his parents about his deal with G-d.

"The baby is going to be a boy, and he's going to be born right on my birthday. You'll see!" he proclaimed with complete certainty.

The Gordon parents did not try to disabuse Jerry of this notion. His faith was sweet and pure, and they did not want to tarnish it. Reality would probably do the job for them, they reasoned, so why argue with him now? When they spoke of the baby in front of Jerry, it was always "he." When they discussed possible names, they were always male names. They couldn't discount Jerry's claim altogether, because oddly enough, Mrs. Gordon's due date was around the time of Jerry's birthday. Time would tell.

One day, Jerry arrived home from school to find that his mother was not yet home. With just two weeks to go until her due date, she seemed to always be going to the doctor for a checkup. A short while later, the car door slammed in the driveway. Jerry looked out the window and watched his mother struggling to get out of the car, making a face that he knew must have been accompanied by a loud sigh of exertion. But when she walked into the house, she was full of smiles and energy. The children all hugged and kissed her, for she seemed almost magical these days, like a princess who held magnificent secret powers.

Later that evening, the Gordon parents sat in the living room engrossed in a serious discussion. Apparently, the doctor had told Mrs. Gordon that he would be going out of town shortly, and would not be there for her due date. If she would agree to his plan, he would deliver the baby. Otherwise, she would have to find another doctor. Unwilling to switch doctors at this late date — just two weeks before her anticipated delivery — she opted to have her baby earlier.

On April 4, two days before Jerry's birthday, a healthy baby boy was born to the Gordon family. Jerry saw this as a complete victory, for he reasoned that if his mother had not been induced, she would surely have given birth on his birthday, April 6. G-d had kept His part of the bargain, and Jerry was determined to make good on his promise.

But how? Jerry did not attend any Jewish education classes. He knew nothing about the concept of mitzvos, let alone what they were and how they were correctly performed. The promise remained more of a plan than an actuality for the next few years.

Then, as Jerry approached bar-mitzvah age, things changed. Other boys in his class — all from affluent Hollywood families — were throwing lavish bar-mitzvah bashes complete with big dance bands, infinite mounds of food, outlandish themes and massive expenditures on custom-made clothes and top-notch photography. Jerry wanted a bar-mitzvah too.

Of course, being somewhat traditional, Jerry's parents agreed that he should certainly celebrate his bar mitzvah. But wisely, before they booked a caterer and a band, they booked a rabbi to teach Jerry his *haftarah* and a little about Judaism. This rabbi had one prerequisite for accepting a student; the boy would have to study several books the rabbi would give him and then take a test. Through this means, the rabbi was assured that the boys would have at least one opportunity in their lives to absorb basic information about Judaism.

For Jerry, this was a long-awaited opportunity to start making good on his promise to G-d. The boy's *neshamah* was open, and the information he read in the rabbi's books sank right in. He delighted in discovering that Judaism was the root of so many ideas upon which civilization rested. "Love your neighbor as yourself" came from the Torah, not the Greeks or Shakespeare, as he had assumed. Roman law and later, English law, was based on the Talmudic system, he was amazed to learn. The Ten Commandments were actually given to Moses and the Jews on Mount Sinai. They belonged to a distinct time and place in history, not the distant mists of legend.

Jerry's bar mitzvah came and went, but his lessons continued. When all the other boys in his bar-mitzvah class had gone on to other hobbies, Jerry kept learning. He would ride his bike every Thursday night to the rabbi's house, even in the cold and rain, because learning with the rabbi was the highlight of his week. Gradually, he began to live what he learned. He began putting on *tefillin* every morning. He started walking to shul — a full five miles — every Shabbos.

The rabbi, although thrilled and touched by the enthusiasm of his young student, couldn't help but wonder. Religious devotion was not common in his congregation, which was comprised large- ly of film-industry millionaires who were firmly entwined with the very icon of the secular world. *What made this boy tick*, the rabbi wondered. *Why, two years after his bar mitzvah, was he still interested?* Finally, one day, he asked.

"All the boys had their bar mitzvahs and went on to other things," he said to Jerry. "You come from the same kind of family as they do. You go to the same school as they do. What makes you so motivated to keep learning?"

Jerry told his story. The big climax was the birth of the baby on April 4, just two days before his birthday. He explained to the rabbi that he had given G-d some leeway on the date, since his mother's labor was induced.

The rabbi's eyes were fixed upon this innocent young man, who believed in the power of his pure-hearted prayer and had devoted himself to keeping his promise to G-d. It was amazing — a true, clear case of Hashem's hand operating right here in the open, for all to see. But one thing bothered the rabbi: Hashem doesn't require leeway to make good on a promise. His work is precise.

"Wait a minute, Jerry," said the rabbi. "Do you think if you make a deal with G-d that something is going to happen on a certain date, He is going to use the secular date? Don't you think He'd use the Jewish calendar?"

"I didn't know there was any difference," Jerry replied. "I thought they were just different names for the same months."

"No, Jerry. That's not how it works. The secular calendar oper- ates according to the sun's cycles, and the Jewish calendar is based on the moon. The days are usually entirely different. Tell me, when was your birthday?"

"April 6, 1959."

The rabbi pulled a thick, leather-bound volume from the bookcase. It was 50-year Jewish calendar that correlated the Jewish calendar with the secular calendar. He flipped through the pages searching for Jerry's birth date.

"O.K. That was the second day of Nissan. Now, when was your baby brother born?"

"April 4, 1970."

Feeling certain that he would find clear evidence of Hashem's Divine Providence, the rabbi stood close to Jerry and searched the correct page together with him. Running his finger down the column of dates, he stopped at April 4 and then carefully slid his finger across to the column of Hebrew dates.

"The second of Nissan!" Jerry cried out. Hashem had heeded his request to perfection. He had heard the voice of a 10-year-old boy and designed a perfect answer, giving Jerry not only his longed-for brother, but a road back to his heritage. It was a road he would now travel with more enthusiasm than ever, taking it as far as it would lead him.

So inspired was Jerry by this clear message from the Master of the World that he embarked on a life's mission of sharing his inspiration with others. Today, Rabbi Shmuel Gordon travels far and wide, opening his fellow Jews' eyes and hearts to Hashem and His constant, loving presence in His children's lives.

From the simple request of a young boy to the impassioned plea of an elderly scholar, Hashem is always listening to our voice. He is, was and will always be there for us.

Not
by Chance

Unexpected Guests

A dark, stormy January day became darker still as the hour grew late. The snow outside was heaped against the sidewalks in dirty mountains that the plows had created. Tomorrow, perhaps, the sun would come out and wash the dreary scene of its grayness, setting aglow the fresh snow that frosted the bare branches and rooftops. But for now, there was no sun, and for Merill Felder, the gloom was nearly unbearable.

"I'm coming, and that's that," she had told her daughter Rivkie just a few hours ago. "I am not sitting here all by myself on Shabbos when I have children and grandchildren I can be with."

"But there's a blizzard going on out there, Ma," said Rivkie. "The driving is crazy. What will you do if you get stuck between there and Brooklyn? You can't make Shabbos on the highway!"

"Queens is already plowed," said Merill. "The highway is probably fine. If I can't get through the side streets, I'll park on the avenue and walk a few blocks. I'm not that old and feeble yet, you know."

"Ma, please, just be careful. I don't want anything bad to happen to you."

It had only been a few months since the children had lost their father, Merill acknowledged to herself. It made perfect sense that they would be overprotective of their mother now. But what they didn't realize was that the worst thing that could happen to her, at least from her perspective, was to spend Shabbos alone. She was filled with dread at the thought of sitting at the big, empty table, left with nothing but the memories of her husband, coming home as he had on every Friday night for the past 50 years, and making *Kiddush* in his rich, warm voice.

She remembered the snowy Friday nights when the boys were still living at home. The door would fly open and they would all come tumbling in as if blown by the gusts. Their hats and heavy black coats would be dusted with snow and their shoes caked with ice and mud. They would be in especially high spirits, like an army battalion that had just won a tough battle. Her husband would bask in the warmth and the sweet aromas of the house. "Smells delicious," he would say as he stamped his shoes and carefully removed his waterlogged coat.

Well, she didn't have to sit home and wallow in memories, Merill decided. She had children who loved her, and she was going to spend Shabbos with them. She took her packed bags and trudged out into the snow. The car sat in the driveway encased in a three-inch layer of white. She turned on the motor and started the defroster, hoping the heat would help clear away some of the snow. The rest she pushed away with a long-handled brush. Luckily, it was a powdery snow that flew away in billows as she brushed.

When the car was clean enough to drive, she got behind the wheel and slowly began rolling out of the driveway. A wheel began to spin in place. She pressed down harder on the accelerator, hoping to muscle her way out of the spot. Instead, she dug herself in more deeply. It would take time to get out of the driveway. It would take more time to drive through the clogged streets to Brooklyn. It would take even more time if she were to get stuck again somewhere along the road. She had to admit it. This was not a realistic plan. In her blind desire to avoid Shabbos alone, she had refused to see just how foolhardy a trip this was.

Defeated, she trudged back inside with her neatly packed bags.

"Rivkie, you were right," she told her daughter on the phone. "I can't come. It's ridiculous. I can't even get out of the driveway."

She went next door to her old friend, Leah Richter, and told her about her misadventure.

"So come to us," Leah said. "You know you're always welcome."

"No, no," Merill replied. "I think it's time I just face the situation head on and get over this fear of being alone."

"Well, you don't have food prepared, so take some chicken and soup and fish and a little kugel. And here's a couple of challah rolls. And if you change your mind, just come over. I mean it."

Merill went home with her "care package" and got ready for Shabbos. With only an hour until candle lighting, her sense of dread began to resurface like a sea monster that had been waiting for its opportunity to strike.

Meanwhile, as all this transpired, another story was unfolding in Manhattan. There, Rena Fischer was having a checkup as her husband Yaakov and their 2-year-old son sat in the waiting room, watching the snow pile up on the street five stories below them.

Rena emerged smiling. Everything was fine, and the doctor said that the baby was due any day. The family made their way to the garage where their car was parked, and cautiously drove onto the sloppy, slushy city street. After progressing just a few short yards, they came to a standstill. Up ahead, a car had spun sideways on a patch of ice, and the entire block was now packed with cars that couldn't move forward, backward or anywhere at all.

"What if we don't make it home for Shabbos?" Rena asked Yaakov. "What are we going to do in my condition with a 2-year-old in tow?"

The family lived in Far Rockaway, a section of Queens that, even under normal circumstances, could be an arduous drive. Under these circumstances, the trip seemed impossible.

"Don't worry," her husband answered in his most matter-of-fact voice. "We'll go as far as we can, and if we see we can't go home, we'll figure something out. My guess is that we will make it home."

By the time the car entered the borough of Queens, it was clear that, had Yaakov made a bet, he would have lost. Traffic was moving at a crawl, and there was less than an hour until Shabbos.

"We'll find a shul," suggested Yaakov. "I'm sure someone will take us in for Shabbos."

"I can't!" Rena exclaimed. "What if no one invites us? What am I going to do, sleep on a bench?"

The 2-year-old, sensing the fear in the air, began to cry, adding to the tension in the car.

"No, no, sweetheart. Don't cry. Everything will be all right. Mommy's just tired," Rena said, faking an assurance she did not yet feel. But suddenly, from the lull in her panic, an idea emerged.

"Wait, Yaakov, here's something that might work out. Remember my friend Toby Felder? Her mother's known me for years, and she lives somewhere around here. Maybe I can call her and see if we can stay there. All her kids have moved out and she lost her husband just a few months ago, so I'll bet she'll be glad of the company."

At the Felder house, Merill sat holding her husband's *becher*, daydreaming about times gone by. Her eyes were moist with tears as she turned to the clock and noted that in just a half-hour, it would be Shabbos. Never had she felt anything but joyful anticipation of the moment she would light the candles. But this evening, she felt a stark fear.

The phone rang, distracting her from her thoughts.

"Mrs. Felder?"

"Yes, who is this?"

"This is Rena Fischer, you know, Toby's friend. How are you?"

"*Baruch Hashem*, Rena, how are you and your family?"

"*Baruch Hashem*. Mrs. Felder, I know this is very last minute, but we are stuck in Queens on our way home to Far Rockaway, and Shabbos is in just twenty minutes. I was wondering if it would be possible for us to stay with you for Shabbos."

"Rena, this is a miracle. Do you know that I have not been home for one Shabbos since my husband passed away? I'm only home now because I couldn't get my car out of the driveway, even though I tried desperately. I was just sitting here wondering how I would get through the night alone. I am thrilled that you called!"

The Fishers parked their car where they were and walked to the Felder house, since they had no way of gauging whether they would make it in time. Yaakov carried his son on his shoulders as they trudged nearly a mile through the cold, icy streets.

As the door flew open and they tumbled in, as if blown by the gusts, Mrs. Felder's heart was warmed by a sudden surge of happiness. "You're here! I was so worried," she told them. Then she ran to her bedroom and found dry clothes for them to wear.

There was still time for Mrs. Felder to make one more trip to her next-door neighbor.

"I need a little more food, if you don't mind," she told Leah Richter happily. "I've got a houseful!"

A day that seemed to promise nothing but disappointment and challenge was transformed into a day of comfort, caring and giving, all carefully orchestrated by the One Above.

The Master Plan

W as it the excitement of moving back into the newly renovated house? Was it some leftover fumes from the paint and polyurethane? Mrs. Straus was feeling a growing, queasy discomfort deep inside. She sat heavily down upon the slip-covered couch and raised her feet upon the ottoman.

"Are you all right?" her husband Yossi asked.

The six Straus children ran noisily from room to room examining their "new" old house, marveling at its clean surfaces and expansive kitchen. The youngest scrambled onto the couch beside his mother, seeking a familiar anchor in this strange setting.

Mrs. Straus looked at her watch. She had been resting for 20 minutes, and the uncomfortable sensation was not subsiding. Rather, it was intensifying. Her weak attempt at denial couldn't change the facts. As much as she had wished to be home to settle the children into the house and prepare for the Yom Tov of Succos that was only three days away, she would have to take care of another priority first — giving birth to her seventh child.

"I think it's time," she told her husband. And with that, the Strauses snapped into action.

Yossi and his wife quickly gathered the items needed for the hospital, called a friend to keep an eye on the children, kissed the children goodbye and were on their way. It was a routine they knew quite well, and even though each birth had its unique circumstances, the couple entered the hospital with the sense of calm conferred by experience. Several hours later, they were holding their new son in their arms.

After a few "get acquainted" moments with the baby, Mrs. Straus turned her son over to the nurses who whisked him away for the mysterious procedures parents never see. All they know is that, sometime later, the baby will return, clean, calm and wrapped tightly in a soft flannel receiving blanket.

With every last drop of energy spent, Mrs. Straus lay motionless on the hospital bed. Her husband sat off to the side saying *Tehillim*. The sweet silence was broken a moment later by the hurried entrance of a slim, dark-haired doctor, someone they had not met before. His heavy brows and dark eyes looked as though they could only express one emotion — sadness. That was indeed the emotion they conveyed now as he introduced himself to the couple.

Neither Yossi nor his wife absorbed much of what the doctor had to say. Their minds were stalled on the first few words: "Something wrong .... testing .... confirmation ...." Finally, his somber voice asked them, "Do you have any questions?" They silently shook their heads and watched him leave the room.

"Yossi, they don't know anything for sure. Maybe it's all a mistake," Mrs. Straus said, speaking to her husband and pleading with Hashem at the same time.

"You're right," he concurred with far more confidence than he felt. "Let's just *daven* and hope for the best. Right now, you need some rest and so do I."

The next day, he returned early in the morning to the hospital, where he and his wife heard their fears confirmed with just two words: "Down syndrome."

It was unthinkable. Mrs. Straus's mind raced in a dozen different directions — the baby, the other children, the time, energy and expenses such a diagnosis represented. A world of therapists and shadows and special schools. Life as they knew it was over. She was frightened for herself and her family, but most of all, she was overcome with sadness at the pain and challenges this little baby would face throughout the life that lay ahead of him.

Yossi's heart twisted as he watched his wife battle the emotions inside her. "It will be all right," he told her. "Hashem will help us. We're not alone. You'll see. Right now it's a shock, but we will get over that part, and we will be able to deal with this."

He drove home alone, repeating to himself the same speech he had given his wife. He knew it was true — Hashem would help them cope. But the news was a deep, raw wound that hurt terribly. Knowing that it would eventually heal did not stop the pain.

When Yossi returned to the hospital on Thursday, the same joyless doctor who had broken the news to them the day before arrived at Mrs. Straus's door for another consultation. He invited

Yossi to sit down, pulled up a chair and informed the couple that their child had yet another problem. There was a hole in his heart that would have to be repaired surgically some time in the not-too-distant future.

For the immediate future, however, this new development had to be filed away in the Strauses' minds. Succos was to begin the next night, and Yossi had no succah, no *arba minim* for himself and his sons, no food for his family and the guests they had invited, and no provisions for the *shalom zachor* that would take place the next night.

Yossi began calling friends and neighbors to solicit help. The kindness and energy that surged toward the Straus family in those 24 hours possessed the power of a tidal wave. By Friday night, all was done. After the meal, the streets around Yossi's house filled with streams of neighbors heading to the *shalom zachor*. The throngs that packed the room sang with all their hearts, conveying in the most eloquent way they could that the birth of this son, like every son, was something to celebrate.

The *shalom zachor* left Yossi with two important pieces of information. One was that he had a great many loyal, wonderful friends. The other was that he would need to find a very large succah to accommodate all these friends, who he now realized would surely be there for him at the baby's *bris* during Chol HaMoed.

On the day of the *bris*, the weather was as dramatic as the event itself. High winds shook the trees and sent debris flying across streets and yards. The gusts did not deter the Strauses' friends, however, and just as Yossi had projected, about 250 people filled the catering hall. As he made an eyeball estimate of the *minyan*, he was glad he had gone out of his way to find a facility with a large succah.

When the *davening* and the *bris* were over, however, the size of the succah no longer mattered. The *schach*, like every other structure that was not bolted down that day, had been ripped apart by the winds. The succah was no longer kosher. The many rabbis in attendance conferred, trying to determine if the rough weather exempted the men from eating in the succah. Meanwhile, dozens of helping hands tried to retrieve the *schach* and put in back in its place. The minutes ticked on and, with no solution in sight, the crowd began to disperse.

Yossi's heart sank. *Even this,* he thought, *had to be fraught with difficulty and confusion.* The few moments of pure joy he had hoped to rescue from this heartbreaking crisis had turned into an unfunny comedy, with trays of lox sitting forlorn on the tables as grown men chased after flying bamboo.

After a while, the wind died down and a loyal remnant of about 50 people — close friends and family — found a long table in the corner of the succah that was still sheltered by *schach*. They took their seats and finally began the meal. As people ate, sang, said *divrei Torah* and showered their blessings on the Straus family and the newly named Moshe, Yossi's heart swelled with joy. He was suddenly struck by a revelation.

"After everything I've been through, why did I have to have the additional problem of this weather?" Yossi related to his rav, who was sitting nearby. "This was what was eating at me all morning. But now I see what Hashem was trying to tell me. I expected to have a large *bris* with all of my friends today. It was going to be an amazing event, and instead, everything was flipped upside down and headed for a total disaster. But in the end, everything worked out beautifully. I had the nicest *bris*. I shared it with my closest friends and enjoyed every moment of it.

"Hashem was sending me a message about my little baby. When my wife went to give birth we expected to walk out of that hospital with a healthy baby. But everything turned upside down when we found out that he was a Down syndrome child. My life seemed like it was headed for a total disaster, and the weather today just brought things to a climax. But now I understand that just as the *bris* had a beautiful ending, so too will my new baby bring our family nothing but pure joy. My son is going to teach me that I am not in control, that life is not always the way you expect it to be. He's going to teach me that whatever Hashem gives me is exactly what is supposed to be."

The lesson was a beacon of light that led Yossi through the difficult times ahead. After Succos, Moshe was taken to Cornell Medical Center in Manhattan for a consultation with the head cardiologist, who was an Orthodox Jew. The tiny patient went through four hours of tests and examinations to assess his situation. Yossi and his wife then met with the cardiologist. They listened attentively as he explained Moshe's condition and advised them on the treatment options. Then it was Yossi's turn to speak.

"I'm sure you meet with a lot of people who are facing difficult challenges," Yossi told the doctor. "I want to tell you what happened to me this Succos, so that maybe you could share it with people who need some encouragement." Now the doctor listened attentively as Yossi told his story.

The Strauses left Manhattan in the thick of rush hour. They haltingly made their way down the FDR Drive heading toward the Holland Tunnel, but the entrance was backed up for miles. Yossi tried to find an alternate route around the worst of the traffic jam. Soon he found himself on the wrong side of the highway, stuck in another line of crawling traffic.

"It's going to take us a half-hour just to get ourselves out of this mess!" Yossi complained to his wife.

"Yossi," his wife said softly, "didn't you just tell the doctor all about how we learned that life is not always the way you expect it to be, and we have to adjust to the situation Hashem hands us? Doesn't that hold for the small aggravations as much as the big things?"

The gentle words hit Yossi like a splash of cold water. These small irritations were indeed part of the same principle. Perhaps if a person could learn to accept Hashem's will when he was stuck in a traffic jam or a long line at the supermarket, he could build the spiritual "muscle" he needed to accept the more difficult challenges. Yossi resolved to remember this ride, and practice the lesson it taught him whenever frustrations arose.

The flash of realization was still bright in Yossi's memory a few days later when he met with a business associate named Eddy Gross. As Yossi entered the office, Eddy was just concluding a phone call.

"If that's the way you want to do business, you'll have to do it yourself," Eddy said sharply into the tiny cell phone. "I don't treat my customers that way."

He snapped his phone shut and looked up at Yossi.

"I'm sorry," he said. "This is one guy that just gets my blood pressure up."

"I know what you mean," Yossi said. "But I have to tell you, this little baby of mine is making me take a whole new look at how I deal with frustration. I'll tell you a story ..." Yossi told Eddy about his trip to Cornell and the "inspirational" traffic jam he endured on the way home.

"You're right," Eddy conceded. "And I should know it, too, because I had a very similar lesson in my own life."

Eddy's story also started a few days before Succos. It was then that he received a phone call from a former business partner, informing him that their mutual friend, Simcha Raskin, was critically ill with a brain tumor. Every doctor who had seen him had maintained that the tumor was located in an area that precluded surgery. Simcha had only a few months to live.

"But there is one doctor, Dr. Whitman," Eddy's friend had told him. "He's at Duke University in North Carolina, and he is supposed to have a procedure that can save Simcha. The only problem is, he's booked for months in advance. It's impossible to see him. What we need is some pull. I called you because I remember you used to do business with a factory in North Carolina, and I thought maybe you could call the manager and see if he could help us out."

"I never had that close a relationship with that guy," Eddy had replied. "But there is someone else I did business with about 15 years ago who I think I could call. His name is Richmond. I'm pretty sure he would do me a favor."

He called Walter Richmond Jr. as soon as he hung up.

Eddy's instincts had been on the mark. Richmond told him, "It so happens that my father just donated a few million dollars to Duke. His name is on the building, and he's on the board of directors. I'll ask him if he can help you reach Dr. Whitman."

On Friday, Erev Succos, Eddy received a call from Dr. Whitman himself. Arrangements were made for Simcha to travel to North Carolina and undergo surgery. It was a success, and Simcha was on the road to a full recovery.

"That's an amazing story!" Yossi said. "But tell me something. What made you remember this guy you had done business with 15 years ago?"

"That's the real point of the story," Eddy replied. "Richmond had gone bankrupt and he owed me a fortune. It almost ruined me! I couldn't forget him if I wanted to, and I knew that he would feel obligated to try to help me. I surely didn't have any way of knowing 15 years ago how Richmond's bankruptcy was going to do anyone any good. But if someone had asked me then to give this same amount of money as *tzeddakah* to save Simcha's life, I would have done it in a second."

Eddy's story added another solid pillar to Yossi's unshakeable belief in the existence of a Divine plan. Down on earth, Yossi, his wife, Eddy, Simcha Raskin and millions of other well-meaning people were struggling to meet the challenges Hashem had placed before them. Meanwhile, up in Heaven, the wheels were turning. The road to recovery was being smoothed for Simcha out of paving stones carved out 15 years earlier.

Today, three years after Moshe's birth, Yossi sees that he and his family were launched on a journey that has revealed itself to be an exhilarating climb to a new spiritual peak. The climb is hard, and sometimes they must stop and catch their breath. But they are seeing wondrous vistas along the way. Their six seemingly ordinary children have found in themselves deep wellsprings of selfless love for their brother. The support from friends, family and community has exceeded anything they could have imagined possible. The patience and sensitivity Yossi and his wife have lavished upon each other have greatly enriched their marriage. And their little boy, their Moshe, has proven with each sweet, eager, loving moment of his life that "perfect" is a word only Hashem can define.

"Hashem is righteous in all His ways and benevolent in all His deeds." Whether our challenges are big or small, when we meet them with faith in Hashem's perfection, they pave a path to growth and fulfillment.

Switching Places

Like a strange snowfall, a steady swirl of chicken feathers filled the air and mounded in piles on the ground. Men, women and children grabbed the clucking, scurrying chickens and stashed them securely in packing cases, which were then loaded onto waiting trucks. It was a messy, cacophonous procedure, but at Moshav Mattityahu, it was the climax of the pre-Yom Kippur week. The Jews of Yerushalayim needed their chickens, and this industrious farming community provided a large percentage of them.

After all, chickens were Moshav Mattityahu's business. The *moshav*, under the spiritual leadership of Rav Zev Leff, was a place where the holiness of the Jewish people and the holiness of the land melded into a simple, beautiful way of life. Besides the thousands of chickens raised there, a healthy herd of dairy cattle provided milk, and a lush vineyard produced wine grapes.

Life on the *moshav* was always busy, but on this day in 1990, the activity was something closer to frantic. This was not the routine shipment of chicken for the Shabbos tables of the city. These birds were slated to be used as *kapparos*. This *minhag* involves swinging a chicken over one's head and proclaiming that the chicken is to serve as atonement for the person's sins, and that the person should be blessed with another year of life. The chicken is then ritually slaughtered and donated to a poor family. With Yom Kippur as the looming deadline for the performance of this ritual, every available hand on the *moshav* was busy loading chickens.

Finally, the task was completed. The last crate was loaded onto the truck and the flying feathers settled to the ground. The next morning, the truck rolled down the dusty road leading out of the *moshav* and rumbled out of sight.

A short while later, somewhere on the *moshav*, a telephone rang.

"Listen!" said the breathless voice on the other side. "The truck flipped over! The chickens are everywhere. We need help, fast!"

A massive chicken-rescue unit was hastily organized and dispatched. This was indeed a major emergency, for the community stood to lose a fortune if the chickens did not make it safely to their destination. The *moshav* could not afford to have them killed on the road or lost in the surrounding expanses of land.

A caravan of cars raced to the scene — a most extraordinary scene. Hundreds of chickens darted back and forth crazily across the highway, flapping their wings, clucking and stirring up clouds of feathers. It looked like a successful poultry insurrection, complete with victory dancing and a flurry of feather confetti. But soon, the escapees were being tracked down by the crowd of *moshav* residents who had come to restore order. The men scattered in all directions, capturing the chickens and placing them back in their cases. In a matter of 25 minutes, all the freed chickens had been caught. Then men counted up the survivors that would make the trip to Yerushalayim and discovered that 127 had been killed in the accident. It was a major loss, but certainly nowhere near as bad as it might have been.

Yaakov and Dovid were two of the men who had responded to the emergency, and now, they were riding home together to the *moshav*.

"Don't you wonder why such a weird thing would have happened to us?" Dovid asked his friend.

Yaakov, who was driving, simply shrugged his shoulders. "Things happen. We don't always know why."

"Well, think about this. How many people live on the *moshav*?" Dovid asked.

The two men began a census, thinking about each house and how many people lived it.

"It's just what I thought!" said Dovid excitedly. "There are 127 people on the *moshav*. There were 127 chickens killed in the accident. Perhaps this will be a *kapparah* for each person on the *moshav*!"

When the residents of Moshav Mattityahu gathered to pray on Yom Kippur that year, it was with a special intensity. As they pleaded for forgiveness for their sins, they felt with certainty that their prayers were being accepted. Hashem had shown that He was right there with them. He had demonstrated His forgiveness by arranging their *kapparah*, and now, they knew He would surely accept their *teshuvah* and bless them with the gift of life.

The "hand" of Hashem is the instrument of everything that happens. Sometimes it's hidden, but sometimes, it's gloriously clear.

Returned to Sender

What happens when Hashem sends a message — not one veiled in obscurity, but one that is obvious, that hits you right on the head? Can you choose to close your eyes and ignore it? In this story, we discover what can be lost when the message is sent, but the recipient refuses delivery.

Bluma Rosenfeld stared at the name she had scribbled down. Betty Davis, Los Angeles. Under the name was the woman's phone number. They were complete strangers to each other, but Bluma hoped that, through the link of Partners in Torah, they would become important people in each other's lives. She hoped that, like many other Partners in Torah mentors she had heard about, she would be able to build her and Betty's weekly telephone learning sessions into a real relationship, and perhaps have the privilege of ushering her partner into a meaningful Jewish life.

It was already 11 p.m. in New York, where Bluma lived. She quickly calculated that the time in Los Angeles would be 8 p.m, long enough after dinnertime, yet still early enough in the evening to receive phone calls.

I guess I'd better just call, Bluma thought. She had been holding the phone number for a few weeks already, but she never seemed to find the right time to make the call. The small surge of nervousness she felt as Betty Davis's phone rang brought her to the quick realization that she had been putting this off, after all.

The ringing was interrupted by the mechanical click of Betty's phone being picked up.

"Hello," said a weary woman's voice.

"Hi, Betty?"

"Yes, who's this please?"

"My name is Bluma Rosenfeld. I'm calling you about Partners in Torah," Bluma said in a warm, conversational tone.

"Oh. I didn't think someone would actually call," Betty quickly confessed. She felt like someone who had made a bid on merchandise she had no intention of buying.

"Well, I should have called sooner," Bluma replied. "But I'm here now, so why don't we just get started?"

There was a moment of silence as Betty tried to frame her response in a way that would be honest yet polite, and decisive enough to bring this conversation to a quick, painless conclusion.

"Listen, Bluma, I don't want to waste your time. I really am not into this," Betty finally stated.

"Then why did Partners in Torah give me your name?"

Obviously, this was going to take a little more explanation, Betty realized.

"Well I'll tell you, I had this experience, and I spoke about it with a rabbi and he told me it was a clear case of Divine Providence and that I really should get involved with Partners in Torah. He said when something so incredible happens to a person, she has to respond. The rabbi thought that my learning about Judaism would be the right way to respond."

Now Bluma's curiosity was piqued. Even if this call ultimately went nowhere, she wanted to hear the story.

"Oh, really? What happened, Betty?"

"Well, my mother lived alone in New York. She got sick, so my sister and I decided to bring her to live with us in California. But the move didn't do her any good. In fact, she got much worse and we had to place her in a nursing home. Shortly after that, she passed away.

"I felt we should bury my mother in New York, next to my father. But my sister insisted that we bury her here. I didn't want to fight, so I gave in and we buried my mother in Los Angeles. Just as we were leaving the cemetery, I began telling my sister how guilty I felt about keeping my mother here. She asked me why it was so important to me, and I told her, we should have buried her next to our father. Here she's all alone."

"In the midst of this conversation, a gravestone caught our eyes. It was engraved with the name 'Gerstein,' which is my mother's maiden name. My sister thought this was a sign that we had buried my mother in the right place. But I reminded her that, given her bad relationship with her father, she would not want to be buried with Gersteins. The very next minute, our mouths dropped open. We looked at the next stone, and it said Drebin. That was my mother's mother's maiden name. So she wasn't buried only with Gersteins, she was buried with Drebins, too. I started to feel a little better about what we had done.

"It was after all that that I agreed to get involved with Partners in Torah. But the truth is, Bluma, I'm not interested in any religion. What should I call you, anyway? Bluma or Blumy?

"Some people call me me Blumy and some people call me Bluma. What's the difference?

"Because my Hebrew name is Bluma as well," Betty answered.

"Really! I can't believe that, Betty. And you're still questioning Divine Providence?"

"Well, Bluma isn't my whole name. My whole name is Bluma Golda,"

"That's really incredible! My mother's name is Golda, and I would like you to know that both names are not very common."

"Oh," replied Betty. She would not allow herself to react any further. After all, what's in a name? Plenty of people have the same names.

But if Betty wasn't impressed with the obvious presence of the Divine Hand in their meeting, Bluma surely was. She felt driven to persist at least a little longer, to see if she could overcome Betty's resistance and open her ears to Hashem's clear call.

"Isn't it amazing, Betty, that Divine Providence was the whole motivation for us getting together? And now we're seeing that in so many ways, we were connected to each other before we even knew it. Isn't it weird?"

"Whatever," Betty responded. But Bluma noted that even in that resigned reply, she seemed a little less resistant.

She dared to try again. "Well, it seems to me that we ought to at least give this a try," she offered. "We can study whatever you want."

"I don't enjoy learning books," Betty informed her.

"Fine, so we'll discuss whatever issues you pick, or maybe we can just go over the Torah portion for each week. There's lots of interesting stuff in there."

"Listen, if you don't mind my attitude, which I admit is kind of negative, I'm willing to give it a try. Give me a call next week."

Bluma felt like she had closed the deal of a lifetime. Surely, as soon as she and Betty would start to learn together and Betty would begin to see the depth and wisdom of Torah, she'd be hooked.

"Take my number," said Bluma. "That way you can give me a call if you want."

"No offense, but don't bother. I'm not going to call," was Betty's dry response. She had already gone further than she wanted, and she certainly did not want to make this bond one notch tighter than it now was. But Bluma insisted once more, arguing that there was no harm in just writing it down, so Betty took the number and tucked it into her personal phone book.

During the next two weeks. Bluma dialed Betty's number several times, but no one answered. It seemed as if the entire family had left town. No answering machine, no forwarding number, just a long series of lonely rings. Bluma felt like reaching out with her hands across the continent and pulling this woman toward her. *Well, she's an adult and she's entitled to make her own decision,* Bluma finally resolved. *But what a waste!*

During the following week, Bluma traveled to Palm Springs, California, on a brief vacation. She left a friend minding her house while she was gone, and checked in occasionally to catch up on phone calls and mail. On one such check-in, her friend gave her the incredible news that Betty Davis had called.

Bluma hung up quickly and dialed Betty's number. A man answered, apparently Betty's husband.

"Hi," Bluma said. "This is Bluma Rosenfeld, you wife's study partner from Partners in Torah."

The man laughed. "Very funny, Judy," he said. "Stop playing jokes. I'm too busy for this."

"Excuse me?" Bluma replied. "My name is not Judy, it's Bluma Rosenfeld and I'm not joking. I'm here in California, and I am really your wife's learning partner."

"What?" the husband sounded sincerely puzzled. "She never told me anything about this." It seemed to Bluma as if he felt he had stumbled upon a dark secret.

"Well, all right," said Bluma. "But why did you call me Judy?"

"Oh, Judy is my sister," he said. "I thought she was playing some kind of joke on me, because Bluma Rosenfeld is my wife's maiden name. I guess I was just confused."

"Her maiden name is the same as my name?" Bluma repeated in disbelief. "Are you serious? This is simply unbelievable!"

The conversation ended with both parties somewhat dumbfounded. To Bluma, the situation was an express mail certified letter, signed and sealed by Hashem and delivered into Betty Davis's hand. But as she found out a few days later when Betty called her back, to Betty it was nothing more than an amusing story.

"Sorry for the confusion with my husband," she said laughingly. "It was kind of hysterical, wasn't it? Well anyway, I know you have been trying to call me and I was not trying to avoid you. I just wasn't home much. But I don't want to go any further with this, really, Bluma. It's just not for me."

Bluma couldn't believe that this was the entire substance of Betty's reaction to what must have seemed to her to be at least an incredible coincidence. "What's really going on, Betty?" she asked. "Why didn't you tell me we had the same name? Didn't that strike you as something remarkable?"

"I'll tell you," Betty replied quietly. "This whole thing is just kind of scary. It's all too weird and I don't want to know any more about it."

At last, Bluma understood what was behind the reluctance, the seeming apathy and casualness that Betty exhibited throughout the entire episode. The confused woman could feel Hashem's eyes, so to speak, upon her, and rather than trying to show Him her best effort, she was trying to hide.

"None of this is weird," Bluma said matter-of-factly. "It's the way the world operates, only we don't usually get to see it this clearly. This is what we call Divine Providence, and it runs everything.

"But you don't have to be afraid of where this will take you, because I'm not here to make you change your life. Let's just talk about the things that matter to us. Isn't there something in your life that that you might be interested in exploring from a different perspective? Even if you're perfectly happy and everything in your life is perfect, aren't there some questions you have? I can tell you that I know many people who have learned more about Judaism and discovered that life has a lot more to offer than they thought. I'll even give you my guarantee that if we touch on a topic that makes you nervous, we'll drop it."

Betty went from casual to cold. She cut off the conversation as politely as possible and Bluma's plea went unheeded. But like any good salesperson, Bluma didn't give up right away. She called back regularly over the course of the next few weeks, but no one picked up the phone. Finally, Bluma made the next logical move.

"I'm sorry," she told her contact at Partners in Torah, 'but it's not working out with Betty Davis. She really is not interested."

While Bluma would have loved for her story to have one of those happy, miraculous *kiruv*-story endings, it was not meant to be that way. However, as a teacher, she began to see in this epi-sode an essential life's lesson for her students. For after all, it's not only the nonreligious Jew who may fail to hear Hashem's call; it's everyone at his or her own level.

"It can be clear as day to the people around you," Bluma tells her students. "But you don't see it, you don't hear it, because you re-fuse to do so. We have to keep the channels open so that when the message is delivered, we can receive it and discover the next step in spiritual growth that Hashem has laid out in front of us. Otherwise, we might just pass it by, and who can tell what we will be missing?"

Those who seek meaning in the events they witness, the words they hear and the people they encounter in their lives are able to discern Hashem's messages.

No Coincidence

"The *sefer*! Of all things to forget!" Rabbi Levy derided himself. Sitting on the runway, secure in his seat belt, he could do nothing about it. He was on his way to Israel to officiate at his former student's wedding, and now he was without the volume he always relied upon for clarifica-tion of the relevant laws.

Oh, well, he thought. *It's not so terrible. The wedding is in Bnei Brak, after all. Certainly there are sefarim stores there. I'll just have to buy another copy.*

What he would not consider, however, was performing the wedding without the help of the *sefer*. It was a complete compilation of the laws and customs regarding the *kesubah* (marriage contract). It even included all the correct spellings of towns and cities, an invaluable aid to correctly completing this essential paperwork. The *sefer's* author, Rabbi Eliezer Stern, was a great Torah scholar and a well-known authority on this particular subject.

The nagging feeling of having forgotten something important began to subside, and Rabbi Levy was able to relax during the long trip. When he arrived in Israel, however, he noticed that the flight had run late. There would be no time to stop at a *sefarim* store before the wedding. He hoped that there would be, among the *rabbanim* present at the wedding, someone he could consult if questions arose.

As he drove to Bnei Brak in a rental car, his mind kept returning to the *sefer*. He pictured it on the kitchen table, where he had purposefully placed it to make sure it would not be forgotten. His wallet and keys had been right beside it, and yet, this one item had become invisible to his eyes. He felt a sense of emptiness, like a person who grasps at something that is suddenly pulled away.

Arriving in the city of Bnei Brak, Rabbi Levy's attention switched decisively to the road. He did not know where he was, nor how to get to the hall. Like a creature caught in a maze, he was turning corners blindly on the hope that they would lead him where he needed to be. As he navigated the narrow, winding streets, he noticed a venerable-looking rabbi standing on a corner with his hand out, apparently trying to catch a ride.

Perfect, thought Rabbi Levy. *I'll give the man a ride, and maybe he can give me directions to the hall.*

He pulled up and opened the door.

"I only need to go a few blocks," the man told him.

"No problem," said Rabbi Levy. "Tell me, do you know where the Ohr Simcha hall is?"

"Certainly," replied the man, and he provided the directions.

Rabbi Levy introduced himself to his passenger.

"*Shalom aleichem*," replied the passenger. "I'm Eliezer Stern."

"Are you by any chance related to the Rabbi Stern who wrote a *sefer* on the laws of *kesubah*?"

"I am the one who wrote that *sefer*. Why, have you seen it?"

Rabbi Levy could not contain the delight that was filling his heart to bursting. Look at what Hashem had arranged!

"Well, I have certainly seen it. In fact, I rely upon it whenever I officiate at a wedding, and this time, I left America without it. I was so disturbed about forgetting the *sefer* that it's all I've been thinking about since I landed. And now, here you are in my car!"

"Unbelievable!" Rabbi Stern exclaimed. "And you should know that I almost never take a ride home from shul. It's just a few blocks to my house, but for some reason, tonight I stuck my hand out to get a ride."

Rabbi Levy asked Rabbi Stern his questions and entered the wedding hall well prepared to handle any situation that might arise. Every wedding is a testimony to the Divine Genius who runs the world, but on that night, Hashem's perfection was as clear as the stars in the sky.

The chances of Rabbi Levy meeting Rabbi Stern at that precise moment were probably one in a billion. From the miraculous events to seemingly simple occurrences, one comes to recognize that there is no such thing as coincidence.

Lost and Found

The bright morning sun lit up the Brooklyn side streets, making each small patch of grass glow like a bed of emeralds. As Meir Simcha Breuer sped along a winding route on his bike, legs pumping hard and cool air slapping against his face, he felt energized. Today was going to be a great day at yeshivah; he just knew it.

He came to a halt in the yeshivah parking lot, a few feet away from the bike rack. Quickly, he chained his bike alongside the others and reached into the basket for his belongings.

Suddenly, his easy smile disappeared, replaced by a look of panic. "Where are my *tefillin*?" he asked out loud.

"Maybe you left them at home," suggested a friend who was standing nearby.

"No way," Meir Simcha responded. "I remember putting them in the basket. They must have fallen out somewhere on the road! How am I going too ever find them?"

The terrible sense of loss stayed with Meir Simcha the entire day. *If only my tefillin would just somehow show up,* he thought to himself. He looked in places he knew they could not be, hoping for a miracle. He organized a search party among those who lived along his bike route, asking them to look for the precious velvet sack on their way home.

Then he faced the worst part of the ordeal — telling his parents. How would they react to the loss of this expensive item that they had given him with so much love? When Meir Simcha arrived home that evening, his mother instantly knew that something was wrong.

Her son dolefully explained the situation. When his father arrived home, the family organized an all-out search strategy. Over the course of the next few days, Rabbi Pinchas Breuer called stores and shops along the route where the *tefillin* might have been turned in. Meir Simcha and his father hung signs in shuls and yeshivos. They even placed an ad in the newspaper. Every time the phone rang, Meir Simcha imagined the voice on the other saying, "I'm calling about the lost *tefillin*." But those longed-for words never came, and his heart sank anew with every disappointment. Weeks passed, and the *tefillin* were not found. Meanwhile, Rabbi Breuer had procured a replacement pair from the *sofer* (scribe).

But where were the *tefillin*? They had to be somewhere, and they were. The same day they fell from Meir Simcha's bike basket, Yelena Markowitz had set out on a grocery-shopping trip. The elderly woman walked slowly, relying on her shopping cart for extra support. As she made her cautious, steady way down the street, she noticed a black velvet bag lying in the gutter, its gold embroidery catching the sunlight. Bending down gingerly, the short, heavy woman picked up the bag, examined it curiously and tossed it into her cart. A Russian immigrant who had grown up without any connection to Judaism, Mrs. Markowitz had no idea what she was holding. She only knew that it was probably something important. *It looks expensive,* she thought to herself. *Maybe I can find out who lost it.*

She went about her errands, piling bags of produce, milk, cheese and meat into the cart, all the while being careful to keep the velvet bag on top of it all, lest whatever was in it would be crushed. At home, she unloaded the contents of her cart onto the kitchen table and put the perishable items away. Then she felt free to indulge her curiosity. She unzipped the bag and drew out what looked like small boxes, bound up in glossy leather straps. From the Hebrew lettering on the front, she knew these must be some kind of religious item, but she had never seen such a thing before.

However, she did know someone who would be able to identify it: her 10-year-old grandson Yuri, who attended Yeshiva Ateres Yisroel. She called him right away.

"Yuri, I want you to bring this to your yeshivah tomorow and give it to your rebbi," she said. "Maybe he'll know what to do with it." Yuri got the *tefillin* from his grandmother and brought them to his rebbi, Rabbi Geller, the next day.

Looking quickly at the bag, the rebbi noticed the owner's first name embroidered across the front. But there was no last name. This would take a little investigation, but at that moment, with 25 boys waiting attentively for class to begin, there was no time for further research. Rabbi Geller gently placed the *tefillin* in his desk drawer, promising himself to follow up on finding the owner as soon as he had the opportunity.

Within seconds, thoughts of the *tefillin* dissipated as the demands of the classroom overtook the rebbi's mind. By the end of the day, Rabbi Geller had forgotten all about the lost, and surely missed, item in his desk drawer. While Meir Simcha's and his family's hopes faded, the *tefillin* sat untouched, unharmed, but unclaimed, only a few miles away.

It was a few weeks later when the subject of *tefillin* reasserted itself, as if the sacred, forlorn boxes were trying to communicate from their spot in the drawer. Rabbi Geller had planned a lesson on the subject, and for his class of Russian Jewish children, a great deal of explanation was necessary. Most of them were growing up in irreligious homes, and few of them had ever seen a pair of *tefillin*.

"Boys, in a few years you are all going to get your own pair of *tefillin* for your bar mitzvah," he explained. Then he tried to describe them and how they are used. He spoke with love and enthusiasm about the mitzvah. "They are beautiful black boxes that contain portions of our holy Torah, and by placing one on your arm and the other on your head you are adding great holiness to your body,"

But it was so hard to convey the message to the boys in words alone. *If only I had remembered to bring my own pair today to show the boys,* he thought to himself. Then he remembered the desk drawer. He opened it up and there, just as he had placed it, lay the *tefillin* bag.

He removed it carefully and took out the *tefillin*, unraveling the straps and holding the boxes high for the class to see.

The students' eyes were riveted to the shiny black boxes with their long, ribbon-like straps. They were an exotic item to those who had never seen them, and even more thrilling to those who understood what they were. The boys begged their rebbi to let them touch the *tefillin* and try them on for size.

"I'm sorry, boys," Rabbi Geller said. "I can't let you handle them. They're not mine. Someone lost them and I have to find the owner." As he returned the boxes to their cases, he noticed that one case bore a sticker from the *sofer* who had last checked the scrolls inside. A clue! He would not forget the *tefillin* this time. He would call the *sofer* as soon as he finished class.

"I have a pair of *tefillin* here with the name Meir Simcha on the bag," Rabbi Geller told the *sofer*. "Do you know anyone by that name who had his *tefillin* checked by you last May?"

"I sure do," the *sofer* responded excitedly. "He came here just a few weeks ago for a pair of replacement *tefillin*. His name is Meir Simcha Breuer, and his family will be thrilled that his *tefillin* were found!"

Rabbi Geller, filled with the fluttering excitement of having good news to share, quickly dialed the number the *sofer* had given him.

"Hello. This is Rabbi Geller. I'm calling to let you know that I have your son's *tefillin*."

"What!" Rabbi Breuer exclaimed. "I can't believe it! *Baruch Hashem*! Just tell me where you are and I will come to get them."

"No need to do that," Rabbi Geller answered. "You're on my way home. I'll be happy to drop them off."

When Rabbi Geller arrived at the Breuer's home, he was treated to a royal welcome. Rabbi Breuer took the long-lost package into his hands and looked at it long and hard, as if to assure himself that it was real. Then he placed it on the bookshelf, where Meir Simcha would be sure to see it as soon as he walked in the door.

Mrs. Breuer dug into her purse and pulled out her wallet. As she opened it up and thumbed through the cash inside, she told Rabbi Geller, "Wait, please. I want to give you something as a reward."

Rabbi Geller jumped back toward the door as if he were trying to escape capture. "No, no, please!" he answered. "I'm just doing the mitzvah of *hashavas aveidah* (returning a lost object)."

"We absolutely must do something for you to thank you," said Mrs. Breuer. "I know. My husband is a Rav and he is often invited to speak at different yeshivos. How about if he comes to talk to your class?"

Rabbi Geller agreed, and a few days later, Rabbi Breuer arrived to address the fifth-grade class. The story of his son's lost and found *tefillin* made a perfect lesson in *hashgachah pratis* — Divine intervention. He knew how to engage the boys' attention, conveying with his expression and tone of voice the full drama of Meir Simcha's loss, the agonizing search and the thrilling return of the *tefillin* — the very same ones they had seen days ealier. "And so you see, boys," he concluded, "no matter what you lose, Hashem will arrange it so that somehow, some way, it will return to you."

Rabbi Breuer noticed a skinny arm raised in the back of the class, with the hand waving frantically for attention.

"Do you have a question?" Rabbi Breuer asked.

"Yes, Rebbe," the boy answered quietly. "What happens if you lose your *neshamah?* Will Hashem also arrange to return it to you?"

The question pierced Rabbi Breuer's heart with its innocence and profundity. He smiled, looking directly at the little boy, who gazed directly back at him. "Just like the *tefillin*, your *neshamah* will never be lost for good," he stated assuredly. "A *Yid* can never lose his *neshamah*. It may be hidden at times, but it is never really lost, and just as the *tefillin* came back, so will the *neshamah* return to a person."

The sweetness of this interchange lingered in Rabbi Breuer's mind. A few days later, when he shared a ride with Rabbi Abraham Levy, the Rav of another Brooklyn shul, Rabbi Breuer was eager to tell his story. He related the entire tale, starting with the lost *tefillin* and ending with the little boy's stirring question.

"That's amazing!" Rabbi Levy responded. Even after he dropped Rabbi Breuer off at his destination, he kept mulling over the details of the story. He kept thinking of the little boy's question: Can you lose your *neshamah*? Sadly, he knew all too many people who believed they had.

An idea flashed in Rabbi Levy's mind. This was *the* speech for the *vort* at which he had been asked to speak that night. The *chassan*, Eli, was a young man who had abandoned his Torah-observant upbringing to try life in the "free world." He had found his way back, and was now embarking on a new epoch, preparing to build his own Jewish home.

That night, Rabbi Levy, who had asked the *chassan's* permission, told the story of the lost and found *tefillin*. "The little boy in Rabbi Geller's class was told that a Jew's *neshamah* will always come back," he concluded. "And tonight we see that our *chassan*, Eli, who had thought that he had lost his *neshamah*, has seen it returned to him, *baruch Hashem.*"

By the time Rabbi Levy had finished, Eli's eyes were overflowing with tears as he thought of his own *neshamah*, like the lost *tefillin*, waiting forlorn and hidden away, until the moment it would be reclaimed. He rose to embrace Rabbi Levy, and then, rather than sitting down again, he announced that he would like to say a few words himself.

Despite the tears that still shone in his eyes, Eli's voice was strong and clear. "After Rabbi Levy's story about the lost *tefillin*, I want to share with you my own *tefillin* story, which brought about my return to Torah."

The hum of conversation died down quickly. Every eye turned toward Eli as he began his story.

"I grew up in Brooklyn and attended yeshivah when I was a boy," he began. "But when I was about 15, I started becoming restless and frustrated. I found the wrong crowd to hang out with, and began to spend more and more time on the streets. Over time, I disconnected myself from my family and from Torah, until I was living a life that was totally not religious. Eventually, Brooklyn held no more interest for me, so I decided to go to Israel. Spiritually, it was a disaster. I spent most of my time on the beach and took small jobs to support myself.

"There was only one thing I held onto from my old life, and that was my *tefillin*. I didn't put them on much, but they were always with me wherever I went.

"One time, I was sleeping on the beach, and I had planned to catch a bus at a certain time. It was late, so I just jumped up and ran to the station. I was already on the road when I realized that I had left my *tefillin* on the beach. It was a terrible feeling. I felt like I had lost my last tie with my old life. But my new life kept me busy, and eventually I forgot about the *tefillin*.

"A few years later, I was walking with a friend in Yerushalayim. He wanted to buy a religious item as a gift for someone, so we decided to go to Meah Shearim where there were many Judaica shops. We entered a small, cluttered store that had shelves packed with all kinds of *sefarim*, shofars, *tefillin* and other Jewish objects. Suddenly, out of all the clutter, I noticed a pair of *tefillin* on a shelf that looked very familiar. My heart was beating so loudly that I could hear it. I reached for the *tefillin* bag and saw to my complete disbelief that it had my name on it. I gave it a big kiss. Then I explained to the owner of the store that these were my *tefillin*, which I had lost a few years back.

"I left the store in awe. Although I had thought my *tefillin* were lost forever, they returned to me, they found me. This brought me to the conclusion that Hashem was showing me that if my *tefillin* could come back to me, then my *neshamah*, which had been lost for so many years, could also come back to me — because a Jew can never lose his *neshamah*. That was how I began my journey back to a life of Torah. I returned to the States and eventually found my *kallah*, and together, with Hashem's help, we hope to build a true Torah home."

For one brief moment, the crowd was silent with emotion. Then people began to applaud. The wave of sound rose to a resounding crest and stayed there for a long time.

Eli's wedding day was a few months later. He arrived at Shacharis surrounded by his father and friends, prepared to pray with all his heart for the future upon which he was about to embark. As he entered the shul, he noticed a blind elderly man collecting *tzeddakah* for himself. Though his eyes were protected by sunglasses, the man looked vaguely familiar.

"Do you know that man?" he asked his father. "He looks kind of familiar to me."

His father studied the man's face for a moment.

"I don't believe it!" he replied. "That man was our *sofer* years ago. He's the one who wrote your *tefillin*."

Eli's father approached the man. "You probably don't remember me," he said, "but you wrote my son's *tefillin*. Those *tefillin* have done more for him than you can imagine, and it is partly because of the *tefillin* that he is getting married tonight. I would be honored to have you as a guest at the wedding." He gave the aged *sofer* a large donation and wished him well.

That night, the joy that accompanied the *chassan* and *kallah* into their new life together was unstoppable. The band took a break, but the guests kept dancing to the sound of their own exuberant singing. Eli had never been more certain of the existence of the *neshamah* that soared inside him. It hadn't been lost. It couldn't be lost. It had only been waiting for him to reclaim it.

No matter how far a Jew wanders from Torah, his neshamah cannot be lost to him forever.

Overdue

L ike soldiers breaking formation, the men in the small Brooklyn shul finished Minchah and began wandering away from their seats, gravitating toward friends and drifting out the door. Rabbi Yisroel Brog, who was visiting from Cleveland, spotted an acquaintance heading his way. The man walked with the purposeful stride of a person tending to business.

"Rabbi Brog," said the man, "I'm hoping that maybe you can help my friend over there." With a slight motion of his head, the man indicated a person standing alone at the other end of the shul. Everyone around him had already left, and he stood in his place like a rock that was too heavy for the tide to carry.

"His name is Srully Frankel," the man informed Rabbi Brog. "He's been going through a very hard time trying to get his son into a yeshivah for the coming year. He's applied to three places and none have accepted him. The thing is, he's very down and bitter about the whole situation. I've made calls on his behalf and so have some other people, but so far, nothing has come of it. Could you speak to him and maybe give him a little encouragement?"

"Sure, I'll do what I can," Rabbi Brog replied.

A few moments later, Srully was telling Rabbi Brog his story.

"They're putting us through a wringer," he complained. "The system is unfair. It's all politics and I just don't know what to do for my son."

By now, the two men were alone in the room. Srully's anger made his edgy voice just a little too loud. Rabbi Brog allowed him to continue speaking until he ran out of bile, at which point he stood silently, searching the rabbi's face for a response.

"Srully, do you believe in Hashem?" Rabbi Brog asked him.

"Of course!" Srully answered. To his mind, this situation was not about the unknowable machinations of Heaven. It was about the power-politics of Planet Earth.

"Well then, you know that Hashem runs the world. If your son didn't get into yeshivah, it's because Hashem is trying to send you a message. There's something He wants to tell you, and you have to answer the phone call. Please tell me a little about your life. Maybe if you think about it, you can think of something you're doing that might be causing your problem."

Srully provided Rabbi Brog with an inventory of his life. "I was a full-time *kollel* man until two years ago, when I went to work," he said. "But I still have a *chavrusa* every night, and I go to *minyan* three times a day, and I'm very careful about every single book, tape, magazine — everything — that comes into my home. I'm doing everything I should be doing as far as I know. I can't imagine what could be so wrong that this should happen to me."

As Srully spoke, the situation was becoming clearer to Rabbi Brog. It was as if the morning fog was dissipating from the windshield, little by little revealing the true picture.

"Let me tell you a little story, Srully," said the rabbi.

"Once, I was giving a class to a group of men in the Telshe Yeshivah. I had talked about how Hashem runs the world, and how everything happens for a reason. There was a *kollel* man named Reb Yankel, who had been standing outside the room listening to my lecture. He came over to me and asked me, 'Do you really think everything that happens is from Heaven? Do you think you can figure out the reason for everything that happens?'

"I told Reb Yankel, 'I can't figure out the reason for everything, but there are some things that anyone could figure out.'

"So Reb Yankel asked me to find the reason for something that had happened to him several months earlier. It seems that he had returned on a flight from Eretz Yisrael, and when he went to pick up his luggage, it was nowhere to be found. The airline had lost his luggage, which contained about $3,000 worth of valuables. All the airline gave him in compensation was $500 and an apology.

"I asked him the same thing I asked you. Could he think of anything he might have done that would cause Hashem to let this happen to him? But I knew this young man, and I was pretty sure I knew why he had been forced to take such a loss.

"I asked him if he gave *tzeddakah*. He, of course, said he certainly did, and that he kept it in a certain account. So I asked him if he had distributed anything from this account while he was in Eretz Yisrael. After all, if you have some money put aside to give to the poor, that's the ideal place to give it. There are so many needy people there.

"Well, it so happens that he did not give away a penny in Eretz Yisrael. The money was still sitting safely in his account. I told him to go right away and find out how much was in the account, because he had no idea.

"About 20 minutes later, he returned to me to tell me that there was $2,500 in his *tzeddakah* account. So I said to him, 'Isn't that interesting? You lost a suitcase worth $3,000, and the airline reimbursed you for $500. So you lost exactly $2,500, the same amount you have in your account. Why don't you give that money away and see what happens?

"But he couldn't do it. He felt possessive of the money. I had to push him a little. 'It's not your money,' I told him. 'You have a debt to pay. You have to fulfill your obligation!'

"So he went home and wrote out $2,500 worth of checks to various *tzeddakos*. Two days later, he received a phone call from the airline. They had found his luggage. They told him it was very unusual to find it once so much time had elapsed.

"That night, he called me to tell me the good news. He was still in shock. Meanwhile, he figured that he might as well get some help in solving another riddle in his life. His wife had given him gold cuff links six years earlier, right after they had gotten married. He didn't have them long when one of the cuff links had fallen off somewhere, and it had never been found. So Reb Yankel wanted to know what I thought he should do.

"I told him to find out how much his wife had paid for the cuff links, divide the amount in half and give that amount to *tzeddakah*. That night, he wrote out a check for $300, which was the cost of one cuff link. A few days later, he was in yeshivah when he noticed a sign on the bulletin board looking for the owner of a lost cuff link.

"It probably won't surprise you to find out that it was Reb Yankel's lost cuff link. Apparently, what happened was that it had fallen off while he was walking up the very large hill from the Telshe *Kollel* housing up to the *beis medrash*. On the side of the hill there is some gravel and some grass. A *bachur* had been walking there, kicking the gravel as he walked, and suddenly he noticed that he had kicked up something shiny. It was the cuff link, which had apparently been buried in the gravel for the past six years.

"After all this, Reb Yankel was ready to do anything I asked him. He called me and said, 'Rabbi Brog, just tell me what to do next and I'll do it. If you say jump, I'll jump!'"

By the time Rabbi Brog's story ended, Srully's eyes were wide with wonder; he was a man who had witnessed a revelation.

"Rabbi Brog, that's me! I'm the same way. I have a hard time parting from my money."

"What does your wife think about this?"

"She tells me that I should give, but somehow I just can't make myself do it. I'm afraid to let go of the money."

"Do you have a decent job?" asked Rabbi Brog.

"Yes! *Baruch Hashem*, I have a very good job."

"All right, then," Rabbi Brog said, "let's figure out about how much you should be giving."

The two men sat with pen and paper going through the numbers. Their calculations showed that Srully owed many thousands of dollars in *tzeddakah* for that year.

"Let's go, Srully," said Rabbi Brog. "We are going to remedy this problem today. I want you to go home now and write out checks for what you owe, and send me receipts of the amounts made out."

"It's never going to work," Srully responded. "Because once I leave you, I am never going to send out the checks. You don't know me."

"Fine, so let's go right now to the bank and take out the money while I am with you, and you'll give it immediately to *tzeddakah*," Rabbi Brog replied.

There didn't seem to be any way out. Srully saw the truth, had the opportunity to act upon it and now he had to rise to the challenge.

"O.K.," Srully said. "Let's go."

They traveled together toward the bank, but as they neared their destination, Srully began to feel physically sick. His forehead was shiny with sweat, although he felt cold to the bone. He began to pant, to become dizzy and weak in the knees as if he were walking to his doom, rather than his salvation.

"Rabbi, I just can't do this," he finally said. Rabbi Brog looked at the panicking young man standing next to him and quickly understood that the patient could not stand such a radical treatment. He would have to coax him to take the medicine in smaller doses.

"I'll tell you what," Rabbi Brog said calmly. "Let's do it a little differently. Go home now and write out head checks for the amount you owe that will come due over the course of the next 10 months. You'll send them out to the *tzeddakos* month by month, and hopefully things will turn around for you. Just to make sure you don't back out, we'll have your boss, who spoke to me about you in the first place, take responsibility for making sure the checks are mailed."

Srully agreed.

"But listen," said Rabbi Brog. "This whole problem of being unable to part with money is a problem of *emunah*. If you believe Hashem takes care of everything, you can give your *tzeddakah* with an open hand and know you'll still have what you need. You need to work on your *emunah*, and the source of *emunah* is Shabbos. So I want you to learn a *sefer* on Shabbos at every Shabbos meal this week. You'll see, it will be a Shabbos like you've never had before."

That *Motzaei Shabbos*, Rabbi Brog received a phone call from Srully. He had done exactly as he was instructed. The checks were written out, sealed in envelopes and ready to be mailed at their appointed times. He had learned from the *sefer* the rabbi had recommended, and felt as if he had experienced Shabbos for the first time in his life. The edgy, aggressive voice Rabbi Brog had first heard coming from Srully's lips was now a warm and happy voice. It was as if Srully had been rewired.

The next morning, things got even better. Srully received a call from the yeshivah that had been his first choice, informing him that there would be a place for his son in the incoming class.

A few nights later in Srully's home, there was a special occasion — a *seudas hoda'ah* — a feast of thanksgiving. The guests were all those who had tried to help get Srully's son into yeshivah. He could think of no better way to thank them than to invite them to join him as he thanked Hashem for steering him toward someone who could help open his eyes, and for allowing him to catch a glimpse of the great wheels of Heaven turning the machinery of life.

As he spoke to the friends assembled there, he asked out loud, "How is it possible? How can one go to yeshivah his entire life, serve Hashem in every way he knows how and still not see this basic fact? We blame the school, we blame politics, we blame people. Meanwhile, Hashem is banging us over the head with a message — look into yourself! Until we do that, nothing changes. But as soon as we do it, everything changes."

Emunah needs constant nurturing to stay strong. It is only by working on it every day that we can internalize the fact that nothing happens by chance; for everything there is a plan and a purpose.

Playing by Heart

"And now, presenting the guitar sensation of the decade
.... ERIC MOYAL!" Blinded by the spotlights, Eric
could only hear the roar of the crowd that filled the
stadium. Thousands of frenzied fans swayed at his
feet, primed for the moment they would hear the first electrifying
chord of his performance ....

Some day, it could really happen, thought Eric. He was only
15, but he knew he had what it took to make it big in the music
world.

Eric's high school years passed in a blaze of masterful, intri-
cate riffs that flowed from his guitar. He spent every spare minute
practicing with his band or practicing on his own, perfecting his
technique. The garage of the Moyals' San Diego home became
band headquarters, and the music that emanated from it grew
more polished each day.

It wasn't long before the band emerged from the garage and
began making its mark on the local music scene. First, they played
only at private parties and small events, but their reputation quickly spread. By the time Eric was 20, he had made a name for himself in the music world. He could turn on the radio and hear a cut
from one of his band's CDs. He could open the newspaper and
see an ad for one of their performances.

Ostensibly, he was fulfilling his dream, and yet, he often wondered, where was the exhilaration he had expected to feel? He was
like a mountain climber who had strained for weeks to reach the
summit, only to find that, after the momentary thrill of achieve-
ment had passed, he felt no different than he had felt on the
ground. The only way to keep the adrenalin pumping, Eric found,

was to keep setting his sights higher — bigger crowds, louder cheers, better sales, more money.

One day, a possibility that was even grander than Eric could have envisioned suddenly landed upon his lap. He received a call from I.K.M., a multinational music giant that handled many of the world's megastars. I.K.M. was interested in signing up Eric and his band. The deal required the band to prepare a showcase concert, which would be recorded by I.K.M. and turned into an album. The audience would include many of the biggest names in music. If all went well, Eric and his band would step from that stage directly into a life of boundless wealth and fame. This was the golden ticket — the chance every musician dreams of, and only a chosen few attain.

The band shifted into overdrive, practicing until the early hours of morning and working out new material. Then, giddy with fatigue, they'd kick back and dream about their future: the cars they'd own, the trips they'd take, the expensive gifts they would give their families, the parties they'd throw, the way their old friends would fawn over them. They would savor every imaginary detail, tasting its sweetness over and over again.

Eric fantasized along with them, but he felt that something was missing. It was as if he were talking about someone else's future rather than his own. His mind was busy planning and dreaming, but his heart was just a bored spectator.

Meanwhile, as this drama unfolded in Eric's life, a different plotline was developing in his mother's life. The Moyal family had been fairly traditional in their Jewish observance. In fact, Eric had attended Jewish day school throughout his elementary school years, switching to public school only when he reached high school age. However, the Moyals did not abide by any halachic guidelines. If they went to shul on Shabbos, it was by car. They didn't bring pork or shellfish into their home, but they didn't buy koshered meat or separate meat from milk. Their observances were mostly weak echoes of what might have been practiced in their families two or three generations earlier.

All this began to change one day when Eric's mother found herself sitting in a seminar in Los Angeles, run by a *kiruv* organization called Arachim. There, she heard astounding things about Judaism, things that took it out of the comfortable realm of legend and tradition and transformed it instead into a compelling fact of life. Mrs. Moyal posed every tough question she could think of — questions to which she was sure there were no answers. She not only walked out with answers, but also with an entirely new view of the world and her place in it. After a few months of involvement with Arachim, Mrs. Moyal made a midlife leap into the world of Torah and mitzvos.

It was as if Eric and his mother were two planets on separate orbits that had carried them to the point of greatest possible distance from each other. She was speeding toward holiness and spirituality while he careened at full speed toward the ultimate in worldly pleasure. Mrs. Moyal, however, was first and foremost a mother, and her love for her son was enough to enable her to reach across the distance. Now that she understood what life was about, how could she stand idly by while her cherished child poured his energy into nothingness?

Eric's mother tried to share some of what she had learned with him, but her excitement met with a bewildered shrug. "It sounds great, Mom," he said, as if humoring a child. "But it's not for me."

She knew better than to press the matter. One day, however, she decided to try again. *If only Eric could hear what I heard, he would understand what I am trying to tell him,* she thought.

"Listen, what would it cost you to spend a few hours at one of these seminars?" she suggested. "I'm telling you that at the very least, you'll learn a little something and it will be interesting. I promise you won't be bored for a second. What do you say? For me, would you just give up one day and go?"

Reluctantly, Eric agreed to sacrifice a precious day of rehearsal to attend an Arachim seminar. His mother asked so little of him, and it seemed to mean so much to her. Why not make her happy?

A half-hour into the seminar, Eric was entirely absorbed. The speaker's words were the only reality he perceived, and they penetrated his mind like nothing else he had ever heard. Hashem was not "out there somewhere." He was the Creator and the Architect of everything that happened in life. Serving Him was the only rational way for a Jew to live his life. Eric felt as if someone had suddenly flipped on the light, revealing a path he had been stumbling down in the dark for the previous 20 years.

Life changed. Eric began learning, and the more he learned, the more he became convinced that Torah was the only truth the world had to offer. His lifelong dreams of fame and fortune in the music world began to seem like empty mirages, and he finally understood why they could not fill him.

During the next few weeks, Eric's heart was in turmoil, heaving with confusion as two mighty, opposing tides crashed into each other. Here he was, a rock star making piles of money, but when he would play with his band on a Friday night, the guilt he felt drained every bit of joy out of the experience. How could he walk away from everything for which he had worked? But how could he not walk away? There was only one certainty in his mind; if he did not extricate himself quickly from his old life, he would never be able to do it.

One day, Eric sat in his room thinking about his situation and suffering with the gnawing pain of indecision. Finally, he decided to take some action. He rose to his feet, squeezed his eyes shut and said, "G-d, I don't know what to do with myself. I have invested the last five years of my life in my band. This is my life. What is it that You want from me? Am I just supposed to pick up and go to a yeshivah now and become a religious Jew? Please answer me!"

A sharp thump made his eyes snap open. There on the floor, in front of his bedroom bookcase, was a volume that had fallen off the shelf. As he bent to pick it up, he saw that it was his ArtScroll *Chumash*, which he had received as a bar-mitzvah present. The book had fallen open, and as Eric lifted it from the floor, he discovered that it was turned to his *haftarah*, which was a portion from the prophet *Isaiah* (Chapter 55).

Slowly, Eric began to understand. Perhaps this was the answer from G-d that he had just a moment ago begged to receive. He eagerly sat down with the *sefer* and, for the first time, sought the meaning of the words he had recited so many years ago.

"Everyone who is thirsty, go to the water. Even one with no money, go, buy and eat; go and buy wine and milk without money and without price," the first verse urged. Eric understood instantly. The prophet was speaking to him, sending him to seek out the Torah for which he was thirsty. It was free and available, and his for the taking.

"Why do you weigh out money without getting bread and (exert) your efforts for that which does not satisfy? Listen well to Me and you will eat well, and your soul will delight in rich food." The prophet told of the emptiness with which Eric had suffered for years. The words stirred his heart like a poker in a pile of embers, releasing the smoldering emotions that lay latent inside him. Tears coursed down his face as he internalized the message. The days of his life had been devoted to acquiring "bread" that could never satisfy him. True satisfaction was within reach, and yet he held back his hand.

He continued reading, *"Incline your ear and come to Me; listen and your soul will be rejuvenated. I will make an eternal covenant with you, the enduring kindness (promised to) David."*

This was Hashem's promise, spoken by Isaiah's mouth centuries ago on the other side of the world, and received by Eric right there and then, in a suburban San Diego bedroom. Eric knew that Hashem was directing him to choose a new path for his life. With trembling fingers, he dialed a phone number he had been keeping in his wallet; it was the number of Shofar, a *kiruv* organization in Israel. From there, he received a contact in America, who led him to Rabbi Bachrach, director of a *baal teshuvah* yeshivah in Monsey.

Eric told Rabbi Bachrach his story, and from the warmth and wisdom of the rabbi's questions and comments, it became clear that this was someone to whom Eric wished to draw close.

"Hashem has presented you with a tremendous test," Rabbi Bachrach told Eric. "You know you will not be able to change your life unless you cut off all your ties with your old life. But you have the strength to pass the test. You are welcome to come to my yeshivah and I will help you in any way possible."

"I understand that I have to break away," Eric explained. "But that's just the problem. We're supposed to do a showcase concert for I.K.M. It's not just me. It's the whole band and everything we've been working for for the past six months. If it goes well, we'll be instant stars. What am I supposed to do?"

"Eric, I'm afraid in a situation like this, it's usually now or never," Rabbi Bachrach explained. "If you take this next step, you'll become much more deeply involved in your other life. It will become almost impossible to extricate yourself. But you are right that this isn't just about you. It's about your children and grandchildren and generations you'll never even see. You're creating their future with the decision you make now."

That day, Eric changed his cell phone number and wrote a good-bye letter to his band. "I'm truly very sorry that I have to disappoint you at this critical time in your career. However, my life has taken a very different path, and it is impossible for me to pursue that path while remaining part of the band. I relinquish to you all my rights in the band, our music and contracts."

After mailing the letter, he booked a flight for New York. The next day, Eric began a new life as a student in Rabbi Bachrach's yeshivah. Although Eric changed his name to Ariel, one does not change from rock star to Torah scholar overnight. Ariel faced a difficult adjustment, but with his own valiant effort and Rabbi Bachrach's unwavering support, he succeeded. After a year and a half in Monsey, he boarded a plane to Israel and began the next chapter of his life.

One night, Ariel attended an event hosted by Shofar, and the great Israeli *kiruv* rabbi, Rav Amnon Yitzchak, invited him onto the stage to tell his story. It was a very different kind of performance than he had ever given before, but not even his finest guitar riff could have moved the audience as he did that night. When he finished, Rabbi Yitzchak blessed him that he should soon find his life's partner.

Among the crowd at the Shofar event was a group from a women's *baal teshuvah* seminary. One of those women thought that her friend back at the seminary would make the perfect match for Ariel. She introduced them, and one week later they were engaged. In another two months, the couple was married. Life was busy and sometimes difficult, but never again was it empty.

Today, Ariel studies in Kollel Yoshevet Tzion in Modiin Illit. He has mastered knowledge of all the materials Arachim uses to prove the veracity of the Torah, and uses his knowledge to illuminate the lives of other Jews, just as his life was illuminated for him. But his message is made all the more powerful because he stands as living proof that even someone who "has it all" can only find real joy and contentment in a life of Torah.

Ariel hopes to take his guitar out of retirement some day and produce a CD of Jewish music. He'll once again be able to rouse the hearts of thousands, but this time, he'll be rousing them to reach out to their Father in Heaven.

"Hevel havelim," the pleasures of this world are nothingness, King Solomon says in Sefer Koheles. "The sum of the matter, when all has been considered: Fear G-d and keep his commandments, for that is man's whole duty." The moment a person opens his eyes, this is what he sees, for there is no other truth.

Loving-kindness

The Extra Mile

itting at his father's hospital bed, Rabbi Shlomo Gissinger waited patiently. His father was stirring, showing signs of awakening
from his restless sleep. Perhaps he would wake up feeling stronger. Perhaps today, this lingering illness would finally loosen its
grip and free his father to embark on the road to recovery.

The bustling entrance of a nurse, who was pushing a squeaky-
wheeled medicine cart into the room, roused the patient out of his
last moment of sleep. She pushed past the father and son to the snor-
ing man occupying the bed on the far side of the room. Downstate
Medical Center, a busy urban hospital in a run-down Brooklyn neighborhood, offered little in the way of peace and quiet.

Rabbi Gissinger's father woke up fully. His eyes lost their cloud
of sleepy disorientation and lit up with happiness at the familiar
sight of his son. He cleared his groggy voice as if preparing to
make an important announcement.

"I want you to do something for me," he stated. "I want you to go
to your rebbi, Rav Pam, and ask him to come visit me here. I feel
that if he would come and give me a *berachah,* I would get better."

Rabbi Gissinger had been a *talmid* at Yeshivah Torah Vodaath
for many years, and he had built a close, warm relationship with
Rav Pam, his rebbi and Rosh Yeshivah. Nonetheless, his father's
request would not be simple to fulfill. How could he ask the re-

vered *talmid chacham* to make the arduous trip to the hospital? Rav Pam's days were filled from beginning to end with learning and teaching. His office and his home were both magnets for Jews from all over the world who sought to benefit from just a spark of his wisdom, or to have their worries soothed with the balm of his wise and kindhearted words. A trip to Downstate seemed a terrible imposition.

Perhaps his father would forget about this idea. Rabbi Gissinger began speaking to him about a different subject, and nothing more was said about Rav Pam's visit. That is, until the next day.

"*Nu?* Have you spoken to Rav Pam yet?" his father asked expectantly. "What did he say?"

Clearly, this was a desire that would not soon be forgotten. It was obviously something that had come from deep within his father's heart, and Rabbi Gissinger knew he had no choice but to try to fulfill it.

The next day, upon returning to yeshivah, he found Rav Pam in his office.

The rebbe invited his *talmid* to take a seat and discuss what was on his mind.

"My father is a patient at Downstate Medical Center," Rabbi Gissinger explained. "He asked if it would be possible for Rebbe to come visit him there."

"I would love to visit your father in the hospital," Rav Pam replied. "But I'm sorry to say that I cannot, because I'm a Kohen. [A Kohen is bound by special rules of ritual purity that prohibit him from being in the same building as a dead body.] My own relative called recently and asked me to visit him in the hospital, and I had to say no to him."

But Rav Pam's expression signified that this was not the end of the matter. He gazed down at his desk, as if searching there for an idea.

At last, he looked up at Rabbi Gissinger. "Is there a window in your father's hospital room?" he asked.

"Yes."

"Does your father have the ability to get to the window?"

"I think so."

"Wonderful!" said Rav Pam with the excitement of someone who has just made a remarkable discovery. "I have a plan. At 2 p.m. on Tuesday, bring your father to the window and I will be right outside on the street across from his room. I'll look up at his window and wave to him and give him a *berachah*. That way, I can fulfill your father's request."

That Tuesday, at precisely 2 p.m., Rabbi Gissinger helped his father out of bed and make his way to the window of his hospital room. Standing out on the street, many stories down, was the great Rosh Yeshivah, who was looking directly at the window, waving and smiling and uttering a *berachah* for the patient's recovery. Despite the windowpane and the distance between them, Rabbi Gissinger's father basked in the warmth of Rav Pam's presence.

Rabbi Gissinger testifies that shortly after Rav Pam's visit, his father's condition began to improve. He had finally obtained a healing dose of the only medicine that could really help him.

Rav Pam's love of chesed motivated him to find a way to help, even when he had every justification for denying the request.

First Class

Although he hadn't planned on it, Rabbi Yanofsky was going to France. The one-night stopover was an unavoidable part of the flight that would get him to his real destination — Eretz Yisrael — and he decided that he might as well make the best of it. After all, as principal of Machon Bais Yaakov high school in Boro Park, Brooklyn, he had not exactly led the life of a world traveler. Surely there must be some worthwhile places to visit in France, the rabbi decided. He would simply find someone who knew the country and get some good advice.

Among the thousands of girls who had passed under Rabbi Yanofsky's tutelage over the decades, one suddenly came to mind as he pondered his trip to France. Sarah Gruss,* a student perhaps 20 or more years earlier — when Rabbi Yanofsky was serving as *menahel* in Rebbitzen Vichna Kaplan's Beis Yaakov High School — had been born in France. She had close relatives living there, and often spoke about life in her native country. She had been in touch occasionally over the years, and would surely be eager to offer some guidance.

Rabbi Yanofsky had indeed chosen just the right person. Sarah was honored to have the opportunity to lend her expertise to her former principal. She provided him with a lengthy list of places to visit, both of historic interest and Jewish interest, as well as places to dine and relatives' phone numbers in the event he should be in need of help or hospitality.

Stepping out of the cab at Kennedy Airport in New York, Rabbi Yanofsky was looking forward to his trip. With his expertly planned stopover in France, this trip would be something different. He piled his luggage onto a cart and entered the cavernous, well-polished interior of the departure terminal. Bright sunlight shone through the huge wall of windows, illuminating the throngs of passengers who crisscrossed the hall with the determination of a league of worker ants. Each found the appropriate line in which to wait as the slow wheels of the airport bureaucracy moved them forward toward their gates, their planes, their destinations.

The rabbi looked around him at the great diversity of human beings about to set off for points around the globe. There was a tiny baby, only a few months old, sleeping blissfully in his infant seat. He would awaken perhaps in a different hemisphere, totally unaware that anything had happened. There were business travelers checking their watches and cellphones, families bouncing with excited anticipation, and a group of college students sitting in a corner on the floor. Some were stretched out, napping on pillows of rolled up coats and sweatshirts.

Sooner than he would have imagined, given the length of the line, Rabbi Yanofsky was at the check-in desk, displaying his ticket and watching the clerk tap endlessly on her computer keyboard. It seemed as if she were entering his entire biography into the system. Finally, she looked up pleasantly and said, "Rabbi, your ticket has been upgraded to business class."

"Oh, no," said Rabbi Yanofsky. "That must be a mistake. I didn't purchase a business class ticket. Look, you see, right here on the itinerary it says Economy."

"Yes, I understand," she replied patiently, looking over his shoulder at the long line of waiting passengers. "But someone has paid to upgrade your ticket. Your seat will be in the business section."

"Can you tell me who paid for the upgrade?" the Rabbi asked.

"I'm sorry, but we're not allowed to give out that information. Enjoy your flight," she said, ending the conversation and leaving Rabbi Yanofsky with no other choice than to make way for the next passenger.

Settling into his wide seat, stretching out his legs in the ample space in front of him, and noting the serene quiet that would allow him to learn, rest, maybe even sleep, he silently thanked his anonymous benefactor. He arrived in France feeling like a pampered millionaire, rested, well fed and ready to embark on the itinerary Sarah Gruss had provided.

The scene at the check-in counter repeated itself for the continuation of his trip to Eretz Yisrael, and once again when he checked in for the flight home. At each juncture, he asked the clerk to reveal the name of the person who had provided the upgrade, and finally, as he boarded for his return to New York, the clerk relented.

"A woman named Sarah Gruss paid the difference between coach and business class for you," the rabbi was informed.

The flight home, like the rest of the trip, felt like a pleasurable visit to someone's plush living room. Rabbi Yanofsky completed a pile of administrative work he had brought along, had plenty of time for learning and got a fairly normal night's sleep as well. Only one thing troubled him during the entire trip. Why had Sarah Gruss done this for him?

As soon as he arrived home, he dialed the Gruss home. Sarah's husband answered.

"Hello, this is Rabbi Yanofsky. How are you?"

"*Baruch Hashem*, Rabbi. How was your trip?"

"It was, *baruch Hashem*, a wonderful trip. Is your wife at home?"

"I'm sorry, she's out at the moment. Is there something I can do for you?"

"Well, perhaps you could answer a question for me. Everywhere I went, I discovered that my tickets had been upgraded from coach to business class. Finally, after questioning every clerk I spoke to, I found one who was willing to reveal the name of the individual who paid for the upgrade and, as I'm sure you know, that was your wife. Now, I have to tell you first of all that I am overwhelmngly grateful for the gesture. It really made the traveling so much more enjoyable. But why? Why did you go to this expense?"

Sarah's husband smiled as he listened to the rabbi's bewildered query. Rabbi Yanofsky obviously had no idea what he meant to Sarah and, by extension, to her husband and their family.

"Rabbi Yanofsky, the reason is simple. It's *hakaras hatov* (gratitude) for everything our family owes you. You had an immense impact on my wife when she was your student. For the 25 years that we've been married, whenever she doesn't know how to handle a situation, she asks herself, 'What would Rabbi Yanofsky do?' and whatever that is, she does it. This approach has never failed; it's never steered her in the wrong direction. So when we heard you were flying to Eretz Yisrael, we wanted to find some small way to repay you for everything you've done for our family. This was truly nothing, just a small fraction of what we owe you. I hope you enjoyed your trip!"

Words said or left unsaid. Deeds done or not done. You never know what impression you are making on a student, a friend or a member of your family. You may even serve as an inspiration for that person for years to come, and the gratitude that he feels toward you may linger in his heart forever.

No Laughing Matter

The contented, full feeling of a good Shabbos lunch gave Yecheskel's face a glow. But it was more than the simple, hearty food that drew him to his grandfather's house. It was the wondrous atmosphere that hovered over these family meals. It was his grandfather's wise words, rich with insight and yet clear and direct enough to penetrate his 12-year-old mind. His grandfather, Rabbi Shlomo Halberstam, was the world-renowned Bobover Rebbe who presided over a Friday-night table crowded with hundreds of Chassidim. But on Shabbos afternoon, it was just family, and Yecheskel relished each opportunity to be a part of it.

On this particular Shabbos, Yecheskel had brought along his friend Reuven. On the other side of Yecheskel sat a distant relative named Michoel, an older boy who was visiting from his hometown. Yecheskel wasn't sure where that was, but it seemed as though it must be very far away, for Michoel didn't wear the Chassidic garb of the Brooklyn branch of the family, nor did he pronounce his Hebrew with the Chassidic accent that Yecheskel was accustomed to hearing. With his short suit-jacket, stubby *peyos* and fedora, Michoel was an anomaly at the Rebbe's table. But he was the Rebbe's esteemed guest nonetheless.

Aside from Michoel's unusual presence, the meal had been like all the others Yecheskel had enjoyed at his grandfather's table. He and his friend had listened intently to the Rebbe's tales of *tzaddikim*, many of whom he had known personally. They sang along with the lively Bobover melodies, tapping the beat on the table and letting their voices blend and rise on the waves of joyful sound. Now, after dessert, the Rebbe's unwavering custom was to sing one more song and proceed directly to *Birkas HaMazon*. The boys opened their *bentchers*, ready to start, but the Rebbe departed from his usual agenda.

"Before we *bentch*, boys, I want to tell you an important lesson that I learned from my father," the Rebbe said, looking at his grandson and his friend. "He taught me that even if someone does something that you find very amusing, you have to hold back your laughter so that you don't hurt the other person's feelings."

Yecheskel was puzzled. Why was his grandfather inserting this lesson into the usual order of things? Who was laughing? Who was hurt?

The Rebbe continued. "When I was younger, I was once with my father at a *sheva berachos*, and it was time to *bentch*. There were many great *rabbanim* at the head table. One of them was asked to lead the *bentching* that night. Right before they *bentched*, someone brought *mayim acharonim* (water used for washing after a meal) to the head table. The small pitcher of water was passed from one person to another; finally it reached the end of the table.

"In that last seat sat the rabbi who was supposed to lead the *bentching*, but in the time that it had taken for the water to reach him, the rabbi had dozed off. His head rested on his hand, his eyes were shut tight and he had no idea what was going on around him. They put the *mayim acharonim* down in front of him. He didn't move a muscle. Someone said, '*Nu, nu?*' to awaken him so that he would wash and take the cup of wine for *bentching*. But he had fallen so soundly asleep that he awoke disoriented, jarred by the sight of everyone looking at him, waiting for him. He quickly picked up the *mayim acharonim*, thinking it was the cup of wine, and began, '*Rabbosai, mir villen bentchen.*'

"Now, this was such a ridiculous mistake that people could not hold in their laughter. I found it funny, too, and I began to laugh. But my father grabbed my hand and in a stern voice, he said, 'We do not laugh at the expense of others.'

"It wasn't long after that incident that I was in shul, and someone made some very silly mistake. I wanted to laugh, just like everyone else was doing, but I kept a straight face. Someone asked me later how I was able to do it, and I told him what my father had told me, that we are not allowed to laugh at someone else's expense."

With those final words hanging in the air, the Rebbe poured a cup of wine and set it before Michoel, signifying that he would lead the *bentching*. Soon, the meal was concluded. Michoel thanked the Rebbe for a wonderful meal and headed out the door.

Yecheskel now had the chance to satisfy the question that had been gnawing at him since his grandfather first launched into his story about the sleeping rabbi.

"All the times I've eaten here, Zeide has never spoken after singing the last Shabbos song," he said to his grandfather. "Why was today different?"

The Rebbe explained. "Many times, when people meet someone who dresses differently or speaks differently then they do, they find it very amusing, I was afraid that when you heard Michoel *bentching*, and using a different pronunciation than you are used to, you and your friend would find it funny and burst out laughing. Of course, this would have hurt his feelings. Before that could happen, I wanted to teach you that even if something strikes you as very funny, you have to hold back from laughing so that you don't hurt another person's feelings. *Baruch Hashem*, Yecheskel, I see that you and Reuven are good students, and you learned the lesson well. I hope you will always remember it."

The Bobover Rebbe illustrated how deeply we must love our fellow Jew. It is not enough to restrain yourself from hurting someone's feelings; you must go so far as to plan ahead to prevent others from causing hurt.

The High Road

You shoot up out of bed and open your eyes and realize it was all a bad dream. You shake your head awake and go on with your life. That's what Rabbi Sholom Holtzman hoped would happen at any moment. But it didn't. After so many years as a successful, popular rebbi, he was really being fired.

"We're making some changes in the yeshivah for the coming year," the principal told him in a tone far too matter-of-factly for the content of the conversation. "Unfortunately, we are going to be looking for a new rebbi for your class. I'm very sorry to do this, but we've given it a lot of thought and this seems to be the best move for the yeshivah."

Rabbi Holtzman felt the blood rushing to his face. How could this happen? How could he tell his wife? What would they do for money? He muttered a few words of goodbye and walked away from the yeshivah that had been his job, as well as his joy, for the past five years.

There was little time to nurse the wound. Rabbi Holtzman began calling every rebbi and every principal he knew, hoping to find a new position before financial disaster closed in around his household. Two weeks later, still without a job, he was surprised to receive a phone call from his former principal.

"We've managed to find someone to take over your class for next year," the principal told him. "However, we haven't found anyone who could give a Navi class in your place. Would you, by any chance, be willing to give the Navi class every day?"

Rabbi Holtzman felt a sensation that he had always assumed was only a figure of speech. His jaw dropped. His mouth hung open in stunned disbelief as he entertained what he considered to be the most audacious offer ever presented to him. After firing him from the job he loved and had performed devotedly for years, this man was now calling to ask a favor. Now, suddenly, Rabbi Holtzman's teaching talents were up to the job — but it wasn't even a half of a job. It was a bone thrown to a man desperate for some source of income, while the meat had been taken from his hands and given to someone else.

For a moment, Rabbi Holtzman felt he would laugh out loud. But at the next moment, he realized he had a dilemma. If he refused the job out of resentment for being fired, he might well be committing the sin of revenge, a motive that is directly forbidden by the Torah.

"Let me think about it and get back to you," he found himself saying.

Of one thing Rabbi Holtzman was quite sure; there was no way he could objectively determine the correct way to handle the situation. His heart still burned with resentment over the loss of his job, and anything he decided to do regarding the Navi class would be in reaction to the pain of that still-fresh wound. He decided to seek the advice of Rabbi Aron Dovid Dunner, the renowned halachic authority of London.

"This is indeed a difficult question," the Rabbi commented when Rabbi Holtzman related the story to him. "I will bring it to Rabbi Chaim Kanievsky for you when I travel to Bnei Brak next week."

When Rabbi Kanievsky heard the question, he stated that Rabbi Holtzman would not be committing an act of revenge against the principal if he should decide to turn down the offer. There was more, however, than the yes or no answer at stake in this question. There was the power of being *maavir al middosov* — the trait of overlooking a wrong that is done to oneself. *Chazal* teach that a person who refrains from exacting his due has a special claim on Heaven's compassion. Rabbi Kanievsky then related two stories for Rabbi Dunner to take back to Rabbi Holtzman:

One night after Maariv, an elderly man named Reb Yitzchak emerged from shul, limping slowly along the sidewalk. He scanned the crowd of men leaving for home, hoping to find someone to give him a ride. At last, his eyes fell upon a young man about to get into his car.

"Excuse me," he called. "Could you give me a ride home?"

The young man was hesitant. "I'm in a bit of a hurry," he replied. "I couldn't take you all the way home because it's a few blocks out of my way. But if you want, I can give you a ride until the corner."

With no other option available, Reb Yitzchak got into the car. He hoped that once the young man had gone part way, his heart would direct him to complete the act of kindness and take a few minutes to bring him to his door. Soon, they were approaching the spot where the driver had determined to drop off Reb Yitzchak.

"You know, young man, it's a very hot night. It's hard for me to walk and it's all uphill to my house. Do you think you could do me a favor and take me the extra few blocks?"

"Listen, I'm sorry but I told you I don't have time to go out of my way. I did what I said I would do, and that is all I am going to do." The young man pulled over to the side of the road and waited for his passenger to get out.

"Please! What's the big deal? Just take me three more blocks and it will be a really big help to me. You see, I have trouble with my feet. Have a little pity on an old man."

The young man's face turned stone cold. He gazed squarely into Reb Yitzchak's eyes and, in a voice that barely contained his irritation, he said, "Open the door and get out of my car."

Reb Yitzchak got out of the car and painfully walked the three blocks to his house. More painful still was the memory of the look on the young man's face, the tone in his voice, the complete lack of respect he demonstrated toward an elderly man.

A few months later, Reb Yitzchak's granddaughter became engaged. Family and friends were called together for a *l'chaim*, and Reb Yitzchak arrived right on time, dressed in his Shabbos clothes and ready to celebrate. The guests eagerly sought out the proud Zeida, clapping him on the back and shaking his hand. Slowly, Reb Yitzchak wove his way through the crowd to where his granddaughter's *chassan* sat. He was practically upon the young man when he caught a close look at his face. At that moment, the blood drained from Reb Yitzchak's cheeks.

They stared at each other in obvious astonishment. Reb Yitzchak could not mask his disapproval.

The boy was now face-to-face with the elderly gentleman he had rudely thrown out of his car. His eyes dropped to the floor and his face burned with humiliation. The cruelty he had displayed that night came back to haunt him at what should have been a peak of happiness. The engagement was called off.

Rabbi Kanievsky explained that the boy's mistake had been in insisting on exactly his measure. Had he gone beyond the limits he had set and given a little extra for the old man's sake, he would have been saved the terrible shame that fell upon him.

Then Rabbi Kanievsky told a second story. Shlomo had gone out with Chavi several times, and at that point, they decided the time had come for Shlomo to meet Chavi's father. This was not the usual meeting between father and potential son-in-law, because Chavi's father was in the hospital. Shlomo took it upon himself to go alone to the hospital and introduce himself. After their meeting, the father called his daughter and expressed his disapproval. He had the strong feeling that this boy was not right for his daughter, nor for his family. Chavi sadly broke the news to Shlomo, who well understood that the young lady would not go forward without her father's approval.

Although Shlomo was disappointed, he respected the father's wishes. Nevertheless, Chavi had become a major part of his life in the few weeks they had been dating, and her love and concern for her father had touched him. He decided that before the relationship was severed for good, he would pay a visit to the father in the hospital, to let him know that harbored no resentment toward him, and to wish him a complete recovery.

A few days later, the father was surprised to find Shlomo standing in his hospital room. The young man had come to wish him well, despite the disappointment the father had caused him. The generosity of this boy's spirit turned the father's initial impression upside down. He asked the boy's forgiveness for his unjustified rejection, and the engagement was announced a short while later.

In this story, Rabbi Kanievsky explained, a person who had every reason to wallow in resentment rose above those emotions. He trusted Heaven to determine whatever justice was due, and in turn, Heaven repaid his trust.

When a person feels that someone has wronged him, he often feels the urge to respond in kind. Chazal teach us to take a higher route — to be maavir al middosov, to rise above the insult and, in doing so, come closer to Hashem.

A Favor Returned

"Hey, Yitz," Dovid called in a voice that was just a little too loud. "I've been waiting for you. I thought we were going to meet here after lunch!"

Yitzy's soft heart became heavy with guilt as he met Dovid's broad, buck-toothed smile. Dovid thought they were best friends, and why wouldn't he think so? Yitzy was the only boy in this bunk of 21 11-year-olds who treated Dovid like a real human being. Most of the other campers avoided him altogether. Some took pleasure in mimicking him behind his back or playing the kind of pranks that can only be played on someone who thinks a little more slowly than everyone else.

Those tactics were not for Yitzy. He simply could not endure seeing another person humiliated. As a result of his empathetic nature, however, Yitzy's eagerly awaited first summer in sleep-away camp was becoming a nightmare. Instead of making new friends, he had become ostracized as "Dovid's best buddy." Instead of starring on the baseball field or in the pool, he found himself dragged into the sidelines of the action where his "friend" Dovid was doomed to dwell.

None of this would have been so terrible for Yitzy if not for the fact that Dovid's deficits were not just in ability, but in simple social graces. He had no sense of personal space. Like an overeager puppy dog, he was always just a little too close, always touching Yitzy, tapping him, slapping him and, most annoying of all, touching his personal belongings. Yitzy knew Dovid could not help the way he behaved, but this did not make the situation any less irritating. Yitzy wished he had never come to camp.

One night, after a particularly difficult day with Dovid, Yitzy lay in bed unable to sleep. He had tried speaking to their counselor, the head counselor and even the camp director. They each praised him for his patience and kindness, but none of them came up with a solution that would put some fun and excitement back into Yitzy's summer.

It's up to me now, Yitzy thought. *This is my summer and my camp too, and I can't even enjoy it because of Dovid. I just have to protect myself. I have to let him know that I'm not his friend.*

The next morning, Yitzy embarked on his new strategy. To assure himself of the support he would need to behave in a way that was so far out of character for him, he aligned himself with the worst of the bunk's Dovid-bashers. Whatever they did and said, Yitzy did and said, all the while struggling to ignore the betrayed look on Dovid's face as he began to absorb the new truth. Dovid became lonely and depressed. His wide smile and loud voice faded into grim silence.

The boys' counselor quickly realized that something had changed in Yitzy. He walked beside him on the way to lunch one afternoon, guiding him along a slight detour where there would be more privacy.

"What's going on with you, Yitzy? Why are you all of a sudden so mean to Dovid?"

"I'm not the only one," Yitzy replied. "If you're going to yell at me, you have to yell at the whole bunk. I'm just doing what everyone else is doing."

"I see you are," the counselor replied. "But you know better."

"Well, maybe now I don't," Yitzy said. The subject was clearly closed.

Later that afternoon, while the boys were taking their rest period, the counselor phoned Rabbi Horowitz, Yitzy's father. He described the treatment Dovid had been receiving from Yitzy.

"This is just not my son," Rabbi Horowitz replied. "Let me speak with him and see if I can get to the bottom of the situation."

Yitzy was summoned from the bunkhouse, where he was reading a new book he had bought especially for camp. Nevertheless, he put it down and walked to the office to speak to his father on the phone.

"The kid was making my life completely miserable," Yitzy told his father. "I wasn't having any fun at all at camp. I just had to get rid of him. I know it hurt his feelings, but what else could I do? Give up my whole summer?"

"Listen, Yitzy," his father advised, "I see it's not such a simple situation. But do me a favor. You don't have to be friends with the boy, but don't antagonize him. Don't insult him. I'm coming on Sunday for visiting day. We'll talk about it more then. O.K.?"

On visiting day, Yitzy took his father on the "scenic route" around the camp — the long wooded trail that Dovid had always insisted they take to the pool. On those occasions, it had been annoying, but now, Yitzy was grateful to have a fairly quiet path to walk with his father. The tall pine trees made a cool shelter for them as they strolled along, deep in discussion about the Dovid situation.

Another family was coming along in the opposite direction. Yitzy began to look around tensely, as if trying to find an escape route.

"That's him!" Yitzy whispered harshly to his father. "He's there with his whole family!"

Yitzy's attention shifted suddenly from his own discomfort to the shattered look on his father's face.

"No, Yitzy, this cannot be the boy you've turned against!" his father said with a trembling voice. "That boy's father is Rabbi Reich, and I can never be the cause of any pain for him or any member of his family. When I tell you this story, you'll understand why."

From the corner of his eye, Yitzy noticed that Dovid's family had veered off the path back to the main campground. The father and son sat down on a broad, flat boulder wedged between two towering pines. Tears welled up in Rabbi Horowitz's eyes as he searched the deep past for the words that would convey the emotions churning in his heart. Yitzy looked expectantly at his father, like someone waiting for a mystery to be revealed.

"After the war, my mother and I were living in a DP (Displaced Persons) Camp in Germany," Rabbi Horowitz began. "The Klausenberger Rebbe had set up a makeshift yeshivah there, in which I studied. A few months later, we arrived at the docks of New York. We were homeless and penniless, but my mother had a plan. She hoped to get some assistance from some government agencies so that we could live. She was going to send me to public school in the morning and hire a rebbi for me in the afternoon.

"But when we got off the boat, a young man with a mustache and hat approached my mother with a pen and pad in hand. 'Greetings, and welcome to New York,' he said. 'I see that your son is of yeshivah age. Where are you planning to send him?'

"My mother explained that she would be sending me to public school, since we had no money for yeshivah.

"The man told my mother to forget about public school. There was a wonderful yeshivah that had just opened in Manhattan and it was being run by the great Rav Shlomo Halberstam, the Bobover Rebbe. He told my mother that I would have a spot in that yeshivah, and she didn't have to worry about anything. 'I'll take good care of him,'" the man told her.

Yitzy imagined his father as a public school graduate instead of the *talmid chacham* he was. What would that have meant? His whole family would have been different. His family as he knew it probably would not have existed at all! His father continued.

"Yitzy, who knows what I would have become if not for that great man who met us at the docks and convinced Bubby to allow me to go to that yeshivah. Whatever I am today is thanks to him. Yitzy, do you know who that man that helped me was?"

"Who?" asked Yitzy.

"He was Rabbi Reich — Dovid's father," Rabbi Horowitz replied. "I owe him the world. I need you to do me a favor and try your utmost to make this boy happy. Give them back a little of what they gave me and, ultimately, you."

Yitzy's empathetic heart was now wide open. "Tatty," he assured his father, "don't worry. I know just what to do."

For the rest of the camp season, Yitzy and Dovid were the inseparable twosome — a big brother and little brother doing everything together. At the picnic bench under the oak tree, you could count on finding Yitzy and Dovid learning together. At cocoa club in the morning, you could be sure Yitzy would be pulling along a proud but sleepy-eyed Dovid. At the pool, on the ball-field, walking along the "scenic route" around camp, the two could be found together. Dovid's grin and exuberant voice returned in full force, displaying to all that he was having the world's best summer. Yitzy was finally having fun too. It was better than the fun of slamming the winning run or beating the fastest swimmer. It was the fun — in reality, the deep, indescribable joy — of single-handedly reviving the spirit of another human being.

When we adjust our perspective, the impossible can become doable. It all depends on awakening in ourselves the realization that the task is worth doing.

Forget About It

"Devorah is a good girl in a bad situation," the man explained to Dov Burtman. "Her family life is complete chaos. We've gotten her into a Bais Yaakov here, but we need a place for her to live. You and your wife are just the kind of people she needs to be around. Put her in a nice, healthy, upbeat Jewish home, and I'm sure she'll thrive. What do you say?"

The Burtmans owned a lovely new home. There was a spacious guest suite where this girl could stay. Reb Dov and his wife discussed the situation and decided to open their home to Devorah.

A few days later, Devorah arrived. She was a pretty young lady, neatly dressed with silky dark hair pulled back into a small, low-set ponytail. Her long neck and high cheekbones gave her a regal appearance, but with one glance into her eyes, the image was shattered. They were the eyes of a troubled girl, a girl who had seen more of the dark side of human nature than a child could possibly absorb. In her young face, her eyes looked old.

Mrs. Burtman led Devorah to her new quarters. It was a small, private suite with a neat, coordinated bedroom in soothing shades of beige and peach. Soft carpeting and fresh linen created just the restful oasis Devorah needed. She had her own bathroom, a desk, a comfortable armchair and a window overlooking a backyard garden.

"This is unbelievable, Mrs. Burtman," she said earnestly. "Thank you so, so much."

Each day, as Devorah emerged from her room dressed for school, her books neatly stashed in her briefcase, Mrs. Burtman's felt the joy of real accomplishment. She and her husband were privileged to provide this lovely Jewish daughter with a home, a life and, they hoped, a bright future.

On Devorah's part, the arrangement seemed to be working out perfectly. She was pleasant and helpful around the house, and she got along well with the Burtman children. School was also going well. Having an orderly household, reliable meals and routines gave her the peace of mind she needed to attend to the business of being a high school student. But Devorah's eyes belied her smile, her good grades and her polite manners. Her eyes told a different story — a long, unresolved story of conflict and pain.

One evening after dinner, Reb Dov and his wife sat down together to plan some major purchases they would be making for their house the next day. Mrs. Burtman's mother had given them a gift of $1,000, designated for the purchase of new kitchen appliances. They had only recently moved into their house, and the kitchen was clearly in need of renovations. As they discussed the various ovens and refrigerators that were available, Reb Dov reached into his pocket to take out the money. The pocket was empty. He checked another jacket pocket, and that was empty too. A cold, clenched panic gripped his gut as his fingers danced frantically from one pocket to the next — jacket, shirt, overcoat, pants — and found nothing there.

"It's gone!" he finally cried out to his wife. "What could have happened? Could it have fallen out? Could I have been robbed? I can't believe this!"

The couple reviewed all the possibilities, but in the end, they had to admit that the money had probably been stolen. It was gone; they just had to get used to the idea, and get used to the outdated refrigerator and oven, too.

Later that week, as Mrs. Burtman straightened out the house, she found some coins lying on the dining-room table. Automatically, she carried them with her into the kitchen and opened the cabinet. Without looking, she reached up to the high shelf where she kept a long row of *pushkas* (charity boxes). Feeling nothing there, she reached back a little further. Then, she rose on tiptoes to see where the *pushkas* might be. To her surprise, there were no *pushkas* on the shelf. Later that evening, when she reported the mystery to her husband, they concluded that their house must certainly have been burglarized.

A few weeks later, with winter well underway, all the schools closed down for a week of vacation. Devorah used this brief break to return home for a visit. A few days into the vacation week, the Burtmans noticed a foul smell in the air. By the next day, it had grown into a terrible stench. They followed the odor to the closed door of Devorah's room.

"Is it right to go in there?" Mrs. Burtman asked.

"What choice do we have?" her husband replied.

He opened the door and stepped into a room that was no doubt an accurate reflection of Devorah's turmoil. It was a mess of piled up papers and clothing, books and half-eaten snacks. On a greasy paper plate on the desk was a salami sandwich, from which one single bite had been taken. The bread was spotted with green mold, and the salami was covered with thick, gleaming slime. It looked as if it had been there for centuries.

But more shocking than the mess and the stench was the refuse on Devorah's bed. Ten *pushkas*, ripped into shreds, lay empty on the crumpled quilt.

Instantly, both Reb Dov and his wife realized that the girl they had taken into their home had robbed them, not only of their *pushka* money, but very likely of their $1,000 as well.

Unsure of how to handle the situation, Reb Dov decided to consult someone he knew would have the insight to guide him — Rabbi Shlomo Freifeld, the Rosh Yeshivah of Sh'or Yoshuv in Far Rockaway.

Dov Burtman told the tale of his and his wife's kindness to this lost young lady, how they had opened their home and made her part of their family. He related their very real need to replace their kitchen appliances, and the generous gift his mother-in-law had given them to purchase what they needed. Then, he described his startling discovery of the stolen *pushkas*, which clearly pointed to Devorah's guilt in the theft of the $1,000.

"Rav Freifeld, I don't know what to do!" Reb Dov concluded.

"Don't do anything. Forget about it, Reb Dov," the Rosh Yeshivah answered simply.

"But it's a thousand dollars! How can I forget about a thousand dollars? That's a lot of money to me."

While Reb Dov raged, Rabbi Freifeld softly smiled.

"I know what you're feeling," he said. "I had a very similar incident myself once. Let me tell you the story, and then maybe you'll understand why I say to forget about it.

"When I was young man learning in Chaim Berlin, on my 18th birthday, my mother bought me a beautiful leather wallet engraved in gold with my initials, S.F. It was my most prized possession and I always kept it in my coat pocket. One day when I was leaving yeshivah, I put on my coat and placed my hand in my pocket, as I always did, to check for my wallet. I was shocked to find that it was missing. I was devastated.

"Well, two years passed and I had just about forgotten about my wallet. Then, one day, I was getting my coat in the coatroom at Chaim Berlin. I noticed a familiar-looking wallet sticking out of someone else's coat. When I looked more closely, I discovered that it was my wallet with the gold initials on it. I couldn't believe that someone had taken my wallet. I put the wallet back in the coat pocket and waited to see who came to claim the coat. A few minutes later, a boy came in and took it. This was a boy who everyone knew had problems at home. He also came from a very poor family, and now I caught him stealing.

"I simply didn't know how to handle the situation, so I ran to the Rosh Yeshivah's office, Rav Yitzchok Hutner. I explained my situation to him and told him how much I had loved that wallet. I asked him, 'Rebbi, what should I do?' and do you know what he said? He said, 'Don't do anything, just forget about the wallet.'

"'But Rebbi,' I said, 'the wallet means a lot to me.'

"Rabbi Hutner, in his great wisdom, said, 'That boy who took your wallet has his share of problems. He is at a crossroads in his life. If you confront him about this wallet, then that might be the last we ever hear of the boy. He might just leave *Yiddishkeit* forever. He'll be totally embarrassed and won't want to show his face here anymore. But if you refrain from rebuking him, then he still has a chance. If we will show him love at this point in his life instead of rebuke, then who knows? He may turn out to be a fine Jew after all.'"

Rabbi Freifeld continued. "I followed the Rosh Yeshivah's advice and forgot about the incident. It is many years later and, *baruch Hashem*, that boy changed his ways. He developed into a fine *ben Torah* and built a wonderful family. My advice to you is the same, Reb Dov. This young girl is at a very delicate stage in her life. If you rebuke her now and accuse her of stealing, then she may be lost to the Jewish people forever. But if you forget about the money and instead of rebuke, you shower her with love, then who knows? She may develop into a fine young woman and may build a Torah home."

Reb Dov followed these words of wisdom and never mentioned the money to Devorah. Instead, he and his family did all they could to let her know that they cared about her and wanted her happiness. Devorah had a happy, successful year, which became the foundation for many years of continuing growth. She stayed in touch with the Burtmans, and they were privileged to see Rabbi Hutner's prediction come true. Devorah became a fine young woman and, with her husband, raised a beautiful Jewish family in a home filled with harmony and happiness.

Sometimes the best way to handle misbehavior is to shower love upon the perpetrator, because it is sometimes the only force powerful enough to penetrate to the core of the problem.

Well Worth the Time

oving gingerly through the toys strewn on the floor, Golda Adelman cleared a path to the ringing telephone. It was already 10 o'clock at night, but 5-year-old Yossi was still wide awake, crunching on animal crackers as he played with his toy cars. There seemed to be no hope of ever getting the house quiet, neat and settled for the night.

"Hello?" Golda answered the insistent ring. Her heart squeezed tight with anxiety when she heard the voice on the other end. It was Chayala's babysitter. No doubt, her next words would be "Sorry, but I'm not going to be available tomorrow."

Indeed that was the case. There stood Golda, casting about and desperate, like a passenger who had lost her passport at the boarding-gate. Now what would she do? If she took another day off from work tomorrow, her boss would have a fit. But it was already after 10 o'clock. Who could she call to care for her 2-year-old daughter?

Tears stung her tired eyes as she sank into a chair at the kitchen table. Seeming to stare up at her with a smirk, there lay an unpaid electric bill. Ever since her divorce, life was an endless round of challenges — an overwrought adventure story with a new dragon to slay the moment the old one was laid to rest.

The next day, after ironing out yet another wrinkled mess of a situation, Golda confided in one of her co-workers that she was becoming overwhelmed with the demands of single parenthood.

True, the strains of a terrible marriage had been relieved, but Golda's heart remained weighed down by worry and exhaustion.

"I have to admit to myself that it's too much for me," she said. "It's not so much the physical work of dealing with the kids and the house and a full-time job. It's the mental strain. There's no one for me to discuss things with. I have to decide everything alone. I have to solve every problem myself. That's the really exhausting part. And it's scary, too. My kids have no one else to depend upon but me."

"Golda, you need someone you can turn to," her friend replied. "And I think I know just the person. His name is Reb Chaim Mordechai Polatsek. He's a real *tzaddik*, someone who just lives to help other people. And he has tremendous *chachmah* (wisdom). You can rely on his advice."

For the first time in months, Golda felt the weight on her heart lift a little, like a balloon that had dropped a little bit of ballast. She imagined the comfort of picking up the phone and having on the other end an answer to a dilemma. This vision was in contrast to long, sleepless nights of reviewing her problems, replaying the facts with the jarring persistence of a broken CD.

Reb Chaim Mordechai was exactly as Golda's friend had described him. He was a Holocaust survivor who had seen everything life could possibly deliver to one's doorstep. Yet he was in no way jaded; his heart was as open and penetrable as a child's. His typical day was filled with visits to the elderly and the sick, collecting money for other people's pressing needs and anything else he could do to lift another Jew out of the depths of distress.

And now, Golda Adelman was on his agenda. She became a regular caller, tapping into his compassion and wisdom whenever the need arose. Just the sound of his welcoming voice on the other end of the phone was enough to defuse the tension building up within Golda. She affectionately referred to him as "my *Yid*," and everyone who knew Golda knew that there was no problem he couldn't ameliorate.

Within a few months of establishing a connection with Rabbi Polatsek, Golda's sense of despair had melted away, and like the snow of winter, it was gone without a trace. Golda could hardly believe that it had lain in a thick, cold layer upon her emotional landscape. Now, she was a vibrant, optimistic woman once again — busy, challenged, sometimes lonely, but always filled with confidence that she could deal with whatever life handed her. She wasn't alone.

A few days before Rosh Hashanah, a major crisis arose in Golda's life. She instinctively reached for the phone to call Rabbi Polatsek, but as she began to poke the familiar buttons of his number, her fingers stopped in midstream. He was a rabbi, after all, and this was the day before Rosh Hashanah. She could only imagine how busy he must be. How could she bother him with this complicated mess she now had to untangle?

After a moment's thought, she continued dialing. There was no choice, for the situation simply had to be resolved.

"Rabbi, I'm so sorry to bother you right now," she said as he greeted her. "I'm sure you must be very busy."

"Don't worry about me being busy," he told her. "That's not your business. You should just know that for you, I always have time. This is something I learned as a child — that for some things, you can always make time. Do you have a few minutes? I'll tell you the story."

Golda laughed to herself. *Do I have time?* she thought. *Now he makes it seem like I'm doing him a favor!*

"Please, I'd love to hear the story," she answered.

"In a *shtetl* in Poland, before World War II, there was a very great Rav who led the town. One Yom Kippur night, he got up before *Kol Nidrei* and made an impassioned plea to the congregation to do *teshuvah*. After he finished, everyone stood up to begin *Kol Nidrei*. But the Rav, instead of going up to lead the shul in prayer, turned to his *shammash* and said, 'Come with me.'

The Rav left with the *shammash* and everyone sat down. They wondered what urgent matter he could possibly be taking care of right before *Kol Nidrei*.

Meanwhile, the Rav and his *shammash* hurried down the road to the old tailor's house. The Rav knocked on the door and was greeted by the tailor's 12-year-old daughter. Naturally, she was very surprised to see the Rav at the door. Unfortunately the girl had been very ill and weak for the past few weeks, and she wasn't able to go to shul with her family.

The Rav asked her, "How are you feeling?"

"Oy, I'm feeling terrible! My stomach hurts and I have bad headaches as well."

"You should have a *refuah sheleimah* and a good year. Now tell me, my daughter, did you get any new clothing for Yom Tov?"

"Oh, Rabbi, how could I think about clothing when I feel like this?" she answered sadly.

"Yes, but tell me anyway, did you get something new for Yom Tov?"

The girl's face brightened a little. "Well, yes, yes, I did get something."

"So what is it that you got?"

"I got a new dress."

"Can you describe it to me? What color is it? Who made it for you?"

The young girl began to describe the dress, and with each new detail she described, her voice grew stronger and more animated. Her blank eyes began to sparkle with enthusiasm.

"It sounds so beautiful," the Rav said. "Maybe you wouldn't mind showing it to me?"

The girl's limbs were suddenly light with energy. She ran to her room and emerged with her lovely new Yom Tov dress, displaying it proudly for the Rav.

"You know," he said, voice filled with admiration, "I can't remember the last time I saw a dress this beautiful. This is certainly something very special!"

Now the girl's face was beaming with joy.

"You'll be sure to wear this on Yom Tov, won't you?" he asked her. She promised that she would.

"May Hashem seal you for a good, healthy, sweet year," he blessed her, and then turned with his *shammash* to dash back to the shul full of waiting congregants.

Naturally, the *shammash* was bewildered by the Rav's actions. As soon as the two were out of earshot of the tailor's house, the question he had been tightly restraining broke free of his mouth.

"Rebbe! Of all things to do before *Kol Nidrei*, why do you go to speak to a girl about a dress? What's so important about a dress?"

"Listen carefully," the Rav answered. "I'm going to explain something to you. When a Jew cries out to Hashem, his cry pierces the Heavens. But when one helps to remove that cry, if he actually takes away the sorrow from the Jew who is in anguish, that pierces all the Heavens and reaches all the way to the Heavenly throne.

"This girl is a very sick child. She is home all alone while everyone in her house and in the entire *shtetl* is in shul. She knew that nobody would be coming home for a few hours, so her spirit was down. All she had to think about was her pain. I came to visit her and asked her all about her dress so that she could cheer up a little — and she did. This good feeling that she now has will keep her company until everyone gets home. Every time she thinks about our visit, it will take the place of a cry of anguish that she would have otherwise had. This certainly pierced all of the Heavens! Now I am ready to go and *daven Kol Nidrei!*"

Rabbi Polatsek, having concluded his story, told Golda, "If I can help remove a cry of anguish on your behalf, then I can go into Yom Tov a little easier as well."

There was no doubt left in Golda's mind. The Rabbi was willing — even eager — to help her. She laid out the details of her problem.

Rabbi Polatsek patiently guided her to a solution. One Jew lifted a painful burden from another, and in Heaven, the scales tilted a little further toward a year of blessing for the Jewish people.

Giving one's time, a listening ear and an encouraging word to a person in need might seem like nothing more than a little courtesy. But in reality, it is a powerful form of chesed that has an impact in the highest spheres of Heaven. And anyone can do it.

To Sanctify His Name

Smells Heavenly

F rom the landing outside the front door, Rabbi Sussman could hear the steady, rhythmic banging of hammer against wood echoing from somewhere in the house. He rang the bell, hoping its chime would be heard. Meanwhile, Shalom Horowitz was enjoying his home-repair project, securing some loose molding to the wall with a steady tap-tap-tap square on the heads of the tiny nails. Today was the day to get it all done — the molding, the dead outlet, the leaky faucet and anything else he could find that needed to be banged back into shape.

Reb Shalom heard the bell. He laid his hammer down on the floor and hurriedly stood up from his crouching position. As he bounded down the stairs to the front door, he realized that his hands were grimy with dirt and oil. He wished he had a moment to wash them before greeting whoever was waiting.

Instead, he opened the door as he was, delighted to discover that his guest was the holy Rav Pinchus Sussman.

"Rav Sussman, it's so good to see you. I can't believe it's already that time of year again! Please come in."

Rabbi Sussman came each year to collect money for a yeshivah in Eretz Yisrael. Reb Shalom was always glad to see him. Rabbi Sussman was clearly a *tzaddik*, and the *berachah* he gave upon receiving Reb Shalom's donation seemed a far greater treasure than any amount of money that changed hands.

"I'm sorry," Reb Shalom told his guest, "but I can't shake your hand." As he spoke, he brought his hands out in front of him and turned his palms up. "My hands are all dirty from the repairs I've been doing."

Quickly glancing down at Reb Shalom's hands, Rav Sussman smiled. "Let me tell you," he said in his thick Yiddish accent, "there's dirty dirt, and there's clean dirt. Your hands have clean dirt on them."

He waited a moment to see if Reb Shalom had understood the riddle, and then offered a story that explained it:

"My father was a true Torah Jew who grew up in Russia, where a person had to have great *mesiras nefesh* to uphold the Torah. When he was growing up under the Czar's rule, there was a death penalty for studying Torah. He lived in a small village in an apartment building that was shared by many Jewish families. For those families, living without Torah was not an option. So they devised a plan to smuggle in a rebbi who could teach their children the heritage of their fathers.

"That rebbi was Reb Hershel. This great *tzaddik* with a long flowing white beard would slink into the building, gather the boys in a small room in the basement and transmit the words of the *Chumash* to his *talmidim*. They, in turn, would chant out loud the sweet sounds of Torah.

"But of course, they always had to be on guard for the Czar's officers. There would always be a watchman whose job was to stand at the entrance of the building and warn them if they saw any officials in the vicinity. The watchman would send a signal to the boys, and they would all scatter upstairs to their apartments while Reb Hershel would sneak out the back entrance. It was a risky venture, but Reb Hershel willingly accepted the risk rather than allow the Torah to be lost to the next generation.

"One Friday morning, the boys were learning in the basement with Reb Hershel when the lookout came running in with a warning.

" 'The soldiers are here!' he yelled. 'Everyone run!'

"The boys disappeared instantly, and Reb Hershel dashed to the back door. But when he peeked out through a small crack, he saw to his horror that there were soldiers there. In fact, the building was completely surrounded. He didn't know what to do.

"The lookout, whose name was Yankel, returned to make sure everyone had vanished, and saw a panic-stricken Reb Hershel standing there, unsure of which way to turn.

" 'You'd better hide, Reb Hershel!' Yankel whispered desperately. 'If they find you here, they'll kill you.'

" 'But Yankel,' Reb Hershel replied, 'there is no place for me to go.'

"Yankel considered for a moment. He had an idea, but it was so awful an idea that he didn't want to say it. Yet, this was no time for doubt. Any idea was better than nothing.

" 'Rebbi, I have a suggestion. I know this is a terrible suggestion, but at least it can save your life. In the middle of the courtyard, there is an outhouse. There are planks on the floor that cover the cesspool. If we lift those planks and lower you into the hole below them, you'll be safe. No one would look there; of that you can be sure.

"Seeing no alternative, Reb Hershel agreed to Yankel's plan. They ran to the outhouse, and lifted the board and Reb Hershel lowered himself into the filthy cesspool full of waste. Yankel carefully replaced the board over the hole, and a moment later, the Czar's soldiers burst in screaming, 'Where is that rabbi? We know he was here. We'll find him, and we'll kill him!'

"Yankel looked at them as if they were crazy, bursting in on a man in an outhouse.

" 'What are you talking about?' he answered confidently. 'You can certainly see that I'm in here, and no one is with me.'

"The soldiers searched inside and out, all around the courtyard, while Reb Hershel suffered in the choking stench, waiting for the moment he would be set free. At last, the soldiers admitted defeat and left the building. Families poured out of their apartments to help bring Reb Hershel out of the pit. They brought buckets of water to wash him as well as they could, and fresh water for him to drink. Then they escorted him into one of the apartments to rest and clean up for Shabbos.

"That night, as always, there was a secret Friday-night *minyan* in the basement. Everyone was waiting to begin Minchah, including Reb Hershel, who had managed to regain his composure and some of his strength. He stood in the back of the shul getting ready to *daven*, but he couldn't help noticing that a commotion was erupting in the front of the shul.

"The Rav, Rabbi Pollack, asked his *shammash* what everyone was getting so excited about.

" 'Rebbe, there is a problem. We are not allowed to *daven* where there is a *ruach ra* (a bad odor), and there is a *ruach ra* in this room. It's coming from Reb Hershel, the *melamed*.'

"The *shammash* related the entire story of Reb Hershel and the raid by the soldiers. Unfortunately, despite all his efforts, Reb Hershel had not been able to rid himself completely of the odor that permeated his foul hiding place. It seemed that the *minyan* would not be able to *daven* unless Reb Hershel left the room. By now, of course, Reb Hershel understood that he was the cause of the storm that was brewing. He, and everyone else in the room, turned to the Rav to hear how he would handle the controversy.

" 'I hold that we are indeed allowed to *daven* in this shul with Reb Hershel. I hold that this odor does not fall into the category of *ruach ra*. Rather, it is considered as the smell of *Gan Eden* because of the *mesiras nefesh* involved in Reb Hershel teaching Torah to our children.' With that, they began Minchah.

"From this story," concluded Rabbi Sussman, "I learned that there is something known as clean dirt."

Reb Shalom couldn't argue with the logic. Pleasant and unpleasant were not realities of their own — whatever one must do to serve Hashem takes on the scent of *Gan Eden*, and no *ruach ra* can cling to it.

Reb Shalom gave Rabbi Sussman a donation for his yeshivah. And as always, he had received far more than he gave.

Sometimes, we endure unpleasantness in the course of doing a mitzvah. If we could view it as Rabbi Pollak did, we would perceive the hardships as the sweetest, most wonderful treasure, because of the Kiddush Hashem involved.

Rapid Rescue

Along with the hearty food he prepared for the yeshivah, Chaim Lipshitz served up something else — delicious morsels about the Land of Israel. Every event in Jewish history was linked to some location on the map of Israel, and Reb Chaim was a self-made expert on this topic. Gradually, his obsession became his profession. He left behind his cooking career and became one of Israel's most popular tour guides.

It was an odd position for a Yerushalmi man born and bred in Meah Shearim. However, his combination of Torah scholarship, knowledge of the land and charismatic personality was the perfect mix. His reputation spread, and those who wanted an authentic, Torah-infused tour of Israel flocked to him.

On one tour, Reb Chaim was leading a group of *chareidi* rabbis on a tour of the Galilee. They arrived at the Banyas River, which is mentioned in the Talmud as a particularly dangerous waterway. Even today, boating is prohibited there. The wise person enjoys the awe-inspiring beauty of its rushing rapids and frothing white water from a safe distance. Therefore, before Reb Chaim stopped to point out notable landmarks in the surrounding mountains, he warned the group to keep its distance from the river.

On the opposite bank, a group of teenagers from a non-re-ligious kibbutz were laughing loudly and playfully taunting each other at the water's edge. Suddenly, the laughter turned to screams of terror.

"She fell in! She fell in!" voices were crying.

Reb Chaim saw them all standing, paralyzed with fear, as the rap-ids brutally swept their friend downriver. Her small head bobbed in and out of the whitecaps as her tiny hands flailed about, catch-ing the glint of the sun. From Reb Chaim's viewpoint, she looked like a small plastic doll that had been cast into the rushing water.

The burly Reb Chaim instantly threw off his shoes and dove into the water. The groups on both sides of the river looked on in horror as a second person bumped downstream. It seemed as if both would be lost, but there was nothing to do now but watch the story unfold.

After a few minutes of frantic swimming, Reb Chaim reached the girl. He grabbed her with one arm and used the other to some-how pull against the rushing water and bring them both to shore. When he finally boosted her up onto dry land, she was gasping and spitting out plumes of water, but she was alive. She was breathing. Reb Chaim had saved her life.

The teenagers quickly surrounded their friend. They cleared the way for a frightened young man who ran to her and squatted by her side, asking with a mixture of tenderness and panic,

"Rina, Rina, are you all right?" Rina was clearly someone special to him, and all the others in the group stepped aside so that he could tend to her. However, as soon as he ascertained that she had survived the ordeal, his attention turned to the hero who had saved her. He strode over to Reb Chaim and stood directly in front of his face, with only inches between them.

"Is it permitted for you to touch a woman?" he challenged.

Reb Chaim was still trying to catch his breath.

"The Gemara has a word for people like you," he replied hoarsely. "It says that a person who does not save a woman because he is not permitted to touch her is called a pious fool. There is nothing more important than saving the life of another Jew. But let me ask you something. Why didn't you jump in?"

The boy retreated a few steps back from his attack position. His arrogant gaze shifted downward, and he turned and walked away. He rejoined his group, which was getting ready to head back home. Rina, who was back on her feet at this point, broke away from her doting friends and approached Reb Chaim.

"I know there is no way I can ever thank you for saving me," she said. "I really don't know what to say except thank you."

Reb Chaim brushed aside the accolades. It was nothing any Jew wouldn't have done for another, he assured her. Before they parted ways, Rina asked for his phone number, and he gave it to her.

The incident began to fade from memory until two weeks later, when Reb Chaim got a phone call from Rina.

"Rabbi Lipshitz, for the past two weeks, I have been having nightmares about my terrible accident," she told him. "And then I have one recurring thought which I can not get out of my mind. All of my life I have always been told that *chareidi* Jews are no good, that they only care about one another. But when I think of how you risked your life and jumped into the water and saved me, I realize that I have been making a huge mistake all of this time. I see that I really don't know anything at all about *chareidim* or how they live. I would really like to experience a Shabbos in your home, Rabbi Lipshitz. I'd like to see for myself what it's all about."

Reb Chaim agreed, and arranged for his wife to pick her up at the bus station before Shabbos.

Rina arrived as scheduled, and proceeded like a wide-eyed tourist through the rituals of the day. The meals, the songs, the contentment and joy that saturated every moment gave her a taste of spiritual delight — a taste she had never experienced before. When *Havdalah* was finished, Rina made no move toward going home.

"I want to stay here," she told Reb Chaim. "This is the first time I have ever felt Jewish in my life. I don't want to lose it."

"You'll hold onto it, Rina. You'll take it home with you," Reb Chaim said. "It's not possible for you to stay here. You know as well as I do that people will say that you've been brainwashed and that we're not letting you leave. You have to go home. But while you are home, I want you to think about whether this is the kind of life you want to lead."

"I'll do what you say," Rina agreed. "But I know that I want this. I know I want to find a school where I can learn more about Judaism."

Several weeks passed and then Rina contacted Reb Chaim again.

"I can't stand my life here," she told him. "Can you please find me some place to learn?"

Now it was Rina's *neshamah* that was flailing about and screaming for help, and once again, Reb Chaim dove in. He found her a school that catered to Israeli *baalei teshuvah*. Rina was soon happily engaged in her studies, changing and growing at an astounding rate. It was as if this were all she had ever wanted.

After a year of learning, Rina had become a devoted, knowledgeable Jewish woman. The next step was marriage, and Rina's teachers were eager to help her find a worthy young man with whom she could build a Jewish home. Their inquiries led them to the *baal teshuvah* yeshivah Ohr Somayach, where there was a kindhearted, learned young man named Yonatan.

The two met. In fact, they had met before, for Yonatan was the boy who had failed to jump into the Banyas to save Rina's life. "Why didn't you jump in?" Reb Chaim had asked him. He could not answer the question. More perplexing still was the question of why this complete stranger — a *chareidi*, no less—would risk his life for a secular girl he had never seen before.

These were questions that required answers, and Yonatan set about finding them. His search led him to Ohr Somayach, where he discovered the Torah, and in it, the secret of the courage and compassion displayed by the Yerushalmi rabbi who had stood on the opposite bank of the raging river.

A year after their reunion, Rina and Yonatan were married. A near-death experience blossomed into a whole new life and a new Jewish family. Reb Chaim had made quite a rescue.

There is one ingredient that has the power to erase any ill will one Jew might have toward another. That is the love each Jew is required to feel for everyone in Klal Yisrael.

Best Learner

The final days of the camp season are always a challenge for the *rebbeiim*. Even though the crispness in the air hints at the school year soon to begin, the boys are always a little less focused, a little easier to distract as the routines and activities wind down. My sixth-grade learning group at Camp Morris was no exception, but I was well armed for the occasion with plenty of cliff-hanger stories, contests and incentives to keep my students' minds on their learning.

The boys' voices blended in a loud, enthusiastic chorus as they recited a *perek* of Mishnayos together. Just as they finished, there was a sharp knock on the classroom door.

Standing there at the entrance was a well-dressed woman, and behind her, partially out of sight, stood a boy who was apparently her son. The woman spoke in a sweet, almost singsong tone. You couldn't imagine anything angry or mean ever coming out of her mouth. She spoke to me quietly about her son. The class strained to hear the conversation, but I'm sure they couldn't hear more than a murmur.

At last, the woman stepped back and the boys could see her son. He was about their age, but his face showed signs of a condition most of them had seen before. He had Down syndrome. The boy stepped forward and shook my hand, and the mother turned and walked briskly away.

"Boys, I want you to meet Dovi. He'll be joining us for the last three days of camp," I said with the kind of enthusiastic voice I usually reserved for announcing a special trip.

Deep down, I was concerned. Dovi's mother thought that three days in a mainstream class would give her son a stronger connection to the world of learning. He functioned well, and she was sure he would relish the chance to sit in a class with regular yeshivah boys. But I wasn't so sure. *These kids could make this boy miserable if they want,* I thought. *I hope this goes well.*

It was a fleeting thought, shattered by the sound of the class's shout of greeting. "Hi, Dovi!" they said in unison, as if they had been rehearsing it all morning. All at once, I understood down to my core the meaning of the word *nachas.* My boys did not see a target; they saw a fellow Jew. They saw a vulnerable little boy who was hungry for their love and attention, and instinctively, these golden qualities began flowing out of them.

Before Dovi had even settled into his chair, a boy named Shimmy had run to the bookshelf to get him a Gemara. He opened it on Dovi's desk and pointed.

"Here's the place, Dovi," he said.

Meanwhile, Mordechai was rummaging through his knapsack. His hand emerged grasping a small, unopened bag of potato chips and a box of fruit punch. These he brought to Dovi, resting them shyly on his desk with the simple explanation, "Just in case you get hungry, O.K.?"

I seized upon the momentum. "Dovi, you can be part of our learning contest. Tell me, what is the *berachah* you make on grapes?"

"*Ha'eitz,*" he answered confidently.

"That's right!" I announced. "And what *berachah* do you make on grape juice?"

"*Borei pri hagafen,*" Dovi responded.

"Right again! Dovi, you have just won Best Learner of the Week! You win a snack from the canteen, and right after class, I'll take you to get it."

The class broke into a chant. "Dovi! Dovi! Dovi!"

As his name filled the air, the child's expression grew radiant with happiness. His smile was almost too wide for his face as he looked around the room at his newfound fan club.

"Rebbe, can I go to the canteen and get Dovi's snack right now, please?" asked a camper.

I nodded and the boy ran out the door. He was back moments later with an ice cream for the fortunate winner.

That afternoon, the championship baseball game got underway. Mendy, a member of the sixth-grade bunk, was the captain of his team. Slim and quick, Mendy was a competitive player who was accustomed to winning. He planned to win today, too, and in fact had been thinking about his lineup since class that morning.

Dovi stood with a group of boys as Mendy began giving out positions for the game. I stood on the sidelines looking on, feeling sadly certain that Dovi would not be given a spot in this critical championship game. I wondered if Dovi would realize that he had been left out. Was he used to it, or did it hurt him anew every time?

"Hey, Dovi, what do you play?" Mendy asked.

"I like to be in the outfield," Dovi answered carefully.

"O.K., then, outfield it is," Mendy called. "Get out there and get ready to catch!"

I stood there, stunned, as I comprehended the exquisite gesture of kindness I had just observed. Dovi could have been consigned to the catcher's position, where the potential for mistakes was relatively slim. He could have been given a noncompetitive job like batboy or water boy. Instead, Mendy had knowingly risked this all-important game to give Dovi his chance to be a regular kid, playing a regular game of ball.

In the end, Mendy's team lost, and Dovi's performance was undeniably part of the equation. But the loss was only in terms of baseball. In terms of life, the championship title was securely in Mendy's hands.

We have to love our fellow Jew more than we love the game, more than we love fame, because this is the precise way in which Hashem wants us to sanctify His great Name.

Lifeblood

"I need a rabbi," said the voice on the other end of the phone. For Rabbi Avrohom Alter of the community institute of the Telshe Yeshivah, Chicago, such a call was all in a day's work.

"Well, I'm a rabbi," he responded. "How can I help you?"

"My name is Rick Pennington. I'm not a religious Jew, and

frankly, I don't know anything about being a Jew," he bluntly declared. This was his disclaimer, the subtext of which was, "Don't expect anything from me."

Then there was a moment of silence. Rick obviously thought there would be some reaction to his introduction, but Rabbi Alter merely waited for the story behind the phone call to unfold. He had been involved in *kiruv* long enough to know that nobody calls simply to inform him that they're not religious.

"But anyway, I do believe in G-d," Rick now continued, "and I'm going through a very difficult time in my life right now. I need to figure out what's going on. You see, my wife gave birth to a baby boy two weeks ago, and he has major health problems. It's doubtful that he will even survive. I just have to know, why is G-d doing this to us?"

Even for Rabbi Alter, this was an unusual question. The pain and bewilderment in Rick's voice made his heart well up with pity, as if he were watching a lost child wander the street searching for his father. Difficult as the question was, however, it had the same answer as the other more typical questions that came his way, and that was to start learning Torah. This was the key to beginning to understand what it means to be a Jew in the world G-d created.

"Rick, I can't tell you why G-d did this to your son," Rabbi Alter answered softly. "But you've already taken one big step in dealing with the situation, because at least you realize that this is coming from G-d. Why don't you come down to the community center and we will learn some Torah together and try to explore the possibilities?"

The first time Rick appeared at the community center, he looked like a tourist who had been stranded in a strange land. Rabbi Alter noticed him and immediately knew who he was. He guided him to a table, got acquainted and, soon, they began to learn. By the second time Rick appeared, he was a native. He settled right in with Rabbi Alter and the *sefer* they were learning. Soon, he was a weekly regular. Torah was providing him with an

188 / Stories for the Jewish Heart

anchor, something to keep him stable in the rough seas of his baby's ill health.

The baby, named Kevin, had been born with a defective heart. In fact, it was constructed backward. Normally, the chamber that pumps blood into the adjoining chamber is a weaker muscle, and the chamber that pumps the blood into the body is stronger. But in Kevin, the chambers were reversed. It was the weak chamber that was connected to the vessels that circulated the blood throughout the body. Because it was not able to perform the task efficiently, the child's body was starved for the oxygen and nutrients his circulatory system should have carried. Kevin's limp limbs were tinged blue and his organs could not function properly. He would need many open heart surgeries to repair the defect.

One night, after Rabbi Alter and Rick finished learning, Rick remained in his seat, obviously not yet ready to leave.

"I need some advice," he told Rabbi Alter. "My son is scheduled for open-heart surgery next week. We're going to need a considerable amount of blood to keep my son going through the surgery. However, there is one major problem. The only source for blood is the city blood bank and I am very frightened to use it. You hear so much about diseases and contamination, I just can't let them give that blood to my son. The blood bank told me I can use blood donated by family members, but that's not going to be simple. It has to be the right blood type, and I don't think I will be able to get enough from my family. Rabbi, what do you think I should do? Should I take a chance on the city blood?"

As Rick laid out the problem, he became increasingly agitated. Every solution presented a new host of problems in his eyes. Rabbi Alter put a reassuring hand on his shoulder.

"Don't worry about a thing," he said confidently. "I'll just round up a bunch of yeshivah boys and they'll go down and donate. I'm sure that from all of them, there'll be enough blood of the right type."

"Yeshivah boys?" Rick repeated. "Why are a bunch of yeshivah boys who I don't even know going to take the time to go down and give blood for my baby?"

"You'll see," said Rabbi Alter. "They'll be glad to do the mitzvah. I'm telling you, there's nothing to worry about on that end. I'll get them a ride to the hospital blood bank on Tuesday at 2 o'clock, during their lunch break. Now, just let the surgery be a success."

"All right, if you say they'll be there, I guess they'll be there," said Rick. "Thanks!"

On Tuesday afternoon, Rick waited on a seat outside the blood bank, which was at the end of a long hospital corridor. It was 1:56 p.m. He peered down the empty hall hoping to see the boys coming, but still wondering if they really would. The minutes ticked by, and as they did, a little seed of cynicism began to sprout in Rick's heart. Who was the rabbi kidding? Why would a bunch of teenage boys spend their lunch break donating blood to a stranger?

At 2:10, still hopeful, he got up from his seat and strolled a little way down the corridor. *Maybe I'll meet them as they come in,* he thought. But all he saw before him was an empty, lonely length of polished linoleum. He went back to his seat. Finally, at 2:25, he gave up. Disheartened, he walked to the reception desk and began speaking to the clerk.

"I'm sorry," told her. "I guess the rabbi wasn't able to round up enough guys to ....."

Before he finished the sentence, he heard the drumbeat of footsteps coming down the corridor. He turned toward the sound and was greeted with the sight of a mass of black-hatted young men, already beginning to roll up the sleeves of their white shirts, marching down the hall like the cavalry coming to the rescue.

"We're looking for Mr. Pennington," one of the boys said to Rick.

"That's me," Rick replied.

"Sorry we got here so late," said the boy. "Where do we go to give the blood?"

As Rick pointed the way, his eyes filled with tears. Never had he

seen a sight as beautiful as these boys, rising up to help him, to give
their time — their blood — for no other reason than their love for a fellow Jew. All the Torah he had learned over the past few months sprang
to life in that moment. He knew he had to learn more and more.

Today, 23 years later, Rick is known as Mendel. The seeds planted
by Rabbi Alter have grown into a full tree with many branches. All
of Mendel's children are Torah-observant Jews. Two have spent many
years learning in *kollel* in Israel, and Mendel, true to his awakening in
the hospital corridor, has indeed learned more and more. Kevin, now
called Yehoshua, requires a pacemaker and must carefully monitor
his health, but he does not let that stand in the way of his learning.
He is known as a fine yeshivah student with a bright future.

The boys who showed up at the hospital that afternoon had no way
of knowing the impact of their deed. They thought they were just helping a baby survive an operation, but instead, in just one afternoon, they
changed the face of an entire family and all its future generations.

*One can never know the impact a kind gesture, a helping hand, a
simple good morning can have on the life of a fellow Jew.*

The Best Place

The hospital bed-table was stacked with *sefarim.* So was the
dresser, the night table and a small storage shelf. When
Daniel Zafler felt up to the task, he would get out of bed
and sit in a large, vinyl upholstered armchair near the win-

dow, where he would immerse himself in learning. Sometimes, he could only manage to sit propped up in bed. But wherever he stationed himself, a *sefer* would be before his eyes. True, his illness had taken him away from yeshivah, but he would not let it take him away from learning. At only 16, he still had far too much to accomplish to let any time go to waste.

Like the legendary saints and scholars of previous generations, Daniel exhibited a burning desire for Torah and mitzvos from an early age. This passion is what sustained him now as he faced the tedious hospital routine and the suffering brought on by his illness. His *tefillah* and learning were everything to him; they were his comfort, his intellectual stimulation and, most of all, his hope. One day at the beginning of his hospital stay, he had slept through the time for saying the morning *Shema*. This loss distressed him so that he began to cry. From that time on, he insisted that he be awakened on time, even if he was deep in a medication-induced sleep.

Through all the dreary days of treatments and pain, one dream kept Daniel afloat; that someday, he would again sit in his accustomed spot in his yeshivah's *beis medrash*, face-to-face with his *chavrusa*, learning Torah with all the energy and joy in his heart. But as the summer wore on, Daniel's condition continued to deteriorate, and he had to content himself with the little *beis medrash* he had created around him.

Outside, the season was changing. Lush green summer foliage began to turn into rich shades of orange and gold. Darkness descended earlier each day and the air felt fresh and cool. Children went back to yeshivah and Jews began to prepare themselves for Rosh Hashanah. In Daniel's world, however, the air remained the same — a depressing potpourri of medicines, disinfectants and human suffering, He grew weaker, and he understood that he would not be leaving the hospital for Rosh Hashanah or Yom Kippur. Daniel's family went to work organizing a *minyan* for him in the hospital. While there was no doubt that this was a poor second-best option, Daniel made the most of it. His *tefillos* were saturated with the yearning in his heart as he begged Hashem to redeem him from his personal exile.

As Succos rapidly approached, Daniel's mind was overtaken with one thought; he needed a succah in which to eat. At first, the hospital officials balked at the idea; the president of the United States, Bill Clinton, was scheduled to visit the hospital on Simchas Torah, and a succah would present a security risk. Finally, the hospital relented on the condition that the succah would be disassembled before the president's visit. The succah went up. It was small and simple, but to Daniel it was perfection. It was another mitzvah that he was able to perform — another golden opportunity to serve Hashem.

As the week of Succos progressed, Daniel was filled with a longing to spend Simchas Torah at his yeshivah. He imagined the fiery dancing, the booming voices, the unbridled joy of the Yom Tov and wanted nothing more than to be immersed in that atmosphere.

"It's just what I need," he told his parents, and they set about making it happen.

On Simchas Torah day, Daniel's brother Avigdor arrived at the hospital on foot to escort his brother to his yeshivah a few miles away. Daniel sat in a wheelchair, his heart filled with happiness like a traveler preparing to embark on his dream vacation. His luggage, however, spoke of another reality, for it included an oxygen tank and a plastic box filled with medications he would require during the hours of his leave.

As they made their way down the labyrinth of corridors, they noticed security guards stationed every few feet. Hospital staff members were murmuring excitedly to one another, and patients kept emerging from their rooms to peer down the corridors. The president was coming.

As Daniel and Avigdor arrived at the exit, they nodded to the security guard at the door.

"Have a good day, boys," he responded. "But, hey, where are you going, anyway? Don't you want to stick around and see the president?"

"We'll be back a little later," Avigdor answered. "Maybe we'll be able to catch him then."

Outdoors for the first time in many weeks, Daniel reveled in the fresh air and sunshine. Nevertheless, the day was uncharacteristically hot. As Avigdor began the three-mile trek to yeshivah, he became concerned about his brother's ability to endure the heat.

"Are you sure you want to do this?" he asked.

"Are you joking?" Daniel answered. "I'm fine. I'm just sorry you have to push me all this way in the heat."

"Don't worry about it."

As the two drew near to the yeshivah, Daniel felt a tingle of joy inside him, as if a new channel of energy had opened up. The familiar contours of the building filled him with a sense of homecoming. Friends and *rebbeiim* surrounded him as Avigdor pushed him through the front door. Daniel was where his soul wanted to be.

The *davening* and dancing on that Simchas Torah rose to the highest heights, fueled by the inspiration Daniel's presence provided. His pure joy, even as he sat there in the center of the circle stuck in his wheelchair, pried open every boy's heart. The sound of their united voices was the roar of a lion, carrying a message of strength and courage for those who love Hashem's Torah. Their dancing seemed unstoppable. But at last, it all did stop. It had to. And it was time for Daniel to return to the hospital.

The three-mile return trip might have been sad for him had he not been overflowing with the joy his trip to the yeshivah had provided. There was no room for despair, for he had performed the mitzvos of the day in the very best way he could, and they satiated his soul.

As the brothers entered the hospital, they felt as though they were entering a separate reality. All conversation revolved around the president's visit. "Did you see him shake my hand?" "Did you see how he played with the children in pediatrics?" "I didn't know he was so tall." Something that had barely registered in the brothers' minds had completely taken over the minds of everyone in this building.

When they entered Daniel's room, his roommate, Bobby, nearly charged at them.

"Where were you? The president came right into our room. He was standing right by your bed! I can't believe you missed it!"

"I didn't miss anything," Daniel answered serenely. "I was back at my yeshivah, the greatest place in the world. There isn't anything better than that for me."

This was Daniel's simple truth. For him, Hashem's Presence was all that mattered. Wherever it could be felt most deeply was the place he wanted to be. Presidents and celebrities could not stir even an ember of the flame in his heart, a flame that burned exclusively for Hashem and His Torah.

Daniel eventually succumbed to his sickness. Those who knew and loved him were bereft of a special light in their lives, but the lessons his life taught continue to shine brightly.

There are special, sublime souls who, just by the way in which they live their lives, teach us what truly matters in life, and how we can best fulfill our Divine purpose.

A Connecticut Connection

onnecticut. On the map, it's not a very large state, but when one is traveling from New Jersey to Boston with a car packed with small children, the map cannot begin to describe the length of the journey.

It was a pleasant early spring afternoon in 1980 when the Moskowitz family's Connecticut saga began. Hours earlier, Rabbi Moskowitz and his wife had loaded up his war-torn old car with their brood of small children and all the paraphernalia the family would need for their Pesach in Boston. Cribs and infant seats, snacks, pots, pans, food, luggage, games and toys were all crammed into the trunk and wedged between the children's dangling feet and the floorboards.

At first, the car was noisy with excitement. Before they had even left the boundaries of Lakewood, the children were begging to dip into the travel snacks that had been packed for them. It was only fifteen minutes since they had finished breakfast, but they claimed to be starving.

Now, four hours later, the car was quiet. A few children colored and a few slept soundly, lulled into slumber by the cranky car's asthmatic motor. Rabbi Moskowitz sped along an open strip of I-95, which could take a person all the way from Maine to Florida.

Suddenly, the massive tractor-trailer that had been far in the distance loomed just a few yards in front of him. The free-flowing traffic had slowed to a crawl, but the Moskowitz car was still traveling at full speed. The rabbi slammed the brakes to avoid hitting the truck. His car came to a jolting stop inches from the truck. The family was safe.

As the traffic began to move again, Rabbi Moskowitz shifted his foot from the brake to the gas and prepared to resume the journey. The car did not budge. The motor had stopped wheezing and instead commenced with a pathetic death rattle, and then, silence. Fortunately, the car had chosen to die in close proximity to a rest stop. The rabbi shifted the car into neutral and pushed it — an overburdened, balky beast — into the gas station.

A firm believer in the power of prayer, Rabbi Moskowitz took a moment to silently beseech the Heavens that his car would have a speedy recovery and that he and his family and his big pile of stuff would make it to Boston in time for Yom Tov. Meanwhile, a mechanic, whose pocket was embroidered "Bob," was bent under the hood, emitting the kind of "hmmm" a dentist emits as he views the site of an impending root canal.

"Well, sir," the mechanic somberly pronounced, "looks like your transmission."

"Really?" the Rabbi asked.

"Yup," Bob confirmed. "And there is no way for me to fix it today."

"Now what am I going to do?" Rabbi Moskowitz wondered out loud. Then, with a spark of hope, he asked "Bob, how much would you give me for the car?"

"This piece of junk isn't worth more then 25 bucks, tops," Bob answered without a moment's hesitation.

"Well, that's not going to help. How long to have it fixed?"

"Give me a couple of days and I'll have it all fixed."

"All right, Bob, you just take care of the car and make sure to have it ready as soon as possible. I'll have to find another way to get to Boston. Do you have the phone numbers of some rental-car companies?"

Bob supplied the numbers and Rabbi Moskowitz began calling the car rentals in the New Haven vicinity, where they were stranded. The effort turned out to be futile, however, since the rental companies all required a credit card, and he didn't have one. Neither was he carrying enough cash. All he had was his checkbook full of New Jersey checks which, for some reason, were not regarded as legal tender by any of the rental companies. There had to be a way out of this mess, but at the moment, the rabbi could not imagine what it might be.

Then, out of the dark came a flash of inspiration. He asked Bob for a phone book. If he could find a shul, he thought, perhaps he could get some help from a fellow Jew. Skimming the "synagogue" listing, he found what he needed. Soon he was on the phone with Rabbi Willner.

"Don't worry," Rabbi Willner told him. "I'll be there in a half-hour and I'll cash a check for you so you can get a rental car."

A short while later, Bob witnessed a sight that was unbelievable to his eyes. Rabbi Willner drove up, the two men introduced themselves to each other and within minutes, Rabbi Willner was exchanging Rabbi Moskowitz's check for cash.

"You'd cash this guy's check even though you never met him before?" Bob asked.

"I never heard of anything like it!"

The two men then began shifting the contents of the Moskowitz car into the Willner car. Out came the pots and pans, boxes of matzah and wine, suitcases, hat boxes, toys, a portacrib and much more.

"Looks like the Jews are leaving Egypt!" Bob joked.

Once the transfer was completed, Rabbi Willner drove Rabbi Moskowitz up the road to the car-rental outlet. The deal was done, the family was retrieved from the service station and they were back on the road to Boston at last.

On Chol HaMoed, Rabbi Moskowitz called the repair shop to find out if his car was ready.

"Got it here waiting for you, Rabbi," Bob confirmed.

"Can I pick it up Sunday?"

"Sorry, closed on Sunday."

Once again, Rabbi Moskowitz was at a loss. He had to be back in Lakewood by Monday morning. There was no way to delay the return trip.

"Listen, I know it's a little unusual, but could I ask you to leave the car for me with the keys somewhere inside, and I'll mail you a check when I get home? Monday is really too late for me to come."

"Normally, Rabbi, I would never do that. But I see that you guys trust each other, so I guess I can trust you too. Your car will be waiting for you on Sunday. Have a safe trip."

The love one Jew has for another has no counterpart among the nations of the world. Because of our connection to each other, we are never alone in a time of need. We always have someone on whom to count, and when the rest of the world witnesses this loving bond, it creates a powerful Kiddush Hashem.

I Can

Suri Jacobs walked slowly in her leg braces. A fair-haired girl with soft green eyes and a pretty, round face, she radiated an almost angelic quality. Her beauty, however, was often overlooked as eyes honed in directly on her spindly, metal-encased legs. To the little girls in her class, her slow, heavy movements looked peculiar. Why couldn't she run and jump rope like all the other girls? There was something wrong with Suri, and in their childish insensitivity, some of her fellow students at B'nos Yaakov in Brooklyn made sure to point it out.

What they could not understand was that Suri's ability to walk — even slowly and supported by braces — was a miracle. Born with spina bifida, a disease of the neural cord, Suri was expected to spend her life in a wheelchair. It was only the child's overwhelming will to succeed that gave her the strength to stand on her own two legs.

Besides the outward challenge that all could see, Suri suffered from yet another, hidden problem. When she was only a week old, she underwent surgery for hydrocephalus, a dangerous buildup of fluids in the brain. The surgeons had inserted a drainage tube that led from her brain to her stomach, where the excess fluid could be absorbed into her system.

All of these medical difficulties, however, did not defeat Suri. Self-pity had no place in her personality. She surrounded herself with good friends, worked hard in class and created a happy life for herself.

One day in fifth grade, Suri was walking home from school along her usual route. Knowing she could not go quickly, she moved cautiously along the Brooklyn streets, giving herself plenty of time to cross the busy avenues. On this particular day, she began crossing when a car turned quickly from a side street and rammed into her frail body, sending her sprawling on the pavement. There had not even been time for her to scream.

Immediately, a crowd began to gather around the fallen girl. Fortunately, the injuries didn't appear to be serious — just a superficial cut on the forehead. Although stunned and in pain, Suri was alert and fully aware of the commotion around her.

"Get an ambulance!" people were shouting. Within a few moments, help arrived and Suri was transported to a nearby hospital.

"You just need a few stitches on your forehead," the doctor assured her. "It's nothing serious." Within hours, Suri was back home, her bandage giving her the heroic look of a wounded warrior.

The school year ended, and sooner than any child would like, a new one began. Suri worked hard in sixth grade, striving to keep up with the faster pace and the greater levels of responsibility the students were given. Several months into the year, she began having difficulty seeing the blackboard. The teacher moved her to a desk closer to the front of the room, but her ability to see did not improve. One day, Suri's teacher observed her taking notes.

"Why are you writing so big?" she asked her student. Suri was bewildered. She hadn't realized that she was writing in anything but a normal script.

It was only a short few days later that Suri found herself undergoing a CT scan to determine the cause of her rapidly deteriorating eyesight.

"It seems that when you had the accident last year, the impact of your fall caused the tube in your head to crack," the doctor informed her. "Fluid has built up there and damaged the optic nerve."

Surgery was performed to repair the tube, but the doctors were unable to reverse the damage that had already been done. When the operation was over, Suri could not be brought back to consciousness. She lay in her bed in a state of deep sleep for an entire week. No one could explain why this young girl with the indomitable will to achieve and thrive would not open her eyes.

Finally, after a long and frightening week, Suri awoke, but the world to which she had emerged was drastically different from the one in which she had lived before. She opened her pretty green eyes, but they saw nothing. She tried to speak, but her confident, happy voice could not emerge from her throat. Mute and swathed in darkness, Suri could do nothing but listen to the voices — the doctors' concerned mutterings, her parents' heartbroken words of encouragement — that surrounded her.

On the second day after Suri awakened, two doctors stood outside her room. One was a middle-aged man with wire-rim glasses and a gentle demeanor. He spoke to the younger doctor, an intern whose education would now include the unusual case of Suri Jacobs.

"We have not yet been able to pinpoint any reason for her inability to speak since the surgery," the older doctor informed the student. "Today we will be sending in a speech therapist to see if there is any possibility of rehabilitation."

They walked into the young patient's room and found her sitting up against her pillows, caressing a large, soft white teddy bear her classmates had brought her.

"Good morning, Suri. How are you today?" asked the elder doctor. "I've brought Dr. Rosen along with me this morning to see you."

"Guuu maa," came Suri's response.

"Suri! You're trying to speak! Beautiful. This is a great improvement. Are you feeling a little better today?"

"Mmmm."

It wasn't exactly discernible, but it did communicate one fact clearly. In the realm of speech, at least, there was reason for hope. And indeed, within a few days, with the help of therapy, Suri totally regained her power of speech. Her eyesight, however, did not follow suit. It was gone, and would remain gone for the rest of her life.

Now the girl who had faced every imaginable challenge in her young life had a new, unimaginable challenge to overcome. The day she arrived home from the hospital, her parents led her to the living room couch, helped her sit down and brought her a bowl of her favorite chocolate-chip ice cream. There in that spot, Suri remained frozen for hours. She feared moving about the house in the darkness. She envisioned herself tripping over a toy on the floor or walking into a wall. She imagined unseen dangers lurking all around her. The house that had been as familiar to her as her face in the mirror was now a source of stark terror.

"When you're ready," her mother told her quietly, "we'll help you. There is a woman whose special skill is in helping people learn how to get around safely without their sight. I know it seems impossible, Suri. But there are thousands of people who go to school and to jobs every day, even though they can't see."

The thought of learning to live with blindness had not, until that point, even occurred to Suri. But now, her heart began to lift just a little, like a tiny bird making its first fluttering foray off solid ground. She felt the familiar tingle of challenge, hope and the will to overcome.

Within three weeks, Suri had mastered her surroundings and was ready to begin the process of re-entering the outside world. Her chief motivation was the burning desire to get back to school, to be among friends and to rededicate her mind, which had been so utterly overtaken by medical matters, to the pursuit of learning.

It might have taken much longer to achieve her goal of returning to school had it not been for the outpouring of support and encouragement her friends provided. One girl placed herself in charge of bringing Suri up the stairs to their classroom. Another girl escorted her down. They helped her with her classwork, studying for tests, homework and anything else she needed. Likewise, her teachers made every imaginable accommodation. They would convey the written material to her orally, and then give her oral exams. Suri's steely determination to adapt, along with her warm appreciation for all that was done for her, inspired everyone in her circle.

In the summer before seventh grade, Suri learned Braille. When school resumed, her parents purchased Braille editions of her textbooks, allowing her to learn alongside all the other girls. Except for her inability to see the blackboard, she was able to function fully as a student. Her teachers compensated for that one gap by reading the board notes out loud as they wrote them.

In the area of mobility, as well, Suri was becoming independent. She learned her way around school, how to manage the stairs, and even how to cross streets by listening to traffic. Despite the incredible impediments she had faced, she finished her elementary school years as an outgoing, active girl.

Choosing a high school, however, presented a whole new host of issues. Some well-meaning friends advised her parents to send her to public school, where the resources would be available to meet her needs. The family would not even consider that option, however. Suri could not see herself as anything but a Bais Yaakov student, and she was certain that there would be some school willing to accept her — braces, blindness and all.

Bais Leah turned out to be that school. Upon meeting Suri and inquiring about her from her former teachers, the administration was determined to do whatever it could to accommodate this courageous and inspiring young woman. Her years there were blessed with success and friendship — an oasis of growth and happiness after years of struggle. She began at this young age to be sought as a speaker on the subject of disabilities. Girls who were struggling with the mundane challenges of adolescence would walk away from her lectures with a refreshingly new perspective on faith and perseverance.

When high school was over, Suri was face-to-face once more with her disabilities. What career could she pursue? Though she would have loved to teach, she realized that such a career would have been impractical in her circumstances. She attended seminary for a few months, but without a goal to motivate her, it left her unsatisfied. Eventually, she found herself sitting home, waiting for inspiration to strike.

At last, it did. Mrs. Sampson, the principal of a local elementary school, had seen Suri deliver a speech at a summer camp, and was impressed by her dynamic presence. Now she needed someone to test students on the *berachos* they had learned, and thought Suri would be just the person to inject warmth and excitement into the program. So Suri began a career that started with the *berachos* tests and progressed to a responsible position in the school office. Her days were busy, filled with action, conversation and fulfillment.

Her nights, however, were becoming unbearable. At first, she enjoyed attending her friends' weddings. The music, the excitement, the chance to socialize with her old classmates made each occasion something special. She loved getting dressed up, even though she didn't have the confirmation of a mirror image to tell her how lovely she looked.

But the thrill of the wedding scene began slowly to turn into pain. One by one, her circle of friends disappeared into their own married lives — a life Suri knew she would never have. She imagined herself at 30, at 40, even at 50, still occupying her desk in the school office, coming home each night to the quiet order of her lonely life. Attending weddings became too difficult; Suri could not bear to bring sadness with her to someone else's simchah.

Even with this disappointment weighing upon her heart, however, Suri refused to stagnate. Even if she couldn't date, she could still live and grow. One day, when she was 23 years old, she came upon a plan that would broaden her horizons and feed her desire to learn. She would enroll in a one-month post-seminary program at Neve Yerushalayim. Suri contacted another single friend, and the two were soon sitting in a classroom in Eretz Yisrael, relishing the chance to live in the rarified world of Torah learning, insights and ideas for a few short weeks. The two friends took long walks through the Old City, and through the streets of Geulah and Meah Shearim. Suri absorbed the sounds and smells that became her "vision" of Yerushalayim, while her friend described in loving detail all that Suri's eyes could not see.

One night, as Suri lay fast asleep, her phone rang. The shrill sound jolted her out of a dream.

Who could be calling now? she wondered. *I hope it's not an emergency!*

She grabbed the phone and, sounding both sleepy and alarmed, nearly shouted, "Hello?"

"Suri, it's Mommy. I'm sorry to wake you up. I know it's the middle of the night there, but this couldn't wait."

"What is it? Is everything ...."

"Oh, my. I shouldn't scare you. Everything is fine. I'm sorry I didn't say that first. It's just that I'm kind of excited. Listen, Suri, Rabbi Shain called this afternoon, and he has a wonderful boy who would like to go out with you. We checked him out, and we think it's really worthwhile for you to give it a try."

"Ma, forget about it, please. I'm not getting married so fast. We can talk about this when I get home, O.K.?"

When Suri came home, she agreed to one date with Boruch, the young man Rabbi Shain had proposed. Three weeks later, Mrs. Jacobs called Rabbi Shain (the principal of the high school. He had helped Suri find her job) to inform him that they were expecting to announce an engagement within a few days.

"Wait," Rabbi Shain interjected. "Did you check with Dor Yesharim yet?" He was adamant that, despite the difficulty in finding a match for Suri, the couple should use this organization's services to test their genetic compatibility and avoid the tragic outcome of children bearing fatal recessive diseases.

"Truthfully, we never had Suri tested," Mrs. Jacobs confessed. "We never thought there would be a need. But you've changed all that, Rabbi Shain."

"There's an expedited testing service available," said Rabbi Shain. "I'll help them get it done quickly."

Within two days, the results were in, the couple was found to be compatible and the engagement was joyfully announced. Suri felt as though she were living in a dream that she had never even dared to dream. A few months later, she and Boruch were a married couple living in their own home, which had been customized with Braille-labeled appliances to allow the mistress of the house to do everything other housewives did.

After settling into married life, she returned to her office, but now there was one immense difference. When the day was done, she returned to her own home and her own wonderful husband. She couldn't imagine anyone being happier, until one day, several months later, she discovered that she was expecting.

Another page turned in the incredible story of Suri's life, and a new chapter opened. The awkward, disabled girl who had braved school-yard teasing ... the resilient child who had learned to live her life all over again in complete darkness ... the young woman who we prepared to face the prospect of life alone ... and then, with the sudden burst of salvation that only Hashem can deliver, Suri was the joyful mother of an active, healthy little boy.

Suri has continued the career she began in high school, speaking publicly about facing life's challenges. "We all have challenges to overcome," she tells her listeners. "We must not think for one minute that these come as a punishment for something we've done wrong. They are always an opportunity that Hashem is giving us to prod us to reach for our potential.

"Everything is for our benefit. We have to thank Hashem for the good He gives us, and do our best to share our gifts with others. It's all about giving."

Coming from Suri, the truth of this message hits home every time.

One who refuses to become steeped in resentment and despair, and instead concentrates on maximizing his situation, can succeed against the greatest odds.

A World
of Torah
and Mitzvos

Above
and Beyond

enny Davis pulled the heavy black receiver off the phone that hung on the wall next to the refrigerator. With one long, slender finger, she pushed the rotary dial through the "grind-click-click-click" of her brother's home number in Montreal. Pulling the coiled cord across the small apartment kitchen, she sat down at her small, Formica table and sipped a cup of afternoon tea as she waited for an answer.

"Aaron? I'm so glad I got you," she told her brother. "I really need your advice."

Henny's son Shmully was a solid student at Rabbi Jacob Joseph Yeshivah, popularly known as RJJ, near the Davis's apartment on the Lower East Side. But now, both his *rebbeiim* and Shmully himself agreed that it was time to move on.

"I have no idea where to even inquire," Henny told her brother. Aaron had taken a fatherly role in Shmully's life ever since Henny's husband had died 17 years earlier, while her son was just a baby.

"And besides that, will another yeshivah be willing to accept the tuition I can pay? And do I really want my Shmully to be far away from me?"

Aaron Katz heard the confusion in his sister's voice. It hadn't been easy for her to raise her son alone. It was 1958 and, already, the Lower East Side was far different from the neighborhood in which he and Henny had grown up. But as a widow raising her son on her own, Henny preferred to remain there, surrounded by the vibrant streets, kosher shops and shuls she knew so well. It was hard for her to picture Shmully, with his confident smile and gentle brown eyes, living anywhere else in the world.

"There are a few good possibilities," Aaron told his sister. "But I think the best for Shmully would be Yeshiva Rabbi Chaim Berlin. That's Rav Yitzchak Hutner's yeshivah. Let me call and see if we can arrange for a *farher.*"

Instantly, Henny felt the burden lift from her slight shoulders. She was confident that if Aaron had recommended Yeshiva Rabbi Chaim Berlin, Shmully would thrive there.

Soon, Shmully was proving her prediction true. He took to the new yeshivah instantly. Nonetheless, with the devotion of a loving father, his Uncle Aaron traveled to New York every few months to keep track of Shmully's progress. The highlight of these trips was a visit to the Rosh Yeshivah.

On those occasions, Shmully would escort his uncle to Rav Hutner's house and wait in an outer room while the two men spoke. Shmully could always tell when the conversation turned to learning, for a lively debate would ensue that he could clearly hear from where he waited. Though the sounds were muffled by the walls, the animation in their voices as the two men questioned, challenged and offered their rebuttals could be nothing other than the sound of Torah. Uncle Aaron's astute, retentive mind made him a worthy partner for Rav Hutner, who would often tell Shmully how much he loved his uncle and enjoyed speaking to him.

It was a freezing Tuesday afternoon in February when Shmully once more brought his uncle to the Rosh Yeshivah's home. Rav Hutner had not often been seen by his *talmidim* that winter, as he was recuperating from a broken leg. Uncle and nephew marched quickly down the icy sidewalks, heads bowed against a knife-sharp wind, until they arrived at the Rosh Yeshivah's home. There, Shmully warmed up in his accustomed spot in the outer room, while his Uncle Aaron basked in Rav Hutner's company. Shmully heard the familiar music of their voices rising and falling in the rhythm of learning, until nearly one hour later, they emerged together, smiling, shaking hands and wishing each other well.

That week, a blizzard of historic scale brought New York to a standstill. More than two feet of snow choked the roads and made the sidewalks impassable. By Shabbos, people were just beginning to crawl out from under the slushy, mounded mess to resume their normal lives.

The following Tuesday, a week after Uncle Aaron's visit, Shmully sat in the *beis medrash* learning with his *chavrusa*. Suddenly, he received a tap on the shoulder.

As Shmully looked up, the boy who had tapped him moved closer to his ear.

"The Rosh Yeshivah wants to speak with you in his office," the boy told him quietly.

Shmully was perplexed as he sat down in Rav Hutner's office. *What could he want to speak to me about?* he wondered.

The first sentence he heard took him by surprise: "I want to tell you what your uncle did for me this week," Rav Hutner began.

The Rosh Yeshivah's story began with a fact Shmully hadn't known — that on each of his uncle's visits, he had given the Rosh Yeshivah some money toward Shmully's expenses. Aaron knew that his sister's means were very limited, and although the yeshivah had been willing to accept Shmully on that basis, Aaron wanted to provide something extra.

On this most recent visit one week prior, Aaron had left the Rosh Yeshivah with a very large sum of money, much more than would seem to be within his means. Rav Hutner recalled their conversation. "I said to him, 'Reb Aaron, you're a rebbi. How can you afford to pay all this?'"

"He answered very simply: 'A Yid darf zich unshtrengen.' That means that a Jew must stretch himself."

The words resounded in the Rosh Yeshivah's mind. They were stated in a tone so simple, so direct — as if this were everyone's philosophy in life.

On the Friday after Uncle Aaron's visit, Rav Hutner received a phone call from someone who had helped him when he first arrived in America many years earlier. Rav Hutner had not heard from the man since that time, but on that day, he was calling to offer the Rosh Yeshivah a way to repay the favor.

"He was making a melavah malkah for his shul that Motzaei Shabbos," Rav Hutner told Shmully, "and he wanted me to attend."

Despite his desire to fulfill the man's request, Rav Hutner had to decline. It would have simply been impossible, or at least extremely difficult, for him to negotiate the snow and ice with his still unhealed leg. He regretfully explained the situation and the conversation ended.

But it did not fade from Rav Hutner's memory. Instead, it became a greater and greater presence. A Yid darf zich unshtrengen, a voice in his mind repeated. It was true, he knew, but a human being still has limitations.

All Friday night, that phrase kept resurfacing in the Rosh Yeshivah's mind.

"I realized that unless I went to the melavah malkah, I would have no peace," Rav Hutner told Shmully.

Immediately after Havdalah, the Rosh Yeshivah summoned Dovid, a student who lived on his block, and asked him to dig his car out of the snow as quickly as possible. Working with another boy, Dovid dug out the car and the two boys accompanied the

Rosh Yeshivah to the *melavah malkah.*

"The man was so happy to see me," said Rav Hutner. "He seated me at the head table with all the *rabbanim.* And why did I undertake this trip, Shmully? Because of your uncle's words to me ... words I can't forget. *A Yid darf zich unshtrengen.*"

Shmully replayed the details of the story as he walked back to the *beis medrash:* his uncle's behind-the-scenes monetary support, the words he lived by, the impact of those words. It was a lesson for life, all wrapped up in a series of events that had unfolded just that week. As Shmully walked along, he noticed Dovid, the boy who had dug out the Rosh Yeshivah's car, standing nearby.

"So, how did you like the *melavah malkah?*" Shmully asked him.

"How did you know? Who told you?" Dovid responded as if he had been caught with the loot of a bank robbery.

"What's wrong, Dovid?" Shmully asked. "What are you so excited about?"

"The Rosh Yeshivah told us not to tell anyone what happened," he answered.

"Well, I know all about it. Tell me what you know and I'll tell you what I know."

Dovid's side of the story added a sense of the urgency the Rosh Yeshivah felt in living up to Aaron's words.

"He was rushing us to finish," Dovid recounted. "Every five minutes, he was looking out the window to see if it was done. We thought something must have been wrong. Finally, we got in the car and started driving down the streets. The driving was just terrible. The Rosh Yeshivah sat in the front seat shaking back and forth and repeating these words 'A Yid darf zich unshtrengen' over and over and over again."

When a person faces a task that seems too difficult, remembering the words "A Yid darf zich unshtrengen" could transform the impossible into the possible, allowing each person to truly do his utmost for his fellow Jew and Klal Yisrael.

Reborn

The town of Malachaka, outside of Moscow, might have been a pleasant resort at one time. But by the time Rabbi Naftoli Cukier arrived there in 1992, the decline and fall of the Soviet Union had taken the sheen off whatever glamour the town had possessed. Malachaka was a gray, rust-stained, weather-beaten locale. It did have one advantage, however. It was large enough to have been chosen to host a seminar organized by Vaad Hatzolas Nidchei Yisroel.

By 1992, much had changed since the organization's founding 11 years earlier. In those years, the Communists were still in power, and studying or practicing Judaism was a high crime. The little trickles of underground Judaism that had leaked into the country had now, under the new, democratic regime, burst into an open, rushing river. Still, it was not enough to slake the thirst of the Jews who had suffered through seven decades of spiritual drought. They flocked to Malachaka from all over the country, seeking the chance to find their connection with their long-lost heritage.

The organizers of the seminar were accustomed to an overflow crowd, having run seminars in Malachaka since 1988. They had developed their own "triage" method to choose which guests could stay and which would be asked to come back another time. Generally, they relied on the age of the participant as the deciding factor. The older people had been well trained in the Communist ethic. It was difficult to break through to their *neshamos.* Younger people were more open and, therefore, the effort expended on them was more likely to bear fruit. In addition, they would be raising children of their own, offering fertile ground for the seeds of Torah to be planted.

Rabbi Cukier approached a couple who appeared to be in their mid-60's.

"I'm very sorry to do this," he began. "But as you can see, we have more people here than we can possibly accommodate. We have to ask you to come back another time."

The elderly man, named Joseph, stood slim and erect, staring in disbelief at the rabbi. A heavy mustache exaggerated the look of displeasure on his face, providing a thick frame for his frown. In a worn blue jacket and cap, he was the picture of the weary traveler.

"Excuse me," he said with a simmering anger cloaked in politeness. "We have spent two days on the road to get here. After spending 20 hours traveling, how can you tell us to leave? We cannot. We must stay here."

Rabbi Cukier quickly realized he had selected the wrong couple to send home. He smiled amiably, conveying the impression that, on second thought, Joseph and his wife were completely welcome to stay.

"Well, if that's the case, then we will just have to find some way to accommodate you here at the seminar," Rabbi Cukier assured them.

During the next few days, however, the wisdom of the "triage" method seemed to be bearing itself out. The days were packed with Torah lectures, each attended by crowds of guests eager to learn. Joseph and his wife were notably absent.

Twenty-five American yeshivah students had come to the seminar to study, one-on-one, with the Russian men. The guests flocked to the temporary *beis medrash* to learn with them, creating a vibrant electric charge in the depressing, worn-down old room. Joseph was nowhere among the learners. There were three *minyanim* a day, most of which Joseph was careful not to miss. He and his wife took part in the bountiful meals, but when the room came alive with singing and dancing, they sat stolidly in their seats, as if enduring an ordeal.

Rabbi Cukier observed their deadpan expressions in even the most exhilarating moments. *The Communists had really done their job,* he thought. *It seemed as if they had managed to kill even their eternal souls.*

One morning, as Rabbi Cukier waited for the crowd to assemble for Shacharis, he noted with surprise that Joseph was heading toward him.

"Rabbi, I would like you to please give me a *tallis* and *tefillin,*" he stated simply. There were plenty of both on hand for just this purpose. Joseph accepted the loans gratefully, as well as a *siddur.* As the services began, Joseph's bland expression softened and melted. His eyes were squeezed tight with fervor. His mouth moved emphatically, as if he had very important business to discuss with his Maker. A trickle of moisture crept from the corners of his eyes.

Whatever had stirred Joseph was more than the winds of change; it was a full-force hurricane. Later that day, he asked Rabbi Cukier to set him up with a learning partner, and from that moment on, he spent every available moment immersed in learning. He and his wife sat attentively at the classes, soaking up the words of wisdom and inspiration. Joseph's wife now appeared in public with her hair covered by a kerchief and a shawl modestly draped over her shoulders. They had transformed themselves from stone-cold atheists into passionately devoted Jews, all in a day.

The next day, Joseph approached Rabbi Cukier with another astounding request.

"Rabbi, my wife and I unfortunately never had a Jewish wedding. We were hoping that perhaps you could arrange for us to have one here, and we would like you to be our *mesader kiddushin.*"

"I'd be happy to help you out," the Rabbi said. "and I'd be honored to take part in the wedding. But could you just answer one question for me? The first few days, you didn't seem interested in Judaism at all. Now, you've completely turned around. Tell me, what changed?"

"To explain that, I would have to tell you a story," Joseph replied.

The Rabbi listened carefully as a poignant, horrifying story unfolded.

"Sixty years ago, when I was a little boy, we lived in a *shtetl* in Russia," said Joseph. "We had a shul in our town where we used to go to *daven* and learn. One day, soldiers came barging into the shul. They ran up to the *aron kodesh* and began to remove the Torah scrolls. When the people in the town heard what was going on, they all ran to the shul to stop the soldiers. They weren't going to let them take away their Torah without a fight.

"There was a big commotion as the people begged the soldiers to leave the Torah scrolls alone. When the soldiers didn't stop, some members of the shul tried to physically stop them. They were thrown to the ground, the police were called and many Jews were arrested.

"The police wanted to make an example out of these Jews and show everyone what happens when you don't obey the law.

"They took these poor Jews and locked them in a cellar that served as a jail. Then they filled the room up with water, until it reached the prisoners' chests. They left these poor souls there for a few days without any food or water. After a while, most of the people were so weakened that they collapsed into the water or fell asleep and drowned. Most of the men of our shul died in that jail. Those that survived were broken both physically and emotionally.

"The shul was closed down after that, and there was no trace of Judaism left in our town. I was a child at the time. Growing up, it really bothered me that there was no shul even though the authorities allowed Christians and other groups to have some symbols of their religion. The Jews had nothing.

"I completely forgot about Judaism. Eventually, I became a painter and married and lived the life of a real Communist, who just happened to be Jewish.

"My son recently became religious himself, and when he heard about this seminar he convinced my wife and me to attend. At first, I must admit that I wasn't interested at all, but I decided

I would give it a try for my son's sake. Then something amazing happened. A few days ago, I came to Shacharis in the morning and, Rabbi Cukier, if you remember, you asked me to lift the Torah up when they were finished reading from it. I was honored with *hagbah*.

"I stepped up to the Torah with trepidation. I lifted it with all my strength and I was completely moved by the experience. When I came before that Torah, I pictured myself 60 years ago, watching the soldiers taking the Torah scrolls out of our shul. At that time, I believed that I would never see a Torah again. Certainly, I never imagined I would carry a Torah in my hands. Then you gave me *hagbah*."

Joseph broke down, overcome with the pain of memories no words could express. His shoulders heaved with his silent sobs, and for a few moments, the rabbi just looked on, an awed witness to an internal earthquake. Pressing his hands against his face, as if to force back the tears, Joseph again stood erect, ready to resume his story.

"I felt as if there were a tremendous mountain on top of my heart, and there was something buried deep underneath it," he related. "But the mountain could not be lifted, because two black angels were holding it down. Then, when you gave me *hagbah* and as I lifted the Torah, I felt as if two white angels had come and lifted the mountain off my heart and thrown it away. This mountain had been crushing my soul for the last 60 years, but I lifted the Torah, and the mountain was gone. Thanks to you, my *neshamah* was ready to learn again.

"Overnight, I began to remember some of the things I learned as a child in *cheder*, a little about Moshe leading the Jews out of Egypt and parts of the *alef-beis*. And that's why I suddenly had the desire to put on *tefillin* and learn Torah once again. It all started with you giving me *hagbah*."

Shortly thereafter, a radiant bride and groom stood under the *chuppah* that had awaited them for decades. The yeshivah boys poured their high-voltage energy into singing, dancing and bringing smiles of indescribable joy to the couple's faces. Rabbi Cukier served as the *mesader kiddushin*, as had been requested. He presented Joseph with a pair of *tefillin* as a wedding gift.

Finally, this momentous seminar came to an end. Joseph and his wife traveled back to their hometown, but they kept in touch with Rabbi Cukier during the year.

The next year, when Rabbi Cukier returned to Russia for another seminar, Joseph and his wife were among the first to arrive. A completely observant Jewish couple stood where, the year before, a strained and suspicious twosome had refused to be sent home. The rabbi greeted them like old friends.

"You know the *tefillin* you gave me?" Joseph asked the rabbi. "Well, don't think that I am the only one who uses them. Every day, there are six boys who come to my house, and I have them each put on the *tefillin*. They come to my house for Shabbos. We sing songs and learn Torah together. And to think, all this has happened because you gave me *hagbah*."

Today, Joseph is known as Reb Yosef of Beitar, Israel. He can usually be found in a *kollel*, immersed in learning, his head capped with a large black *yarmulka* and his face adorned with a long white beard. He may look like an elderly Torah scholar, but he learns with the energy of a young man, for in his eyes, he was born in 1992.

In 2002, he had the opportunity to see Rabbi Cukier. "I am 10 years old today," he told him. "Because it was 10 years ago that you brought my *neshamah* back into this world." Three years later, at the age of 78, he celebrated his bar mitzvah — 13 years after the day that *hagbah* changed his life.

When Rabbi Cukier handed the recalcitrant Joseph a chance to lift the Torah, he could never have known the enormity of what was really being lifted. And for the rest of Reb Yosef's life, the upward power of that moment will never lose its ability to elevate everything it touches.

Chazal teach that we must not take what we perceive as a small mitzvah lightly, for one can never know what one small mitzvah might accomplish.

Dancing for Joy

T he *beis medrash* of the Telz Yeshivah resounded all morning long with the sounds of impassioned learning. It was not just an undercurrent, it was a full-bodied roar that emerged from the *talmidim's* emphatic arguments and search for true understanding. At last, the time came for a break, and the young men, like exhausted prizefighters, would use their time-out to recoup energy for the next round. Often, this would mean taking a stroll through the neighboring woods and fields.

"Young man, why don't you come and walk through my fields?" the neighboring farmers would often beckon.

"Oh, no, thank you," the students would reply. "We don't want to damage your property."

But the farmers would insist, for they had seen with their own eyes that wherever the Telzer students left their footprints, Hashem's blessings would rest. Those fields would produce crops that were larger, healthier and more plentiful than anything else the farmer grew.

That, said Rav Mordechai Gifter, was the blatant power of the Torah of Telz. He often related these slices of life in his old home of Telz to his students at the Cleveland Telz Yeshivah, where he served as Rosh Yeshivah for 55 years. Like a torchbearer carrying a flame from across the ocean and the decades, he would try to ignite in his students some of the fiery passion that burned within the walls of the Lithuanian yeshivos in their pre-war golden era.

The fuel for that fire was *simchah*: pure, unfettered joy in the ability to connect to Hashem through His holy Torah. One of Rav Gifter's favorite stories revealed the depths of that joy. He recalled that Rav Simcha Zissel Ziv, known as the Alter of Kelm, would occasionally disappear from his *beis medrash*, only to reappear later as if nothing had transpired. This mysterious habit piqued the curiosity of the students, and finally, one of them asked for an explanation. The Alter explained that he would struggle with a piece of Gemara for a long period of time, and finally, he would understand it. He would arrive at a clarity and depth he had not seen before, and this revelation would fill him with a joy so overwhelming that he longed to dance.

"So, I go up to the attic and dance," he explained simply. "And then I come back."

"But why does the Rosh Yeshivah have to dance in the attic? Why not dance here in the *beis medrash*?" the student persisted.

"Why? Because people would think I'm crazy," the Alter of Kelm answered, as if it were the obvious explanation.

A few days after telling his students this story, Rav Gifter was guiding them through a complex Gemara. At last, they reached a point of sparkling clarity, and Rav Gifter declared jubilantly, "Now, this is real *simchah!*"

"Then why don't we get up and dance like Rav Simcha Zissel did?" said Yisroel, one of the students.

He didn't wait for an answer. His idea grabbed every student sitting there, and they all rose to their feet and began dancing around the room, singing with pure joy. The students in the *beis medrash* heard the noise and went to Rav Gifter's room to see what the occasion was; perhaps someone had a *simchah* in the family. But as they came through the doorway, they were pulled into the circle and enveloped in the spirit that seemed to lift the room off its foundations. The circle flew around and around, the rhythmic pounding of feet keeping time with joyful songs of Hashem and His Torah. For this one group of yeshivah *bachurim* in this one classroom in Cleveland, it had suddenly become Simchas Torah — not on the calendar, but in their hearts.

To the degree that a person labors in Torah, he experiences the incomparable joy of learning.

Forever Lost

"Thank you, thank you, Reb Shmuel," said the soft-spoken young man as he backed out the door. "*Tizku l'mitzvos.*"

He stepped out of the air-conditioned home into the simmering heat, which instantly closed in around his head like an enveloping, steaming towel. *All right,* he thought, catching his breath. *"There's just one more stop today, and it's right next door."*

The year was 1970, and Yerucham Pitter and his friend had volunteered to spend a week of their summer break collecting funds for Bais Medrash Govoha, Lakewood's renowned yeshivah. They had been dispatched to Chicago armed with a list of yeshivah supporters, and they had been diligently visiting each one as Chicago's worst heat wave in years lingered on and on.

Most of their stops had been productive, but none had provided the big "jackpot" they had hoped to take back to Lakewood with them. The next house was one that might well yield a substantial donation, judging from the stately elegance it projected from its position set back from the road, partially hidden by the tall, leafy hedge that marked the property's border. This family hadn't been on his list at all, but Reb Shmuel, the last donor he had visited, suggested paying his neighbor a visit.

"He's a wealthy businessman," he had told Yerucham. "Give him a try."

Yerucham made his way along the circular driveway leading to a stone staircase, at the top of which were two tall oak doors. The pavement seemed to breathe waves of heat at his reddening face as he slowly plodded forward. *Look confident, energetic and positive,* he thought as he approached the doorway. It was advice that a successful fundraiser he knew had given him as he prepared for his trip. *I look more like that,* he thought, observing the wilted petunias that edged the well-watered lawn.

Yerucham knocked hard on the heavy door, certain that a lighter tap would never penetrate the inner reaches of the massive house. He waited awhile, and then knocked again, straining his ears for the sound of footsteps. The moments passed slowly as the sun bore down on Yerucham's head, but at last, a slim woman warily peeked out the door. Her thin white hair rested like a cumulous cloud in puffs around her head. Her face seemed ancient, but alive with the youthful sparkle of clear blue eyes and a gracious smile.

"Yes, young man," she asked in a heavy European accent. "Can I help you?"

"I would like to speak to Mr. Jacobs," Yerucham replied, unsure of whether he should reveal the nature of his visit.

The woman, who was obviously Mrs. Jacobs, invited Yerucham inside. She moved slowly, with a sturdy metal cane aiding her cautious steps. Despite her age and European roots, she dressed like an American grandmother in a pair of comfortable, white cotton slacks and a loose-fitting pale blue T-shirt.

She motioned to Yerucham to sit down in the living room, "Please," she said in Yiddish. "Have a seat. I'll go get my husband."

He sat down gratefully on a well-stuffed sofa and scanned his surroundings. It wasn't an ostentatious home at all. Rather, it bespoke quality and refined taste. The furniture was not the stark, modern type that was so popular in 1970, but rather the curved, polished-wood style of an earlier era. The walls were hung with family pictures and oil paintings framed in heavy, gilded museum-type frames. Many of the paintings depicted Jewish themes: a group of men and boys standing outside a small, village shul reciting *Kiddush Levanah*; a *chassan* and *kallah* beneath an outdoor *chuppah* in the moonlight; a rebbi pointing out words in a *sefer* to a small cluster of little boys who crowded around him.

This was clearly a proud Jewish home, but not the type of home to which Yerucham had become accustomed. His eyes wandered to the coffee table, and there, to his surprise, he saw a small pile of *sefarim*. Examining them more closely, he discovered that they were Hebrew commentaries on the *Chumash*. But who were these commentators? In all his years of learning, he had never encountered any of them.

His thoughts were interrupted by the entrance of a man who bore a striking resemblance to Albert Einstein. He was tall and thin, with a wild fringe of gray hair around his bald head.

Yerucham rose to shake his hand. "Yerucham Pitter," he introduced himself.

"Dan Jacobs," the host replied in an accent less pronounced than that of his wife. "Please sit down."

Dan got straight to business, grilling Yerucham about the purpose of his visit and the value of the cause for which he was collecting.

"Who runs this yeshivah?" Dan asked.

"Rav Aharon Kotler founded it," said Yerucham.

"I never heard of him," Dan replied.

"It's a major yeshivah," Yerucham explained. "The people who learn there become rabbis and leaders of Jewish communities all over the country. It's a noted center for learning."

"So, you're a *yeshivah bachur*," Dan interjected, smiling at Yerucham in an almost wistful way. "I, too, was once a *yeshivah bachur*, and I'll bet you've never heard of my Rosh Yeshivah either. But I'll tell you that he was one of the greatest in Europe, a very big *tzaddik*."

"Who was it?" Yerucham asked.

"An American boy would never have heard of him," Dan replied.

"Who? Please tell me," Yerucham urged.

"All right, I'll tell you," Dan relented. "His name was Rav Baruch Ber Liebowitz," he pronounced grandly.

"Well, certainly I've heard of him!" said Yerucham with a surge of excitement, as if they had discovered that they had the same great-uncle. "His *talmid* recorded his *shiurim* in the *Birkas Shmuel*. It's a classic *sefer*."

"No, that couldn't be. His work wasn't published," Dan insisted.

Yerucham quickly realized that the break between this man and the yeshivah world must have occurred before his rebbi's Torah had been published. It had apparently been a break so complete that news of the *sefer* had never reached the ears of his once loyal, admiring student.

"If you have a little time," said Dan, "I'll tell you about my Rosh Yeshivah. I grew up in a small *shtetl*, and everyone knew that I was a very bright boy. They used to call me an *iluy* (genius). My father hired a rebbi to learn with me when I was 12, and we continued until I was 14. At that point, the rebbi told my father that there was nothing more for him to teach me. He suggested that I go to Kaminetz to learn under Rav Boruch Ber Liebowitz. The next thing I knew, I was on a train headed to Kaminetz.

"When I got there, it was the middle of the night. I walked alone down the quiet streets until I reached the yeshivah, but the lights there were already out. There was no one to receive me, so I decided to enter the *beis medrash* and find a bench to sleep on for the night. I was so exhausted that as soon as I stretched out on the hard bench, I fell asleep.

"But in the middle of the night, I was awakened by the sound of the door opening. A short old man with a white beard walked into the room and headed straight to the *aron kodesh*. He opened its doors and put his head inside. I couldn't imagine what he would do next, but I was watching his every move. He began to cry like a child. 'Please, *Ribbono Shel Olam*, please tell me the meaning of the *Tosafos*. Let me understand Your Torah!' A few minutes later, he closed the *aron kodesh* and departed.

"The next morning, I was *davening* with the yeshivah and I saw the old man from the previous night heading to the front of the *beis medrash*. It was the Rosh Yeshivah himself. I introduced myself to him and showed him a letter from my rebbi. He accepted me into the yeshivah and gave me one of the best *bachurim* as a *chavrusa*. His name was Shloimele."

"What was his last name?" Yerucham asked. "Was it Heiman?"

"Why yes, it was. Shloimele Heiman. How did you know?"

"Because Rav Shloime Heiman later became the Rosh Yeshivah of Yeshivah Torah Vodaath in New York."

"There's a yeshivah in New York?" Dan asked incredulously. "I never heard of it."

Yerucham sat across from this man with his bare bald head and eccentric fringe of gray hair and wondered what could have happened to him. How did a man who traveled in the circles Dan described suddenly fall off the face of the Torah world?

Dan had found willing ears for his life's tale — a listener who not only expressed interest, but understood the grandeur of the world and the people he had known. He continued, his words tumbling out as though they had been pushing against the portals of his mind for decades.

"Once, my Rosh Yeshivah had trouble understanding a certain

Gemara, so he decided to travel by train all the way to his own rebbi to discuss it. His rebbi was an important Rosh Yeshivah in Brisk, whose name was Rav Chaim."

"Rav Chaim Solveitchik," Yerucham interjected.

"Yeah," said Dan. "You know about him too?"

"Who hasn't heard about Rav Chaim Brisker?" Yerucham answered. "He wrote *sefarim* on all of *Shas!*"

"Oh, I didn't know that. Anyway, when my Rosh Yeshivah came back, he was bursting with the piece of Torah."

With the memory now fresh in his mind, Dan grew animated. His face took on a different expression, as if he were playing a different character in the play of his life. He began relating the concept from *Mesechta Gittin* that his Rosh Yeshivah had heard from Rav Chaim.

"And when is the last time you said that piece of Gemara?" Yerucham asked him, astounded by the precision of his recall.

"Ha!" the old Dan was back. "I can't remember … it was that long ago. I don't do that stuff anymore." He paused, thoughtfully reviewing some snippet of his past. "I remember one time, I was going back to my parents for *bein hazmanim*. I went to Rav Boruch Ber and asked him if he could write me a letter for my father to let him know how I was doing. A sort of report card. He took a piece of paper and wrote 'assid lehiyos gadol b'Yisrael — in the future, he will become a great leader of the Jewish people.' So, what happened to this *gadol b'Yisrael?*"

It was the opening Yerucham had been waiting for.

"What did happen?" he asked Dan, trying to restrain the urgency in his voice.

"It was really very simple," Dan answered. "You see those books on the table?"

Yerucham glanced once again at the pile of unfamiliar *sefarim*. They were bound in the browns and burgundies of other *sefarim*, the gold embossing of their Hebrew titles dull with age.

"One summer, I went to Kiev for *bein hazmanim,* and I fell completely into the hands of *haskalah*. I can't recall each step I took away from Torah, because it happened so fast. I read these books and learned ideas I had never considered before. I didn't know how to react. In the end, my faith was shattered."

Yerucham left the man's house with an $18 donation, and a profound understanding of the pivotal impact of each step a person takes. Not just the impact on the person, but the impact on the entire world, for clearly Dan would have left his mark as a great Torah leader, just as his Rosh Yeshivah had predicted. Who knew what wisdom would have emanated from his Torah, what learning would have been generated by his pen?

Today, as Mashgiach of the Yeshivah of Long Beach, Rav Yerucham Pitter tells this story to his students as they prepare to depart for *bein hazmanim*. It illustrates with painful clarity that every word, every step and every decision can be a turning point in the story of a person's life.

A wrong move has the power to change the direction of our lives. If we keep in mind the tremendous potential we each bring into the world, we would perhaps make our choices with more faith and courage, avoiding anything that could diminish our ability to fulfill our full potential.

Light
and Happiness

A s Rabbi Braun spoke, he scrutinized the faces of his students. Were they with him? Engaged? Skeptical? Bored? It wasn't just a test of his teaching ability, it was a vital cue indicating whether this group of young Jewish men, none of whom came from religious backgrounds, was absorbing the Torah he was trying to impart. They had come to Ohr Somayach's winter seminar to give authentic Judaism a try, and Rabbi Avrohom Braun was determined to make sure that they found it a perfect fit.

As his eyes quickly moved from face to face, he noticed a completely unfamiliar face — that of a middle-aged woman — peeking in through the door. Outside, the hilly Monsey, New York landscape was covered with snow. The woman was dressed for the weather, with a fur-trimmed hat and a thick fur collar turned up against her neck.

I wonder who that might be? he thought. *Probably one of the students' mothers.*

After his class, Rabbi Braun went directly to his office, where he had arranged to meet with Asher Sokol, a student in the program. Asher was already there, brimming with a story that spilled out immediately.

"Rebbi, I have to tell you about the strangest thing that just happened," he said. "I was sitting outside in my car in the parking lot when I saw a woman going up the driveway toward the yeshivah. She seemed to be lost, so I got out of my car and asked her if she needed help.

"She asked me what kind of place this is. I told her it's a college for Jewish men who are learning various religious subjects like Talmud, *Chumash* and Jewish law.

"Then she asked me, 'What's the name of this school?' So I told her it's called Ohr Somayach. She got all excited and asked me, 'Doesn't *ohr* mean light and *somayach* mean joy?' So of course I told her that she was correct. Then she asked me to show her a sign that has the name of the school written on it. So I pointed to the sign on the building.

"She stared at the sign as if it were some kind of amazing miracle, and she said to me, 'So, there is a G-d after all!' I asked what she meant by that, and she told me this story. You see, her parents are from Monsey, and her father just recently passed away from cancer. She's here visiting her mother. She told me that a few years ago, when her father first became ill, she came here to visit him. One day, they took a long walk together and they came to a road that they thought was beautiful, a road with many large, shady trees. They walked up the road and it was breathtaking. They stayed there for a long while, and then they returned to the parents' house.

"Recently, she had a dream and that she was walking up that same road with her father. As they came up the road again, they saw a beautiful, intense light emanating from the top of the road. Her father was full of joy. She didn't remember ever having seen him so happy. He told her that he felt tremendous joy in this place. Then the woman woke up.

"The dream was so real to her that she felt she had to come back to the place where they had walked and see what was really there. But when she got here, the scene had changed because our building and campus was here. She was confused, and that's why she asked me what this place was. When I told her it was Ohr Somayach, she was completely amazed. There it was — the light and the happiness she had dreamed about, right here in front of her.

"And here's what the woman told me. She said that she understood that the light her father was enjoying was the light of Torah, and that his tremendous happiness came from Torah. He wasn't a religious man, but she feels that he has seen the truth on the other side. I took her number and told her that a rabbi would contact her to talk over her experience."

Rabbi Braun called the woman immediately and set up an appointment for the next day.

The woman arrived at the rabbi's office with her son, a young boy of about 7. She told her story, ending with the only remaining question. "I know G-d wanted to tell me something, and I don't know what I'm supposed to do next. I do know, though, that this is a wonderful place, and I hope some day my son will come here to learn."

"I think you have to start off with something small and practical," the rabbi advised. "I want you to go to the Judaica store and buy Shabbos candles and a calendar. Every Friday, make sure to light candles before sundown, and not any later. Otherwise, it's better not to do it at all. I think for you this is a good first step, because your dream was about light and happiness, and Shabbos candles will bring light and happiness into your life and the life of your family."

The woman listened attentively, as if she were receiving the ingredients to a secret formula.

"Then that's what I'll do," she told Rabbi Braun, and she went back out into the bright, cold winter afternoon.

Ten years have passed and Rabbi Braun has not heard from the woman again. Perhaps she went on to create her own world of light and happiness for her family. Perhaps her son is today sitting in a yeshivah somewhere, forging a bond with the Torah whose light shone from his grandfather's face in his mother's dream. But no matter how the story really ended, this woman did merit to see

232 / Stories for the Jewish Heart

something few others have — the brilliant aura of holiness that emanates from every place in which Torah is being learned.

True light and happiness come from one source alone. It is the acquisition of those who live their lives attached to Torah.

The Long Way Home

Eric was a business major. Jeff was pre-med. But their friend, Mark Sandler, had something else in mind when he entered college. Inside Mark was an urge to know — but it was not knowledge of the here and now he was seeking. He wanted to know the world he could not see. The world of the soul. The world of the cosmos. The world beyond.

Mark became a religion major. His studies exposed him to his own religion, Judaism, and other major world religions as well. Still, his inner hunger was unsatisfied. The more he learned, the more he wondered if he would ever find answers. Finally, his studies led him to the Hindu religion, and he began to feel that his spiritual self was finally coming alive. After awhile, he realized that he needed more than facts and theories to hang onto. He needed visceral experience. He didn't want to know about the Hindus, he wanted to find out what it was like to be a Hindu.

With this quest set before him, he took a leave of absence from college and booked a flight to India. There, he found exactly what he was looking for — a way of life in which the word "spiritual" did not have the negative, fuzzy connotations it had in the West. Mark eagerly sought guidance from the Hindu holy men, learning about the religion's panoply of gods and goddesses, and how to conduct the many ancient rituals involved in worshiping them. He mastered the art of meditation and chanting, and eschewed all forms of meat.

Months later, he was back in Rochester, New York, but he was a different Mark. He was staying at his parents' home for the time being, unsure of what path to pursue next in his life. Sitting at the kitchen table one evening, he watched his mother as she wrapped up some leftover roast and stashed it in a full-to-capacity freezer. She was a practical woman. He knew it was hard for her to understand the spiritual longings that had always pulled at his heart. If she had her way, he would be getting ready to apply to law school now. Instead, he had a duffle bag full of exotic Indian art and incense waiting to be unpacked. It was all so foreign to her, but there was something she needed to understand.

"Ma, I want to tell you something that's kind of important to me."

Mrs. Sandler shut the freezer and sat down at the table across from her son.

"Go ahead, I'm listening," she said.

"Well, while I was in India, you know I was learning about Hinduism and it seems to me that this is really the truth. Everything about it just makes so much sense to me. It's just what I've always been looking for. So I went through a conversion and became a Hindu."

His mother looked into his eyes, a businesslike, unperturbed expression on her face.

"I'm glad you found what you were looking for," she said. "But you have to also live your life, and that requires an education. I

234 / Stories for the Jewish Heart

want you to go back to college and finish your degree. I don't know what a person does with a degree in religion. But at least you will have something."

The new semester was starting in just a few weeks. Mark signed up for a comparative religion class taught by Professor Reginald Smith, a former Catholic priest. He was a tall, angular man with a thin, hooked nose and a mat of lank dirty-blond hair that flopped frequently onto his forehead. He was a professor from central casting who favored worn tweed jackets with suede elbow patches, and owned a seemingly endless number of khaki pants.

Professor Smith apparently held himself to be the world's foremost expert on all things religious. He spoke emphatically, leaving no room for questions and comments. Judaism and the Jews were the topic about which he was most passionate. He hated everything having to do with the religion and its people. He propounded every ugly stereotype that existed, stopping just short of blood libel.

Mark, despite his newfound religion, became agitated whenever Professor Smith launched a discussion of his favorite topic. After all, even if Mark was a Hindu, he had been a Jew for many years, his parents were Jews and so were many of his friends. He could not sit still and listen to the lies and abuse without feeling that he was about to burst out of his seat and fight back.

One day, in the midst of a lecture about the early Christians, the professor digressed onto the topic of Judaism's allegedly wrathful, vengeful nature. Although Mark did not have the theological background to argue, he had the facts. If Judaism preached violence, why had the Jews never oppressed or attacked anyone? If Christianity was so peace loving, what were the Crusades? What was the Inquisition? What was the Holocaust? He rose to his feet and barged into the middle of the professor's lecture — just pushed his way in like a brazen burglar bursting through the front door. The professor stood dumbfounded, his swatch of limp hair hanging foolishly over one eye, as Mark angrily smashed his argument point by point.

The other students stared in awed silence as the face-off reached its climax. Mark threw down his textbook — authored by the professor himself — and marched out the door.

Down the empty corridor, down three flights of stairs, across the campus and into the Student Union building, Mark just kept marching. Finally, he felt his pulse slow. He took a deep breath and settled heavily into an overstuffed chair in the student lounge. *What happened?* he asked himself. *What got into me? Why did I feel like I had to rise to the defense of the Jewish people? I'm not even Jewish anymore. But his words hit me so deeply. Why?*

His next class was a writing workshop, but he skipped it. Introspection was the only item on his schedule that afternoon. He sat and thought, walked and thought, and finally, he came to a conclusion. He needed to explore his connection to Judaism.

From that point on, Mark's life changed quickly. He found a rabbi to guide him, and within weeks, his keen mind was absorbing deep concepts in Torah. He felt as if his entire journey, from Rochester to India and back again, had led him to this juncture. The following month, he noticed an ad for a two-week seminar at a yeshivah in Monsey called Ohr Somayach. It was a program especially geared to people with limited background, and Mark decided to enroll. Once he got to the yeshivah, he never wanted to leave. He delved deeper and deeper into Torah, and at last discovered that the spirituality for which he yearned had been his, as a Jew, all along.

Years flew by as Mark caught up with his lost Jewish education. He married, moved out of Monsey and built a beautiful Torah family. Gradually, he lost touch with his *rebbeiim* at Ohr Somayach, but word would occasionally come back to them that he was thriving.

Ten years later, Rabbi Braun of Ohr Somayach traveled to Israel on behalf of the yeshivah. His itinerary brought him to the pristine hills of Tsefat, where he spent a Shabbos with a group of boys who were part of a *kiruv* program. On Shabbos morning, Rabbi Braun walked the narrow stone streets to a beautiful, small Chassidic shul in the Old City. He entered and took a seat near the front. Across from him, he noticed a traditional *Yerushalmi* with a long blond beard and *peyos*, dressed in a beautiful cloak. Next to him, peering into his own *siddur*, sat a boy who was clearly his son. He had the same gentle blond hair as his father, with golden *peyos* curling alongside his angelic face. The child was praying with such seriousness and emotion that Rabbi Braun had trouble taking his eyes off of him.

At a certain juncture, the *tefillos* stopped and the congregation prepared to read from the Torah. The *Yerushalmi* man leaned over to Rabbi Braun and spoke softly to him in a perfect American English, which seemed so incongruous coming from his mouth.

"Please don't act surprised. I don't want to arouse my son's curiosity. But aren't you Rabbi Braun from Ohr Somayach?"

"Yes, I am, but who are you?" asked Rabbi Braun, trying mightily to follow the man's directions and act nonchalant.

"I don't know if you remember me. My name used to be Mark Sandler," the man said. "Now it's Moshe. I used to learn in Ohr Somayach."

"Sure I remember you, Moshe. What brings you here?"

"Well, I moved here with my wife and became a *sofer*. I write *mezuzos*. This is one of my sons," Moshe said, wrapping his arm around the beautiful little boy next to him and giving him an affectionate squeeze. The child looked up from his *siddur* for a moment and flashed a guileless, innocent smile.

From the mountains of India to the hills of Tsefat, Moshe's journey encompassed far more than the miles. He followed the winding path Hashem laid out before him, and that path led him home.

The Jewish neshamah seeks nourishment wherever it can find it. But it is only when it is connected to Torah that it finds complete fulfillment.

Making Amends

leep would never come, Malky was sure. Not as long as the sick, warm flush of embarrassment kept washing around inside her. Her mind's eye again replayed the last time she had seen Danny. He had walked her into the house, spoken for a few minutes to her father and then said good night, his wide, even smile turning his face into a picture of total happiness.

Malky and her mother had sat in their airy kitchen until 2 o'clock in the morning, sipping tea, eating cookies and talking. The house was silent except for the sound of the young woman's voice, which flowed like a song.

Despite the late hour, Malky's aquamarine eyes were bright. "Now I know what people mean when they say, 'You just know when it's right.' I just know. There's no doubt in my mind that Danny is my *bashert.*"

"Don't jump the gun, Malky," her mother gently warned. "He's only the third boy you've gone out with, and even if everything has been perfect so far, it's not an engagement until it's an engagement. Let's wait and see before we start celebrating."

Thinking back on that conversation, reliving her naïve certainty, she felt like a complete fool. Here she had imagined that Danny went home thinking about nothing but how and when to propose to her, when, in fact, he was set to break it off. How could she have misread things so completely? She thrashed around in bed all night long, trying to put the entire episode out of her mind.

The next day, the heaviness in Malky's heart lingered like a leaden thundercloud. Only Tova, her best friend since high school, could possibly know the words to say that would help the gloom to dissipate.

"I'm trying so hard to accept this and just get past it," she told Tova. "But what I think and what I feel are just two different things. No matter what my head tells me, tears keep coming to my eyes." With those words, she dabbed her smooth, pale cheek with the cuff of her blouse.

"Listen, I know it doesn't make things any better to hear someone else's problem, but I have to tell you, I'm having such a hard time of it, too," Tova said. "The dates go great, but in the end, the guy breaks it off. I don't know what I'm doing wrong."

"And what about poor Chaya!" Malky interjected. "Did you hear that she was almost engaged, and then he broke it off? She must have been heartbroken!"

The girls were quiet for a moment, as if both had to recoup their energy before resuming the discussion.

"Malky, think about it for a second," Tova said in a low, conspiratorial tone. "Not one girl in our class is engaged or married. Out of the eight classes that graduated together, every single other class has at least a few girls that are married. But not ours."

"That's weird," Malky murmured. "Really strange. Do you suppose there's something about our class? Do you think there's, maybe, some kind of Heavenly decree against us for some reason?"

"I don't know, Malky. But we had better check it out. Maybe someone is holding a grudge against us for something we did. If that's the case, we have to find the problem and fix it."

The next day, Malky began her research. She started calling a list of teachers who had taught her class throughout their years in high school. Starting with her 12th-grade teachers, she explained the difficult fate that was befalling her class and asked each of them if they had been hurt or offended, or knew of anyone who had been. After speaking to the entire roster of 12th- and 11th-grade teachers, she was still empty-handed.

Nonetheless, the more Malky thought about the situation, the more certain she became that she was pursuing the correct course. She continued with her phone calls, questioning the 10th-grade teachers. When she reached Mrs. Green, who had taught her class *Chumash* that year, an answer at last emerged.

"Do you remember Avigail?" the teacher asked. "That girl who had moved here from France? Remember how she didn't speak the language well, and was shy about mingling with the class? As I recall, no one made any effort to befriend her. She was basically snubbed by the entire class, and she had a very difficult year. Eventually, she left the school and no one every heard from her again. Is it possible, do you think, that she was so hurt that she's still holding a grudge?"

"I remember her," Malky said. "This might just be the problem. I hope I can find her!"

The next day, Malky went to the school office to find out if there was any contact information for Avigail. To her great relief, she discovered that Avigail had a sister, Dora, who was now a student at the same school. Malky found Dora between classes. With her halo of black ringlets and deep, dark eyes, she instantly brought to mind a picture of Avigail's sad face.

"I was in your sister's class when she came here in 10th grade," Malky explained to the girl. "I'd like to speak to her. Do you have a number where I could reach her?"

Dora knew enough to understand that her sister might not welcome this contact. She smiled pleasantly, but provided no information.

"My sister is married and has moved back to France," she explained. "I will call her and see if she wants to speak to you. I've got to get to my next class," she said, quickly turning to leave.

"Wait, wait," Malky called. "Take my number. Just please let me know if I can call her, O.K.? Thanks."

Two days later, Dora's call came.

"My sister says that she has terrible memories of being in that school," the girl told Malky firmly. "She doesn't want anything to do with anyone from there, so please leave her alone."

Malky felt as if the ground were falling out from beneath her feet. She had to grab quickly at something that would save her. She could not let Dora hang up, for now it was certain that Avigail's pain was the source of the problem.

"Listen to me please for one more minute," she begged. "You have to explain to your sister that not one girl in our class has found a *shidduch* yet, and we feel sure that the reason is because we were so unkind to her. We are really pleading for a chance to ask forgiveness. The whole class is depending on it. Could you please tell her this for me?"

"I'll try again," Dora promised. Her voice had lost its prosecutorial tone. "I'll get back to you as soon as I can."

The night wore on and Malky waited, occasionally staring at the phone and willing it to ring. Finally, it did.

"My sister says that, Heaven forbid, she should cause anguish for anyone. She forgives you all with a full heart," Dora told Malky.

"Thank G-d," Malky murmured. She let out her breath slowly, feeling as if she had been holding it for days.

That night, Malky's former classmate, Hadassah, got a welcome phone call. A boy to whom she had been suggested had finally, after several weeks of delay, agreed to go out with her. Two weeks after their first date, they were engaged. The floodgates of good news were finally opened, and more and more engagements flowed through. Malky knew that when her turn came, her *chuppah* would stand under a clear night sky, sparkling with the pure, starry light of forgiveness.

Sometimes, when we suffer with a stubborn difficulty in our lives, it is a sign that we need to rectify a wrong. When we do so, we clear the obstructions that keep us from receiving Heaven's blessings.

Too Easy

A person who didn't know Jack might be intimidated. Tall, broad shouldered and erect, he appeared as solid and strong as a mighty oak. He had spent his younger years as a sailor, and outwardly, he still looked the part, with his craggy, tanned face and his bone-crushing handshake.

On the inside, however, Jack had changed profoundly since his days as a sailor. Gradually, he had begun to seek a connection to his Jewish heritage and eventually, he became fully observant. He began to channel his warm heart and capable hands into Torah-oriented endeavors, and soon became as proficient at *chesed* as he had once been at overcoming the challenges of the high seas. With that same courage and can-do attitude, he undertook the project of building a shul in his home city of Miami Beach.

As the shul grew, Jack remained involved in every aspect of its operation, tending to it as if it were his own home. His devotion was repaid each year on Yom Kippur, when he received an *aliyah*. To him, this was an honor to be cherished — a chance to publicly bless Hashem and His Torah on the holiest day of the year.

One year, a few weeks before Rosh Hashanah, Reb Mottel, the *gabbai*, approached the Rav, Rabbi Leff, with a dilemma.

"Last year, Mr. Brody passed away on Yom Kippur," the *gabbai* explained. "Now his son, Reb Nosson, has called to find out if he could have an *aliyah* on Yom Kippur, on the *yahrtzeit*. I told him I would discuss it with the Rav. The problem is that there are no extra *aliyahs* available. The only solution I could think of was to ask Jack to give up his *aliyah* and take one on Rosh Hashanah instead. But I hate to do that because I know how much this means to him."

The Rav thought for a few moments, and quickly came to a conclusion. "I'm sure Jack will be willing to switch," he said.

The next morning, Reb Mottel drew Jack aside.

"Jack, I have to ask you for a favor. You see, Reb Nosson would like to have an *aliyah* for his father's *yahrtzeit*, which is on Yom Kippur, and since there are no extra *aliyahs* available, I'm wondering if you would mind switching yours to Rosh Hashanah."

"Sure. If it will help him, it's no problem for me," answered Jack in his typical, good-hearted manner.

Reb Mottel walked away relieved. Jack simply shrugged and began putting on his *tefillin*.

The Shabbos after Rosh Hashanah, Rabbi Leff was walking toward shul. From the distance, he noticed a familiar form — the tall, muscular form of Jack — waiting at the door.

Oh, no, Rabbi Leff thought. *I sense a little remorse here. I'll bet he wants to take back the aliyah he gave away.*

As the rabbi approached the door, Jack greeted him.

"Could I speak with you for a few minutes?" he asked.

Rabbi Leff knew he needed a little time to come up with a solution to Jack's problem. Maybe in the space of a little time, Jack would also reconsider and regain his desire to help out Reb Nosson.

"Why don't we talk after *davening*?" Rabbi Leff suggested.

When the services had concluded, the shul members wandered out, chatting with one another and stopping to wish Rabbi Leff a good Shabbos. As the crowd thinned, Rabbi Leff noticed Jack waiting in a quiet spot off to the side. It was apparent that he was still perturbed. Finally, he approached and asked to speak to both the Rabbi and the *gabbai*. The three men went to Rabbi Leff's office to talk privately.

When Jack began speaking, it was not in the complaining tone the Rabbi had expected. In fact, this brawny, soldier-straight man was beginning to cry. He tried to talk, but his voice was too choked to continue. He tried again.

"Rabbi. I just want to know how I ... why I ... I didn't ...." and he began to sob. His massive shoulders were hunched and his eyes cast to the floor as tears streamed down his rugged face. The Rabbi and Reb Mottel looked on in bewilderment. What words of comfort could they offer when they didn't even know the cause for Jack's grief? They waited patiently until he regained control.

"Jack, what is wrong?" Rabbi Leff finally asked.

"I feel terrible," Jack said, his voice still raspy. "I was asked to give away my *aliyah* on Yom Kippur so that someone else could have it for his father's *yahrtzeit*, and I just gave it away without a second thought. I realized that if the *gabbai* had come to ask me for a $1,000 loan, I would have said I need to think it over. It's a lot of money. But when he asked for my *aliyah*, I agreed right away. Shouldn't I have found it difficult to give away such a great honor? I feel like I disgraced the honor of the Torah. I don't know what I should do!"

A new wave of regret swamped Jack's heart, and he began to cry again.

Rabbi Leff could feel nothing but awe. Here was a simple Jew, an unlearned man, whose regard for the Torah was so pure and wholehearted.

"Jack, Jack, listen," Rabbi Leff said soothingly. "You gave it away out of your love for your fellow Jew. That's not a disgrace to the Torah. That's an honor to the Torah. It's a *Kiddush Hashem* (sanctification of Hashem's Name)."

And with that, Jack was finally consoled.

Although he wasn't a great Torah scholar, Jack set a powerful example of "kavod haTorah," honoring the Torah, from which everyone could learn.

The Minyan Club

People are religious about a lot of different things. Paying their bills on time, for instance, or walking for a half-hour each day or getting all the children's homework done before dinner. This is a story about people who are religious about religion. In other words, they have accepted a religious obligation upon themselves, and nothing stands in its way. Ever.

Jewish men share the obligation to pray with a *minyan*, even if they do not take it upon themselves as a special commitment. There are thousands of men who are careful to pray with a *minyan* three times a day, and the benefits of doing so make this practice clearly worthwhile. But then there is another level of commitment, and that is the Minyan Club. Men who join a Minyan Club create a blanket obligation for themselves, no matter where they go, no matter what they are doing, to never miss a *minyan*.

Staying true to this obligation requires a whole range of personality traits, and those who do not have these traits when they first join up will surely develop them by virtue of their membership. Being a Minyan Club member demands devotion, self-discipline, resourcefulness, optimism and courage, too. One must be the kind of person who does not accept limitations — a living exemplar of the old adage, "Where there's a will, there's a way."

For anyone who enjoys tales of brave, intrepid adventurers who are prepared to surmount every obstacle, here are a few stories from a Minyan Club in Lakewood and another in Flatbush.

The Lakewood Club

Sometimes, a person hears a lecture and the words seem aimed straight at him, even if there are 100 other people in the room.

Yisroel Danzig of Lakewood experienced that sensation one evening, listening to a speech on the importance of praying with a *minyan*. As if suddenly awakening to a reality that had been there all along, he came to a new understanding: Hashem never turns away the prayer of a *minyan*. How, then, could he justify ever missing a *minyan*? There was too much at stake with every *tefillah* to let anything supersede the imperative of praying with a *minyan*. He was determined to never miss this precious opportunity again.

His determination was strong enough to convince his friends, Simcha Laufer and Berel Hassler, that this was a commitment worth making. Thus began the Lakewood Minyan Club — three men with an ironclad obligation to pray with a *minyan* three times a day, come what may.

The Fervent Flyer

When Simcha Laufer was planning a five-day trip to Israel, his commitment was tested on a battlefield upon which many commitments die — the infamous Battlefield of the Wallet. Simcha's travel agent told him that with his itinerary, a ticket on El Al would cost $1,249. Swiss Air, on the other hand, was offering a round-trip ticket for just $649. The obvious choice was the Swiss Air flight, and Simcha was about to book it. Then, he found out that there would be a four-hour stopover in Zurich, which would result in his missing a Maariv *minyan*. Of course, $600 was no small consideration, especially to someone living on a *kollel* budget. But Simcha was a Minyan Club member. He flew El Al.

Going the Distance

One hectic night, Berel Hassler stole a quick look at his watch and noticed that it was already 11:45 p.m., and he had not yet *davened* Maariv. The simplest solution was a visit to the Satmar shul, which is Lakewood's prime spot for catching a *minyan* any

246 / Stories for the Jewish Heart

time of day. A fender-to-fender line of cars is always parked in the front of the shul, and the doors are constantly swinging open as men rotate in and out of the building. That's the scene, except for this night, when Berel discovered only three people waiting for a *minyan* to gather. Usually, it's just a matter of waiting, so Berel prepared to wait. But at 12:15 a.m., it was clear that there would be no *minyan* at Satmar.

That closed off the last option in Lakewood. Berel, however, did not accept defeat. He knew he would *daven* that night with a *minyan*; he had to. The only questions were: Where? How? Suddenly, he remembered the shul in Boro Park, Brooklyn, called Shomer Shabbos. Like the Satmar shul in Lakewood, it housed a continuous rotation of *minyanim* day and night. Unlike the Satmar shul however, it catered to the far larger population of Brooklyn. There literally was always a *minyan* going on at Shomer Shabbos. Berel quickly slipped behind the steering wheel of his car and pointed it toward Boro Park. An hour and a quarter later, he arrived at Shomer Shabbos, *davened* Maariv and headed home. It was after 3 a.m. when he finally sank into his bed. A Minyan Club member never says "can't."

Honorable Discharge

Perhaps one of the most startling Minyan Club stories belongs to the founder, Yisroel Danzig. One night, Yisroel injured his neck and rushed to Lakewood's Kimball Hospital in terrible pain. The doctors ordered a battery of tests and X-rays to determine the nature of the damage. As a precaution, the doctors inserted an intravenous line.

Suddenly, Yisroel cut the proceedings short. Like a guest who had stayed long enough, he told the doctors that he would be leaving for about 20 minutes. He had to take care of an emergency, he explained to their disapproving and shocked faces. Yisroel discharged himself from the hospital, still in great pain, and joined a

Maariv *minyan*. As he had promised, he was back in the hospital 20 minutes later, ready to complete the tests.

The Flatbush Club

The Flatbush Minyan Club was founded by Nosson Kolatsky, who hasn't missed a *minyan* in 10 years. Nosson is a successful businessman who, by virtue of his position, has been able to motivate many other men to become Minyan Club members. It is a pre-condition of working for his company. He may well stand alone in the world as the only boss who not only allows, but insists that his employees duck out of a conference, business lunch or deal-closing to get to a *minyan*.

Nosson himself sets the example. One time, he was returning to Brooklyn from a business trip to Buffalo, New York, when he discovered that his flight would be delayed due to heavy rain. The change in schedule would mean that he would not be able to reach New York in time for Minchah. As a Minyan Club member, his top priority was to make sure that, no matter where he might be at Minchah time, he would be in the company of a *minyan*. With a burst of frantic effort, he set upon the task of finding a more suitable flight, and was at last able to secure a seat on a plane leaving for Newark at 3 p.m. That would get him back to New York with a little time to spare.

The weather threw his plan out of gear once again, causing a one-hour delay on the Newark-bound flight. Nosson, however, would not allow the airlines and the weather to stand in the way of meeting his commitment. He phoned a friend in New York and enlisted him to find eight men who were willing, for $100 each, to come to the Newark airport to meet Nosson and a business associate with whom he was traveling. The offer was apparently too good for people to refuse, and the friend soon called Nosson back with the news that the *minyan* had been arranged.

When Nosson's flight finally arrived in Newark, he was disappointed to discover that the mobile *minyan* had not arrived. Several minutes later, a call from his friend confirmed that they were nowhere near the airport, but rather, were stuck in a mammoth traffic jam on the Garden State Parkway. By the time they would reach the airport, the time for Minchah would have passed. Nosson's nimble mind quickly leapt over that obstacle as well. He and his companion would travel to a designated exit on the highway, and the group would meet them there.

This time, the plan succeeded without a hitch. For an expenditure of $800, Nosson had his *minyan*. To him, it was worth every penny.

Two weeks later, Nosson received an important call from his Florida office. In the aftermath of a major hurricane, Florida's governor had declared a state of emergency. People were without homes and the state was scrambling to find shelter for them. Somehow, a large building owned by Nosson's company had come to the government officials' attention, and they were calling to offer him $80,000 to rent it to the State of Florida. Nosson readily agreed, gratefully accepting Heaven's hundredfold compensation for the $800 he had invested in ensuring that he would have a *minyan*.

Blessed

On another flight, Nosson met a man named Chesky Raider. The two men spoke for awhile, and the fact emerged that Chesky and his wife were still childless after 12 years of marriage. Having seen with his own eyes the power of the Minyan Club to draw blessings from Heaven, Nosson offered Chesky his best advice: If he would pray three times a day with a *minyan*, no matter what circumstances arise, Hashem would certainly answer his pleas for a child. One year and more than a thousand *minyanim* later, Chesky and his wife were blessed with a baby girl.

The next time you are too busy or too tired to go to a minyan, imagine what you would do if you had no option. Then do it.

Reprieve

*S*uch is life, thought Doris Stafsky. *You think you'll always be active, you'll always be full of ideas and energy, able to make things happen. Then, there you are, 80 years old, sitting like a lump on a hospital bed, and your most impressive accomplishment is drawing another breath.*

It was May 2004, and Doris was suffering from an intractable bout of pneumonia. After 50 years of heavy smoking, her lungs could take no more abuse. For the past 10 years, she had been tethered to a portable oxygen tank because of her severe breathing problems. But now, with pneumonia on top of it all, she felt that at any moment, she might draw her last labored breath in this world.

Her room at the Cleveland Clinic was not unpleasant. Several pretty pastel floral paintings brightened the monotonous beige walls, and a dazzling blue sky shone through a large window. *It looked like a nice day outside*, Doris thought. How she longed to be part of that outside-the-hospital world again — the great, big, wide world of life.

Doris's son Morris walked through the door, seeming to carry a fresh whiff of the outside world with him. She was still mildly surprised every time she saw him. His black suit and wide-brimmed fedora gave him quite a somber presence, but when his face broke into its usual, beaming smile, he was Morris again. True, he was a much more religious Morris than the boy she and her husband Harry had raised, but he was still the son they had always known and treasured.

"Hi, Ma," he said as he rushed in and went straight to her bedside. "How are you today?"

He took her hand in his and smiled his cheerful smile. He hoped it was an effective cover for his aching heart, for his mother looked terrible. She was a specter — a thin, ghostly presence topped by a thatch of lank gray hair. Had he not seen her face above the blankets, he'd have thought the bed was empty.

He began to despair. Where was the miracle he was praying for? He spent every spare moment either saying *Tehillim* or searching for a doctor, a treatment, anything that could help his mother. Yet every day, she seemed to get worse. It was so difficult to watch her struggling to breathe, gasping for life while inch by inch, it slipped away.

When he pondered the situation, he realized that he was actually very fortunate. Had he not found Torah, he would have felt all alone in this struggle. Ten years ago, this same situation would have plunged him into a murky pool of bitterness at the unfairness of life. But Morris had found Torah. Now, he held in his hand an unbreakable lifeline. He knew that his mother's suffering, painful as it was for the whole family, had an ultimate purpose. He knew that close by, right within reach, Hashem was there to call upon and lean upon. He had the advice of the many great *rabbanim* of Cleveland and the Telshe Yeshivah to guide him, both practically and spiritually. Hashem had indeed given him the "cure before the illness," as the Torah promised.

Nevertheless, each day he hoped that he would walk through the door and see his mother sitting up in bed, alert and animated as she had always been. He couldn't help but be disappointed anew each time he discovered that his dream had not come true.

For a while, Morris just sat silently next to his mother, watching her stare at the blue sky outside. It was difficult for her to speak. Then he remembered some photos he had brought along for her.

"Look, Ma, would you like to see some pictures of the kids?" he suggested. "I brought you some recent ones."

She turned toward him with a pleased smile. He held the photos in front of her, describing each one as he progressed through the pile. *Baruch Hashem,* he thought, *at least I can give her a little nachas.*

As Morris left his mother's room that day, her doctor sought him out.

"Mr. Stafsky, could we talk in my office for a few minutes?" he asked.

There was no question in Morris's mind; this was not going to be good news. He followed the doctor into his office and took a seat. There was an awkward silence for a moment.

"Mr. Stafsky," he said quietly, "we have done everything we can to try to improve your mother's condition. Unfortunately, she does not seem to be responding to anything we can offer. I feel that it's only right to inform you that her prognosis is very poor, and you should begin making any end-of-life preparations you need to make."

"Well, doctor, I'm sure you are doing everything you can," Morris replied. He felt an aching heaviness inside him, as if his heart had suddenly turned to lead. But at the same time, he would not relinquish hope. Hadn't his *rebbeiim* taught him that life and death are in Hashem's hands alone?

"But I do want you to know something, also, and that is that what happens to my mother is not up to you or me. It's up to G-d, and as long as she's alive, nobody can know for certain that she won't recover."

"Listen," the doctor responded sympathetically, "I'm not discounting miracles. I'm just telling you what I feel I'm obligated to tell you. I hope you're right and I'm wrong."

As soon as Morris left the doctor's office, he called his rebbi, Rabbi Yisroel Brog. Rabbi Brog was the grandson of the renowned Rabbi Avigdor Miller and, like him, he had a talent for transmitting his own passionate love of Torah to his students. Morris was a regular at his weekly classes; he had become very close to him over the years.

Rabbi Brog instantly perceived the urgency in Morris's voice. He was calling to ask the rebbi to come to the hospital to visit his mother, hoping that his presence and his prayers would bring the miracle Morris had been unable to elicit.

The following day, Doris lay in her bed, limp and pale, when a surprise guest appeared at the door. *It must be one of Morris's friends,* she thought. *Why else would there be another man in a suit and hat at my door?*

She made an effort to sit up straighter, but the effort failed and she slid back down against her pillow.

"That's all right, Mrs. Stafsky," Rabbi Brog told her. "I'm Rabbi Brog, a friend of your son. I came to look in on you, and if you don't mind, to say a few prayers for your recovery."

Doris nodded and smiled a resigned smile that said, *Well, what could it hurt?* Rabbi Brog opened a *sefer Tehillim* and recited a few chapters as a merit for her recovery. He spoke to Doris for a few more minutes, telling her how well respected and loved her son was. Then, he left.

Morris caught up with Rabbi Brog as he walked toward the elevator.

"Rebbi, is there anything else I could do for my mother?" he asked. "I have been *davening* for her and saying *Tehillim.* I have been doing whatever I can to help, but nothing has been effective."

Rabbi Brog closed his eyes and thought. An idea came to him.

"Can you convince her to cover her hair?" he asked. "That may be the *z'chus* she needs to save her life. You know, it's brought down in many *sefarim* that if a woman finds herself in a dangerous situation, she should examine whether she has been careful in the area of modesty."

Now Morris really was beginning to feel the situation was hopeless. If his mother's recovery depended upon her covering her hair, she was doomed.

"Rabbi Brog, covering her hair is the last thing in the world my mother would ever agree to. I had discussed this with my mother many times and she always refused to consider the idea. She always said that if G-d gave me my own hair, why would He want me to cover it with someone else's hair? It makes no sense, she'd say. Or she would ask, 'Where in the Torah does it say I have to cover my hair?' Even if she would do it, my father is dead set against it also. There is no way my mother would ever agree to it."

"Listen, why don't we go back inside and give it a try?" Rabbi Brog suggested hopefully.

The two men returned to the hospital room, where they saw Doris, eyes half shut, lying as still as death itself. *Perhaps she was in some semisleep state,* Rabbi Brog thought. He would have to speak clearly and concisely, for the woman was obviously in no condition for a prolonged discussion.

"Mrs. Stafsky," he said loudly, to arouse her attention. "I feel that if you would take upon yourself a commitment to cover your hair, it might be a merit that could save your life."

Doris's face suddenly twisted into a grotesque mask of anger. Her fists were clenched with more strength than anyone could have imagined she possessed, and she pronounced in a loud, clear voice, "No! I won't do it!"

Rabbi Brog and Morris both instinctively jumped back, as if evading an attack.

"But Ma, what if this could save your life? Ma, why don't you at least ...."

"Come Morris, not now. Let's not get your mother upset," said Rabbi Brog as he guided Morris out the door.

"In all my years, I have never heard such a response to that suggestion," the rabbi told Morris. "I felt as if I were speaking to the Satan himself. I would have expected your mother to ask ques-

254 / Stories for the Jewish Heart

tions. Why do I have to do it, or where does it say so? But to say
so strongly that I don't want to do it, especially when you are just
about on your deathbed, that I have never seen. Now I am really
convinced that she has to cover her hair in order to get better.
That was the Satan talking out of her mouth."

Two days later, on Friday afternoon, Morris went to visit his
mother again. She looked worse than ever. He thought, *This may
be my last chance to convince her to cover her hair. Who knows if she'll
even make it through Shabbos. I have to at least give it my best effort.*

Looking straight into his mother's cloudy eyes, he asked her,
"Ma, do you want to live?"

Doris nodded. There was no longer enough breath for her to
form a word.

"Then you know you have to do what Rabbi Brog told you to do.
You have to cover your hair."

She nodded in assent.

"There's a little more to it though," Morris added. "You can't do it
because you feel you are being forced. It has to be out of your own
will to do what Hashem wants. That's the only way it can help you."

Again Doris nodded.

Morris immediately called his wife Dina at her office.

"Could you go home right now and bring a snood over here for
my mother to cover her hair?" he asked. It all had to be done immediately if it were going to be done at all, Morris understood.

Twenty minutes later, Dina entered the room with a snood. She
sat by her mother-in-law's side and helped her place it over her
hair. Tenderly, Dina tucked the stray gray locks underneath the
soft cotton band and adjusted it on Doris's head. Then she stood
back and smiled admiringly.

"It looks beautiful on you, Ma," she said. "You look like a holy
lady from Jerusalem, I'm telling you!"

Doris nearly managed a laugh.

Morris bent over his mother's bed and kissed her goodbye.

"We'll see you right after Shabbos," he promised her, but in his heart he wondered, would she still be here? Could this be the last time he would see her alive?

Throughout Shabbos, Morris could find no tranquility. He felt strongly that something had gone wrong with his mother. As he pictured her lying there in bed, a snood on her head and a hopeful look in her eyes, his heart was flooded with pity. If only Hashem would see her as Morris did, and give her another chance to live out her old age with her family.

As soon as *Havdalah* was finished, Morris ran to the phone to call the hospital. A floor nurse spoke to him.

"I don't know what happened," she told him, "but your mom has taken a definite turn for the better. You should see her. She's got some color back in her face and she's talking a bit more, too."

Morris rushed to the hospital Sunday morning, eager to see the miracle with his own eyes. But when he arrived at his mother's room, she actually looked worse than she had on Friday. Perhaps the merit of covering her hair had earned her a brief respite, but not a full and complete recovery.

The next day, however, the tables turned once more. Each day thereafter, she gained a little more strength. Her eyes lost their dull, filmy appearance and by the end of the week, she was clamoring to get out of bed. At the end of this startling week, Doris was transferred to a nursing home to complete her recovery. When Morris came to visit, it was easy to spot her. She was the only woman in a snood.

After a month of rehabilitation, Doris went home. She was back in the great big wide world of the living, back with her husband Harry, their son and his family. Once again, she could walk under the dazzling blue sky rather than staring at it through a window. Of course wherever she went and whatever she did, her hair remained covered — now with a *sheitel*. It was a new life that she had returned to, for her husband was inspired by the miracle he had seen with his own eyes, and the couple, in their ninth decade, took upon themselves a life of Torah and mitzvos.

"Anyone could see," said Harry, "that this had nothing to do with doctors. G-d, the Creator of the World, made a miracle for us."

For Morris, the episode was his own personal splitting of the sea. It was the biggest, clearest miracle he had ever been privileged to witness. And, it was a heart-stopping, awe-inspiring demonstration from Above of the unbounded power of one single mitzvah.

Each mitzvah is a lifeline that connects us to spiritual as well as physical well-being. We have to grasp each one with all our might.

Pushing It

Imagine being told every day of your life, "There is no such thing as G-d. It's a fantasy, a fairy tale for weak minds." Imagine thousands of people being raised on the same dogma. Imagine that they are Jews.

Given this background, could anyone imagine that these Jews would be likely candidates for Torah observance? Only someone who refuses to accept limits, someone who is undeterred by any obstacle, could see it happening. Rabbi Yitzchok Zilber was such a man — a man who could not say "can't." With that trait as his primary qualification, he led the organization called Toldos Yeshurin, which brought thousands of Russian immigrants in Israel back to their long-lost, cruelly suppressed heritage.

The strength to take on this task was refined in the crucible of Russian labor camps. In 1955, Rabbi Zilber was arrested under false charges and sentenced to hard labor. When he arrived in camp, he quickly discovered that the bleak surroundings and backbreaking work were only a small part of the menu of misery. Besides all that, he was surrounded by common criminals and anti-Semites. He was the camp's only religious Jew.

All of this, though difficult in the extreme, was secondary. The primary problem in Rabbi Zilber's mind was how to carry on as a servant of Hashem when he had been pressed into slavery for the Soviet Union. How would he put on *tefillin* each day? How could he find time for daily learning? What could he do to avoid desecrating Shabbos in a place where labor was the essence of every waking hour? These were his life-and-death necessities, and Rabbi Zilber set about finding ways to fulfill them.

These were the issues on his mind even as he packed his belongings for the sad journey to the labor camp. Therefore, he had come prepared. A small pair of *tefillin*, a *Tanach* and *Mishnayos* were well hidden among his possessions. He only had to find a place and time to use them.

Upon arriving at camp, he learned that his coat was to be kept in a coat room. He decided to keep his *tefillin* hidden inside his coat. Each day, he would come to retrieve it, find a secluded place and spend a few precious moments donning his *tefillin*. Although this arrangement carried great risk to the rabbi's life, to him it was a comfort and a relief. He could wear his *tefillin* every day.

The next challenge was avoiding work on Shabbos. There was no hour, let alone day, of rest at the camp. However, Rabbi Zilber saw a window of hope. He would apply for a job as a water carrier. These were the men who carried buckets of water from the pump outside the camp to a large tank that supplied the camp's needs. It was a backbreaking chore, but it had an advantage. There was a quota of water that had to be supplied for each day's needs. If he could fill the tank on Friday with enough water for Shabbos as well, he would be able to refrain from working on Shabbos. The key to the plan, however, was that he had to work alone. Only then could he be sure that no one would notice his absence.

Rabbi Zilber decided that this was his best hope. Although he dreaded the prospect of drawing any attention to himself and thereby raising questions, he had to ask for the job if he wanted it. He approached the officer in charge of the water tanks.

"I would like to begin working as a water carrier," he said.

"Why should I take you as one of my workers?" asked the officer.

"Because I am a very hard worker. I am willing to do by myself everything that all of these workers did together."

"You think you could do the work of six men?" the officer responded.

"I know I can. Just give me the chance and you'll see."

Eager to see the foolish young prisoner fail at the impossible task he had set for himself, the officer acquiesced.

Rabbi Zilber thus began doing the work of a horse, indeed, six horses. But his work did not break him. Instead, it invigorated him tremendously, because through this job, he was able to keep the holy Shabbos.

Even with these two facets of his spiritual life in place, Rabbi Zilber was not satisfied, for he had no time to learn Torah. To him, this was an untenable situation. A Jew must learn every day, regardless of circumstances. But there was no time on the clock for him to fulfill this obligation. Work started at 5:30 a.m. and wasn't over until 7:30 p.m., and in all that time, there was no free moment. *Still*, Rabbi Zilber thought, *there had to be a way*.

And he found it. He calculated that if he ran with his buckets instead of walking, he would be able to do an hour's work in 45 minutes. With those extra 15 minutes, he would have time to learn. True, 15 minutes was not much time, but with 14 hours in the workday, he would end up having learned three and a half hours a day. Rabbi Zilber was energized by his plan, rushing through the drudgery to reach the fabulous hourly reward of Torah learning. He found a hiding place behind a curtain in a small storage room, and there he engaged in his life-sustaining passion.

One day, all of the inmates were summoned to the dining hall for an emergency meeting. The tables were filling up quickly, and at the front of the room, sitting alone at a long table, was the camp commander. The room, although filled to capacity, was dead silent. The men looked tensely at the floor, at the ceiling, at each other. No one wanted to meet the commander's eyes, for it could never be good to be noticed.

"Yitzchok Zilber, come to the front," the commander's somber voice announced.

Rabbi Zilber sat frozen in place. He could not imagine what he had done to draw this terrifying attention to himself.

One of the camp officers rose to his feet and delivered the withering accusation. "Everyone in this camp is treated equally," he proclaimed. "We all work as hard as we can for our country. We all share in a common goal. However, you ..." and the officer pointed a finger at the rabbi, "think you are different. You think we are fools, and that we don't know that you never work on Saturdays. You are a lazy traitor!"

The word caught like a wildfire. The inmates began chanting "Traitor, traitor," and threatening to kill the man who dared beat the system. Rabbi Zilber feared that the enraged mob of inmates would get him before the authorities even had their chance. Either way, it was in Hashem's hands; he whispered a prayer.

A small commotion broke out in the crowd as two big Ukrainians inmates rose from their seats. These two were known as hard-core anti-Semites, but it wasn't only the Jews who needed to fear them. They were tough, sadistic men whose eyes seemed more animal than human.

"Listen, everyone!" he shouted. "No one had better dare to touch the Kaziner (the name by which Rabbi Zilber was known in camp). If you do, then we will kill you. Do you hear me? We are here for life, so trust me when I say this. I have nothing to lose.

"I have been in this camp for 15 years and there has never been enough water to drink. But ever since the Kaziner has come, we have had enough water."

Their point made, the men sat down. Rabbi Zilber sat in his seat in shock; the most unexpected of saviors had come to his rescue. The inmates, including Rabbi Zilber, were all dismissed.

Rabbi Zilber spent many long, hard years in that camp. One day, he was informed that he would be transferred to a new location. The news was unwelcome, for although life was extremely difficult where he was, he had succeeded in obtaining what he considered the necessities of life. Nevertheless, he was given no choice, and he would have to go where they took him.

As the inmates stood in line to leave, each was told to empty his belongings onto the snow. There, the guards would inspect the items, searching for contraband and valuables. Rabbi Zilber knew that if they found his religious articles, he would be shot right there. He had hidden them under a plate, spoon and cup that he had taken with him to avoid eating from the camp's *treife* dishes. However, if the guard chose to make a more aggressive search, the *tefillin* and *sefarim* would easily be found.

Fortunately, the guard found the tableware enough of a subject of mockery that he no longer felt the urge to look further.

"Look!" he shouted to his fellow guard. "Our plates aren't good enough for the Rabbi! He came with his own!"

His taunting smile turned to a ferocious scowl as he slammed the suitcase shut. He lifted it up high and brought it crashing down on Rabbi Zilber's head.

"Here's your plate and spoon. Get out of here!" he sneered, and walked on to the next inmate.

Rabbi Zilber's head was stinging from the blow, but his heart was laughing. He thanked Hashem for saving him once again. It seemed certain that just as he would never give up on Hashem, Hashem would never give up on Rabbi Zilber, either.

The person who believes all things are possible often finds the wherewithal to achieve the impossible.

Making a Difference

Shalom Aleichem

The car window was wide open and the balmy air of a summer night blew full force at Rabbi Haber's face. A tape was playing a familiar tune, lively wedding music meant to make a person jump up and dance. But neither of these ploys was helping Rabbi Haber stay alert as he sped along Route 17 on his way to Monsey. It was 1 o'clock in the morning; his eyes knew that they wanted to shut, and they kept trying.

This is dangerous, Rabbi Haber thought as he vigorously shook his head in an attempt to wake himself up. *I'd better get myself a cup of coffee somewhere.*

He quickly discovered that despite the fact that he was out and about in the hours after midnight, the owners of the small coffee and snack shops along the road were not. They were apparently all safe in bed while their storefronts stood dark and locked, awaiting a new day's business. Rabbi Haber traveled along like a man lost in the woods, hoping desperately to find some light in the distance. At last, he spotted the unmistakable glow of neon a short way up the road. He pulled into the small parking lot of the little snack shop and was relieved to see a sign for "Hot Coffee" featured prominently in the window.

Just the thought of the steaming hot liquid with its welcome, bittersweet taste was beginning to put some life back into Rabbi Haber's blood. He walked in and noticed the unattended counter, where one could purchase all the necessities of life — deli sandwiches, lottery tickets, travel packs of aspirin, candy, cigarettes and, of course, coffee. The hunks of ham, Swiss cheese and other delicacies displayed in the deli case told the rabbi unequivocally that he was the wrong man in the wrong place. But there was no doubt in his mind that a cup of hot black coffee was a lifesaving necessity at this point, so he looked away from the cold cuts and scanned the store for someone to assist him.

A man soon emerged from behind one of the small grocery aisles and made quick note of the bearded, black-hatted customer who had wandered in.

"*Shalom!*" the cashier shouted. He was the vision of a Sabra — dark curly hair, deep brown eyes, a worn pair of blue jeans and a Yankees' T-shirt.

Well, you just never know who you'll meet, Rabbi Haber thought.

He thrust out his hand in greeting and replied "*Shalom aleichem.*"

"Ha! You Jews in America don't know anything about Ivrit," the Sabra responded tauntingly, as he shook the rabbi's outstretched hand. "Even a rabbi doesn't know. '*Aleichem*' is plural. I am just one person. You just say '*Shalom*' to me, just like I said to you!"

Rabbi Haber felt certain that he was on the receiving end of something more than a Hebrew grammar lesson. The answer with which he responded was, in turn, addressed to something far beyond grammar. Inexplicably, his mind seized upon the Friday-night song *Shalom Aleichem,* and the traditional explanation that it is a greeting for the two *malachim* that accompany a Jew home from shul.

"If I were only speaking to you, what you say would be correct," Rabbi Haber told the young man. "But every Jew has *malachim* that accompany him. The verse says "*Ki malachav yitzaveh lach lishmaracha.*" For he commands His angels for you to guard you. When I am speaking to a fellow Jew, I'm not just speaking to him. I'm talking to the *malachim* that are with him as well. So you see, '*Shalom aleichem*' really is correct."

Now the Israeli was becoming completely exasperated. "*Malachim!* What are you talking about? Do you believe in fairy tales too?" Then he seemed to feel a little remorse for his tirade. His face softened a little. "Here, Rabbi, here's your coffee. Have a safe trip."

The rabbi took his coffee and went on his way. Gratefully, he noted as he drove that the surge of caffeine had conquered his overwhelming desire to sleep. *What was I telling that man?* he thought. *What made me talk about malachim?*"

It was about a month later when Rabbi Haber was once again on a late-night trip to Monsey, feeling the pull of sleep tugging relentlessly at his eyelids. Visions of a hot cup of coffee drew him onward until once again, he found the only snack shop on the road that was open all night.

This time, as he walked through the front door, he was greeted instantaneously by the Israeli. It was as if the man had been lying in wait by the door for the entire month.

"*Atah kilkalta es chaim sheli!*" the man screamed in Hebrew.

"I ruined your life?" Rabbi Haber exclaimed. "What are you talking about?"

"You and your *malachim!*" the young man said accusingly. "Maybe you don't remember how you came in here and said 'Shalom aleichem' and I tried to help you so you would say it correctly, but instead you told me that I was not alone, that there were *malachim* with me always.

"Well, now I can't live the same life anymore. After you left I sliced up some ham and some Swiss cheese and I made myself a big sandwich with lettuce and tomatoes and mayo, and I was about to take a bite, but I couldn't. Your *malachim* were there watching me. I tried again and I still couldn't. I put down the sandwich and now I'm scared. Well, let me tell you it's not easy to scare me. But how can I eat a ham sandwich with these holy *malachim* standing next to me?

"I ended up throwing the whole thing in the garbage. And I haven't been able to eat a sandwich here ever since. Who knows what will be next? What did you do to me?"

The man was still sputtering angrily as he served the rabbi his coffee and took his dollar. Rabbi Haber set out on the road, sipping his coffee and letting his mind drift back over the details of the scene he had just encountered. One offhand comment from Rabbi Haber had caused this Jew, so distant from his religion, to stop eating nonkosher sandwiches at work. The man wasn't happy about it, to say the least, but the fact remained that his *neshamah* was being spared a terrible daily dose of impurity.

Who knows what will be next? he recalled the Israeli shouting at him. *That's what the guy was wondering, and I'm wondering the same thing.*

Our words can have a tremendous impact on other people. When we use this power in a positive way, it can help build a person. Conversely, negative words can break a person. It is up to us to acknowledge the power of our words, and use them wisely.

The Kind Pickpocket

lowly, boys joined the line that formed at the table where Rabbi Yakov Safsel sat inconspicuously, a *sefer* opened before him. The elderly rabbi, known as the Visker *Iluy* (genius), listened intently as each boy came to him in turn, asking their toughest Talmudic questions. He considered each question carefully and returned a thoughtful answer, making the boys feel as if they had asked the world's most insightful questions. Sometimes, when the question required a longer answer, Rabbi Safsel would mail the answer to the boy on a postcard.

There was nothing the *talmid chacham* enjoyed more than engaging young students in a discussion of Torah learning. It was for this purpose that he would leave his customary place of learning, a thriving Lower East Side shul called Agudas Anshei Maamid, to take up his post in Yeshiva Rabbeinu Chaim Berlin's *beis medrash*. The rest of the time, day and night, he could be found in Anshei Maamid, pouring over his *sefarim* and filling notebooks with his great Torah novalae.

Among the regulars at Anshei Maamid was a group of boys from Yeshivas Rabbeinu Jacob Joseph, located right across the street. One of the shul's major attractions for the boys was the heavenly, hot potato kugel and tangy herring served at the *Kiddush* each Shabbos. Avremel was one of the gang — a skinny, fatherless 10-year-old who had come to America with his mother after World War II, and, like refugees throughout the century, had settled in the Lower East Side. With no father to take him to shul, Avremel came by himself.

One Shabbos, Rabbi Safsel approached Avremel. "Tell me, Avremel, what are you learning in yeshivah these days?" he asked in Yiddish.

Avremel answered that he was learning the Talmudic tractate *Gittin.*

"Yeah? Really?" responded Rabbi Safsel. "Listen, do you think you'd be interested in learning a little with me?" The rabbi's tenuous tone implied that by agreeing Avremel would be doing him a great favor.

"Sure, I'd love to learn with you," the little boy replied, flattered by the elderly sage's attention. They sat down at a table across from each other and began. Avremel would recite the passages he had learned in yeshivah, and Rabbi Safsel would listen carefully, correcting any errors the boy would make. Avremel and the Visker *Iluy* became a regular feature of the Anshei Maamid *beis medrash* as they sat, once or twice a week, and reviewed the boy's learning.

One afternoon, Avremel missed Minchah at yeshivah. He ran across the street to the shul, caught his breath and took his place just in time for the start of the *davening*. The shul was packed to capacity with men who were all much larger than Avremel. He felt like a small, skinny sapling surrounded by a forest of tall, dark trees. But when the *davening* was over, the little sapling was quickly uprooted by the mob of men making their way to the door, pushing him along with their momentum. He was wedged in on all sides as the crowd edged through the narrow doorway, but even with the crushing pressure, he felt one distinct sensation. It was a hand, and it was in his pocket.

Avremel couldn't believe someone would try to pick his pocket. What could they expect to find? A marble? A stick of gum? Surely everyone knew he had no money, save the one dime his mother was able to give him each week as an allowance. Not really wanting to know to whom the hand belonged, and yet driven to find out, Avremel slowly cast his eyes along the length of the black-coated arm that disappeared into his pocket, and followed the trail to a familiar face. It was Rabbi Safsel! Avremel quickly averted his eyes and pretended to feel, see and know nothing. He would deal with the situation when the crowd was gone.

Once he got outside, he immediately thrust his hand into his pocket to find out what had been taken. But instead of the linty little treasures he usually felt inside his pocket, his hand touched something crisp and smooth. As he pulled it out, his eyes joyfully beheld a new dollar bill.

Could it be? he thought. *The Visker Iluy gave me a dollar!*

Immediately he began calculating what this huge amount — 10 whole weeks' allowance — could buy. He knew just what he would do. He would go with the other kids on Friday afternoon and rent a bike for 35 cents for an hour. He could even afford two hours for 50 cents! Suddenly, the world held new possibilities.

On Avremel's next visit to Rabbi Safsel, he envisioned a new arrangement for the partners. Instead of sitting across from the rabbi, Avremel suggested, wouldn't it be better to sit side by side? From then on, the two sat on one bench next to each other, leaning their heads together over the *sefer*. And of course, Rabbi Safsel used this proximity to place a new dollar bill into Avremel's pocket each time. The skinny little orphan was beginning to feel like a millionaire.

For many years, the Visker *Iluy* continued to learn with Avremel, and to provide him with the dollar that relieved him of the painful pinch of constant deprivation. The rabbi never mentioned his act of kindness to anyone. He simply placed the dollar in the boy's pocket, leaving it as an open secret between the two of them. With each passing year, Avremel understood more and more deeply the powerful message of love carried in each dollar bill and each session of learning.

The years passed, and Avremel became Avraham, an accomplished rebbi and, ultimately, the *menahel* of a New York yeshivah high school. Among his responsibilities was to administer the entrance exam to boys wishing to attend the yeshivah. Each year, he would be visited by dozens of nervous 13-year-old boys squirming anxiously and silently praying to make a good impression. In order to give each boy the chance to display his best abilities, Avraham always started the meeting by trying to set the candidate at ease. He would ask them simple questions about themselves and their families, and tell them about the yeshivah. Once he saw that the boy was calmer, he would begin the entrance exam.

One day, a particularly nervous boy came to him for an entrance exam. The child was so frightened that his lips were trembling. His thin build and pale complexion added to the image of a young man scared nearly to death. Avraham's heart went out to the boy, and he gently asked the least confrontational question he could think of.

"What's your name?"

"S-S-Safsel. Safsel," the boys stuttered.

"What!" Avraham responded with amazement. "Are you related to the Visker *Iluy*, Rabbi Yaakov Safsel?"

"He was my *zaidy*," the boy replied in a barely audible murmur.

"Well then, young man," said Avraham joyfully, "you have nothing to worry about, and no test to take. You're accepted."

Finally, he had a chance to repay, in some small way, the dollar-by-dollar investment that had so enriched his life.

Although the dollars that the Visker Iluy gave Avremel are long gone, the fatherly love and warmth they imparted would last a lifetime.

Stubborn to Perfection

A vrohom's eyes shifted methodically from face-to-face, scrutinizing each *bachur* seated in the crowded *beis medrash*. His mind weighed the pros and cons of each option: *Is this the right guy? No, too introverted. How about this one? No, the personalities wouldn't match up ... Oh, wait, there's Yitzy Becker! He's the guy,* Avrohom decided.

With all his years of learning in Yeshiva Rabbeinu Chaim Berlin's *beis medrash*, Avrohom knew who was who. He often used that familiarity to arrange *chavrusas* for other *bachurim*. Nothing delighted him more than seeing both partners flourish, knowing he had put together the ingredients that would make Torah learning sweeter for each of them.

Mendy Zucker was Avrohom's focus at the moment. Here was a brilliant boy, a highly successful college student with aspirations for a career in law. Mendy wasn't just smart, he was a good-hearted, generous boy, the kind of person you could trust. With all those assets, however, Torah learning had just never taken off for him. He dutifully spent one *seder* a day in *beis medrash*, but learning was clearly a job for Mendy, not a love. This became all the more obvious as he departed each day for his college classes, suddenly animated and full of energy. He'd pack up his knapsack hastily and stride purposefully out the door.

Now, if I could get Yitzy to learn with Mendy, Avrohom thought, *he wouldn't be in such a hurry to leave.*

One look at Yitzy Becker engrossed over a Gemara told the whole story. He seemed barely able to stay in his seat as he articulated the arguments, the contradictions and questions each page posed. A new insight, whether it was his own or his learning partner's, was to Yitzy like a delicious meal delivered on a silver platter. He greeted it with gusto and dug in, blissfully chewing over every morsel.

"Yitzy," Avrohom approached him. "I have a great *chavrusa* for you!"

"Who is it?" he asked.

"Mendy Zucker."

Yitzy's eyes narrowed incredulously.

"Mendy Zucker?" he repeated. "That's not a *chavrusa* for me, Avrohom. I've got to have someone who's at least somewhere around my level. Otherwise, I'm just wasting my time."

"You have the wrong impression of Mendy," Avrohom persisted. "The guy has a good head. He can learn. He just needs some motivation, and I'll bet if he learned with you, he'd really take off."

"Sorry, Avrohom. Look, it's a big *beis medrash*. I'm sure you can find someone else."

When Avrohom walked away, Yitzy thought he had laid the matter to rest. Therefore, he was surprised to see Avrohom wending his way across the *beis medrash* the next day, sights set on Yitzy.

"Did you think about my suggestion?" Avrohom asked, as if there had been some window of doubt left open from the previous day's conversation.

"I didn't think about it, because it's not a good idea," Yitzy said with finality. What more could he say to convey that this partnership was not to be?

None of this mattered to Avrohom. This match, as far as he was concerned, was made in Heaven. He felt it was right, that it was good for both parties, and that if he just persisted, Yitzy would eventually agree. Therefore, he did persist. During the course of the week, Yitzy began to develop a certain kind of radar that told him Avrohom was headed his way.

"Look, Yitzy, if it doesn't work out for you, you don't have to stick with it," Avrohom reasoned. "Just give it a try."

With the understanding that he could opt out if necessary, Yitzy sat down the next day across from Mendy, and the two began to learn. As Avrohom had promised, Mendy proved a perceptive, intelligent learner. And as Avrohom had hoped, Yitzy's fire for learning began to catch; Mendy walked into the *beis medrash* with the vitality he had formally reserved for walking out.

Thirty years later, Avrohom was known as Rabbi Avrohom Gurwitz, the Rosh Yeshivah of Ner Moshe, a prestigious yeshivah for American students who wanted to spend a few years learning in the rarified atmosphere of Eretz Yisrael. Sitting in his office one day, sifting through the pile of mail on his desk, Rabbi Gurwitz's eyes were drawn to a particular envelope from America. The name on the return address had a familiar ring, but he could not place it. Curiously, he unfolded the letter and read what was, essentially, a profound message from the past.

Dear Rabbi Gurwitz:

My name is Yitzchok Becker. I am not sure if you remember this, but many years ago I learned together with you in Yeshiva Rabbeinu Chaim Berlin. You came over to me one day and urged me to learn with another boy who had been going to college at the time, Mendy Zucker. At first I didn't want to learn with Mendy. I didn't think it was a good match, so I told you that it wouldn't work. But you didn't let up. You kept on approaching me and tried to convince me to at least give it a try. Well, Rabbi Gurwitz, I did end up learning with him because of you, and I enjoyed it very much. It worked out so well with Mendy that I continued to learn with him for a few years.

We learned at night and during the day, during bein hazmanim and on Shabbos as well. We became very close friends, and I must tell you that you were the cause of something amazing. You have no idea what you have done for my life and what you have done for Mendy. Because we became so close, I ended up having a tremendous impact on his life and lifestyle. Mendy became thirsty for Torah and spent his days and nights immersed in the seas of the Talmud. Torah became first and foremost and college was secondary — a means of making a living, but not life itself. Mendy married a girl who likewise appreciated Torah.

Today, Mendy spends all his free time in the beis medrash. He raised a family of bnei Torah. His boys have married and learn in kollel, and his daughters as well have married kollel men. They are a family that lives and breathes Torah, and it's all because you made the extra effort to convince me to learn with Mendy. For this, I have no words to describe my gratitude.

Thank you,
Yitzchok Becker

Rabbi Gurwitz carefully folded the letter and returned it to its envelope. His thoughts traveled back to those days at Yeshiva Rabbeinu Chaim Berlin, to Yitzy and Mendy and his persistent campaign to bring them together. Just a few minutes a day — that's all it took. Altogether, perhaps he had invested a half-hour in selling Yitzy on the idea. From his vantage point now, decades into the future, he was privileged to see, piled high in front of him, the fruits born by that effort. So many lives would have been different had he accepted Yitzy's refusals. But he hadn't.

The Vilna Gaon once said, "Someone who is stubborn in his determination to succeed will have success in life. We can never view stumbling blocks as failures, but rather as stepping stones to further our growth."

Take My Number

Things change at the Shabbos table of Rabbi Dovid Orlofsky. Jews who never thought much about how they spend the seventh day of the week suddenly get a taste of what it is meant to be. Though he is a world-renowned speaker and Torah educator, at his table, Rabbi Orlofsky is the consummate host. With warmth and wit, he embroiders the meal with entertaining stories, deep insights and enthusiastic singing, gently drawing people into a world they would otherwise never have known.

Because his Shabbos table is such a powerful tool for *kiruv*, Rabbi Orlofsky liberally extends invitations to just about anyone he thinks might benefit. There may be hundreds of people who possess a little slip of paper with the rabbi's handwritten name and phone number scrawled on it. The mystery is, who of those hundreds will heed the call? As the stories that follow illustrate, one never knows.

One night, the Orlofsky family enjoyed a rare opportunity to go out for dinner together. As they sat in a busy dairy restaurant studying the menu, their waitress, an American girl named Tamar, came to take their orders. As with many large families, this procedure did not go smoothly. Tamar patiently answered questions and waited for decisions to be made, unmade and remade.

In the course of their friendly conversation, Rabbi Orlofsky found out that Tamar was attending Hebrew University and was working as a waitress to make some extra money. He complimented her on her patience and apologized for the delay his family was causing. But Tamar's sweet expression conveyed no irritation. Her calm blue eyes were fixed on the children as they debated the merits of spaghetti versus blintzes. "I like spaghetti better," she told them with a teasing smile. "It's more fun to eat."

At last, Tamar took the final orders and reappeared a short while later with the food. When the meal was finished, she came with the check. "Did everyone like what they got?" she asked the children, who were clearly flattered by the attention.

"Tamar, I want to thank you again for your patience," Rabbi Orlofsky said. "And I also wanted to ask you something. We always have a full table of guests at our house for Shabbos, and we would be honored to have you come. There's a lot of singing and good food and interesting company. I think you'd have a great time."

As the rabbi spoke, he tore off a corner of the paper place mat on the table and reached inside his pocket for a pen.

"Wow, that sounds great!" Tamar replied without hesitation.

"Good, so here, take my name and number, and just give us a call whenever you want to come." Rabbi Orlofsky scribbled the information on the shred of place mat he had torn off for this purpose.

Tamar took the paper, but she never called. Rabbi Orlofsky had seen it many times before; once the person is left alone to think about going to a rabbi's house for Shabbos, it seems just a bit too strange. But he had done his part. He had reached out to his fellow Jew and offered a chance to experience a Shabbos.

Ten years went by, filled with many more encounters. Some resulted in nothing more than one more Jew who could say he was treated warmly by an Orthodox rabbi. Others resulted in precious *neshamos* returning to their heritage.

Around this time, Rabbi Orlofsky was teaching in a special program of Yeshivah Ohr Somayach called Ohr Lagolah. In this program for *kollel* men who are studying for *semichah* (rabbinic ordination), successful *kiruv* rabbis were invited to lecture in hopes that the students would be inspired to reach out to the estranged Jews they would meet in their own communities.

One night, after Rabbi Orlofsky had finished his class, a new student named Yehuda approached him.

"What can I do for you, Yehuda?"

"Well, do you by any chance remember about 10 years ago, you were eating out in a restaurant in Jerusalem with your family, and you invited your waitress to come for Shabbos?"

Rabbi Orlofsky tried to conjure up some memory of the meal, but nothing would come to mind.

"To be honest, Yehuda, I invite a lot of people every week. I can't say I remember."

"The waitress was a brunette, Tamar. She was a student at Hebrew University. Does that help?"

The young man looked expectantly into Rabbi Orlofsky's eyes, as if certain that no one could have permanently forgotten the brunette Tamar.

"Listen, Yehuda, it was ten years ago. I'm sorry, but I just don't remember."

With a little shrug of resignation, Yehuda reached into his pocket and pulled out a crumpled shred of paper. He held it up in front of Rabbi Orlofsky's eyes — Exhibit A — and revealed the reason for his question.

"That waitress you invited for Shabbos is now my wife, and this is the piece of place mat on which you wrote down your name and number. After you were so kind to Tamar in the restaurant, she began to rethink her entire life. She realized that there was a special kindness about the religious Jews she met, and she thought to herself. *If this is what it's all about, then that's the life I want.*

"She enrolled in Neve Yerushalayim and began studying Torah. She has held onto that piece of paper and cherished it for all these years, even though she never actually used it. She never wanted to forget who inspired her to become what she is today.

"We got married a couple of years ago and now we hope that we can go out and spread the light of Torah to others. That's why I enrolled in Ohr Lagolah. When my wife heard that you were teaching here, she asked me to bring this little paper to you in order to thank you and let you know that your kindness went a very long way."

Rabbi Orlofsky looked silently at the idealistic young man in front of him, and the little shred of history he was holding in his hand. There seemed to be nothing to say. It was as if someone had dropped an acorn on the ground and had come back 10 years later to find a forest growing all around.

Later that same week Rabbi Orlofsky received a phone call at his home. The caller introduced herself as Tova Keller, and said that she had shared an El Al flight to New York with the rabbi six years earlier.

Once again, Rabbi Orlofsky had to apologize for not recalling someone who seemed to recall him quite well.

"Well, Rabbi Orlofsky, that flight changed my life," the woman stated. "You see I had just lost my father and I was really down in the dumps. You noticed me seated a few seats away from you holding tissues to my eyes and realized that I was crying. Then you came over to me and asked me why I was so sad. I couldn't believe that a stranger was interested in my problems — not only that, but a Rabbi. And I wasn't even religious! Then I told you that I had just lost my father, and how I loved him so much and felt I couldn't go on without him.

"But you calmed me down. You began to explain to me how the Torah views death. You told me that my father had accomplished his mission on this world and that he was no longer suffering from his terrible illness. Rather, he was elated in *Olam Haba* and was proud of me and my accomplishments.

"Rabbi Orlofsky, I can't tell you how much your words meant to me. Then you took a little piece of paper out of your pocket and wrote down your name, number and address and gave it to me. You said I was invited anytime for a Shabbos. 'Trust me, you'll really enjoy it,' you said. I thanked you and put the piece of paper in my purse.

"I can't tell you what an impact that made on me. I thought to myself, 'What a rabbi, and what a religion!' I asked myself why I was not like that, and I realized that I only had one option — to become a religious Jew.

"I have cherished that piece of paper with your invitation all these years, and I have come a very long way. Today I am *shomer Shabbos* and I keep all the mitzvos, and it's all thanks to you. I am calling you now because I have a question I need to ask a rabbi, so I figured I would call you."

That Shabbos, Rabbi Orlofsky shared the remarkable events of the week with his family. Twice in the space of just a few days, he had discovered that a simple invitation, offered with friendliness and warmth, had incubated over a period of years and developed into two completely transformed lives. His children got the message; one must show love and concern for every Jew.

During the week that followed, Rabbi Orlofsky had occasion to go shopping at a local mall. As he went about his business, a security guard approached him. The young man's long hair was pulled back into a wavy brown ponytail, and a small gold stud glistened from one earlobe. There was no swagger in the guard's approach; he came to the rabbi in a deferential manner, as if he did not wish to disturb him.

"Excuse me, Rabbi," he said. "Could you tell me why Jews eat dairy foods on Shavuot?"

Too seasoned to be surprised by the contrast between the young man's appearance and his interest in Jewish tradition, Rabbi Orlofsky simply answered the question with his characteristic warmth.

A while later, he finished his shopping and called home to check in. His daughter answered the phone, and he told her about his exchange with the security guard.

"Tatty, Tatty! Did you give him our phone number and address and invite him for Shabbos?" After a week of miracle stories, she was eager to set another one in motion.

"You know, I didn't," said the rabbi. "I didn't think of it. But I'm going back to do it now."

He ran back to the spot where the guard was stationed and scribbled the information on the back of a shopping receipt. A few years have passed since that encounter, and Rabbi Orlofsky has not yet heard from that security guard. Only Hashem knows if that little piece of paper, or the hundreds of others that Jews have planted in their pockets, purses and dresser drawers, will someday take root and blossom into a beautiful life of Torah, mitzvos and acts of kindness.

All Jews are responsible for one other. Extending to our neighbors a simple invitation to our Shabbos table, or even just some sincere warmth, can literally change their lives. Knowing that gives each of us a tremendous responsibility.

Food
for Thought

As he settled into his seat, Rabbi Chesky Travis felt the little tingle of anticipation that accompanies the start of an airplane flight. For a change, the plane wasn't packed to capacity. In fact, there was an empty space between his window seat and the Israeli man who occupied the aisle seat. The Rabbi fastened his seat belt and looked around with a contented sigh. Perhaps he might sleep a little, and arrive back in New York ready to tackle his class of rambunctious yeshivah boys the next day.

Soon, the El Al jet was air borne, heading back to America. The time passed so uneventfully that one could easily forget he was traveling 30,000 feet in the air. The occasional bumps of turbulence felt more like a bus ride on a potholed street. The Israeli, who appeared to be nonreligious, occupied himself with a magazine while Rabbi Travis sat with a *sefer* open on the tray-table in front of him.

After a while, the monotony was broken by the announcement airline passengers love to hear. It was dinnertime. A change of pace. Something to do. No matter how good or bad the food might be, everyone sat up in eager anticipation like children waiting for the recess bell.

El Al offered two types of meals. One, their regular meal, was certified kosher, but did not meet the strictest levels of kashrus. The "*mehadrin* meal," on the other hand, met more stringent criteria. On this flight, the *mehadrin* meals were being distributed first, and an airline attendant soon arrived with Rabbi Travis's portion. Setting it aside on the tray in front of the empty seat, he continued learning.

The Israeli stole a glance at the unopened meal. With a look that said, *Who knows?* he returned to his magazine. But the sight of the forlorn meal, just sitting there getting cooler by the minute, was nagging at him. Finally, he broke the silence.

"Rabbi, why don't you eat your meal?" he asked in Hebrew.

"I'll wait until you get yours," he said. "I'm sure you're hungry too, and I wouldn't want to eat my food right in front of you while you have nothing to eat."

"Forget about it! I don't mind. Please, eat!"

"It's all right," Rabbi Travis responded. "I will wait until you get your food."

Another 15 minutes passed, and the attendants were just beginning to give out the regular kosher meals. The Israeli man was becoming frantic with frustration at this point.

"Rabbi, eat your food already! It's getting cold!" he commanded, sounding like the mother of a picky eater.

"Listen, I'm not doing this for you," Rabbi Travis answered. "If I were to eat now, while you are sitting there hungry, I wouldn't be able to enjoy my meal. So I'm really doing this for myself, so that I can enjoy my meal."

Finally, the man's food came and he began to eat. Rabbi Travis took his cue to open his own meal as well. Not another word passed between them for the rest of the flight.

At last, the plane landed at Kennedy Airport and the passengers streamed out to the baggage area. Rabbi Travis retrieved his bags and moved along to the customs line. As he waited his turn, he heard a voice yelling, "Rabbi, Rabbi! Wait one minute please!"

It was the Israeli, who was running to him now as if he were bearing some urgent message. He arrived a moment later, breathless.

"Rabbi, I want you to know that I am a *chiloni*," he said. "I have always strongly resented the *chareidim* because I viewed them as very selfish people who are only concerned with their own. All

282 / Stories for the Jewish Heart

they do is take the government's money and they don't contribute anything to the country. Yet here I am sitting next to you during the flight and you look like a *chareidi*, and you were so sensitive to my feelings. I must admit, I now have a new outlook toward the *chareidim*. It may even be that I have been wrong all along!"

Rabbi Travis listened to the man's surprising confession, grateful that he had exercised this little bit of courtesy and self-discipline. The two men shook hands and exchanged a friendly goodbye. It had been a remarkably uneventful flight, except for the fact that the Heavens and earth had moved.

When we act in accordance to the will of Hashem, we have the power to open people's eyes to the Torah's beautiful ways.

My Hero

The soil of *Har Hamenuchos* has absorbed torrents of tears throughout the years as family after family has stood upon it, delivering their departed loved ones to their final resting place. On the day of 11-year-old Yossi Katzenbaum's funeral, the air was saturated with bewilderment and grief. Only one day earlier, this lively boy was a shining star at Yeshivah Kol Simcha in Jerusalem. His love of learning inspired even his *rebbeiim*, and his sweet nature enchanted his friends. To his parents, he was a source of constant delight. Now, suddenly, his radiant presence was gone from the world.

The accident had occurred in one tragic flash. Yossi had been on his way home from yeshivah, making his way down the familiar winding streets of Geulah. As he stepped out to cross a street, a car trying to beat a red light sped around the corner and slammed into him. The cloudy winter evening went black, and the sounds of weeping could be heard throughout the neighborhood's narrow alleyways as the news spread.

The very next day, Rabbi Katzenbaum stood disbelievingly in a place he had never expected to stand, amid masses of family members and friends at his beautiful Yossi's funeral. His heart could not accept that it was real, and yet, as he looked around at the tear-streaked faces of those who stood around him, his mind had to acknowledge the truth. The child was gone. There was cousin Avram, Uncle Dovid, his brother Yitzchak, their faces etched with expressions of pain and sorrow. As he scanned the crowd, Rabbi Katzenbaum noticed a man he did not recognize. He was not a relative, nor a close family friend, and yet, his broken sobs spoke of a deep, piercing bereavement. *Who is this man, and how does he know my son?* the father wondered. He watched the man for a few moments, struck by his ardent emotion.

The week of *shivah* began. The Katzenbaum house seemed far too small to contain all the people and compassion that poured into it that week like a storm tide surging past the shoreline. Yossi's rebbi came with his classmates, offering the family deeper glimpses into the precious soul of the child they were privileged to have known for 11 years. Words of comfort flowed and swirled around the family like a soothing bath of solace.

The seamless days of *shivah* drifted by, one into the next, defined by nothing more than the three daily *tefillos*, and the quiet words and gentle faces of visitors. On the third day, Rabbi Katzenbaum's ear was drawn to a sound that broke, ever so gently, the ambient hush. It was the sound of muffled weeping, a cry that wanted to emerge full force, but was being held back in a throat choked with sadness. Rabbi Katzenbaum's gaze followed the sound, and landed upon a man standing nearby; he was the man who had broken down at the funeral. The area around the man had fallen silent.

"Excuse me," Rabbi Katzenbaum addressed him softly. "But did you know my son Yossi?"

"Oh, yes," the man said in a tremulous voice. "I certainly did. He was a great boy."

"And where did you know him from?"

"It's a little bit of a story," the man answered shyly. "Perhaps now is not the time."

"Oh, no, please … I'd like to hear."

The man quickly realized that the bereaved father was eager for any detail that would give him a deeper, fuller picture of the son he had lost. This story was not just a few minor brush-strokes in the picture. It was a true-to-life, complete portrait to treasure.

"My name is Shimon Bressler," he began. "I work as a crossing guard during the afternoons near Kol Simcha. Everyday, I cross the kids from one side of the street to the other and make sure they get there safely. I probably cross 200 kids a day. However, no one ever really speaks to me. They say thank you in an automatic way, but they never take notice of the fact that there's a person doing this job. And on my part, I do the same. I mind my own business, do my job and go home.

"But your son was always different. He would ask me, 'How are you today?' And he'd really seem interested in knowing. I have to say, it made me feel very good inside. It made the job more rewarding.

"Well, one day, Yossi came over to me and asked if I was feeling all right. He said I looked sad. I don't know what made me open up to him. But for some reason, I told him what was in my heart. You see, I've been working for all these years crossing the children coming home from yeshivah, and unfortunately, I've never had a child of my own. Sometimes it gets to me. I look at all these boys and wish that one of them could be mine. It was 10 years already that I had been married, and still there was no child.

"I told Yossi this, but he didn't look sad or worried. He looked at me with this excitement in his eyes. 'Don't worry Shimon,' he said to me. 'I can help you out. I'll say *Tehillim* for you, and I'll round up my whole class to *daven* for you. Hashem will surely answer our *tefillos* and give you a son.'

"I couldn't help it ... I was a little cynical. 'Come on, Yossi,' I told him. 'This isn't a story. It's real life.' But that didn't stop him. He wrote down my name and my mother's name, and he did what he promised. He was so sure Hashem would answer that every afternoon, he'd come over to me and ask. 'Any news yet?' I was touched by his concern, but I didn't think anything would change.

"Then one day, the miracle happened. I couldn't wait to tell Yossi the great news. 'You see, Shimon. I told you I could help,' was all he said to me. Ten months after he started praying for me, I had a baby boy.

"And that is why I'm crying, Rabbi Katzenbaum. Your son meant so much to me. I owe him everything. That boy was my hero."

Shimon's story was an emotional life-raft for the Katzenbaum family. It was the story they held onto, for it showed them that each day of Yossi's short life was enriched with the goodness and light he dispensed around him. He was indeed a hero who had unhesitatingly come to the rescue of a despairing fellow Jew, using the only tool he had — the pure, sweet prayers of the yeshivah boys.

Yossi's legacy is an awareness that each Jew is a person to be valued, whose needs cannot be overlooked. Whatever is within our ability to do, we must do.

I Owe It All to You

The room was packed with women, yet the buzz of voices was low and hushed. Rebbetzin Sara Heiman sat in the center of the crowd, quietly receiving her visitors' comforting words. Her husband was gone. The beautiful rhythm of their daily life had ceased, to be temporarily replaced by the peculiar rhythms of the week of *shivah*. Together, the couple comprised a powerful force in the world of *chinuch*. Rabbi Yisroel Meir Heiman had been a beloved rebbi who had given countless students a taste for the sweetness of Torah learning. His wife was the principal of a large, successful girls' elementary school. The waves of young women who came to be with her in her time of grief were testimony to the bonds she had formed with her students, many of which stretched back over decades.

As Rebbetzin Heiman scanned the faces arrayed around her, she noticed one that was familiar, yet somehow out of place. Was she a former student? The daughter of a friend? Whatever the woman's identity, there was no doubt that she was someone special. She had a refined serenity about her, a quiet modesty that was crowned by a sweet, gentle smile. Dressed in a dove-gray skirt and sweater, she sat quietly, erect in her seat, waiting for the Rebbetzin's eyes to meet her own.

"I'm sorry," the Rebbetzin addressed her at last. "You look so familiar, but I can't think of your name. Could you please remind me?"

"My maiden name was Chava Kessler," the woman replied. "I was one of your students. Do you remember me?"

Rebbetzin Heiman's eyes opened wide in surprise. Chava Kessler? Could this be that unkempt, troubled girl who had managed to hang onto her Bais Yaakov education by the slimmest thread? How well the Rebbetzin remembered this poor child's chaotic family life. The parents fought constantly. Shabbos, Yom Tov and even the most rudimentary routines were nearly non-existent. As a student, Chava had been a mirror image of the anger and confusion in which she lived. The Rebbetzin had done her best to keep Chava close, providing a little island of love and acceptance in her hostile world.

Obviously, something had happened, something wonderful, and Rebbetzin Heiman wanted to know what it was. Chava directed her admiring gaze toward her former principal. She spoke softly, but with certainty. "I want you to know that as soon as I heard the tragic news, I had to come here to be *menachem avel*. I flew in from out of town so that I could be here to tell you that I owe everything I am today to your husband."

"Did you know my husband?" Rebbetzin Heiman asked.

"No, not really," Chava answered.

"Did you ever have the opportunity to meet him?"

"We never actually met," she said.

"How, then, did my husband have such an influence on you?" the Rebbetzin asked.

"Well, if I can take a little more of your time, I will tell you a story," Chava began. "One day when I was in high school, my principal came to me on a Friday afternoon and asked me to bring you a package. Since I lived around the corner from you, I agreed to do it. Anyway, I felt so close to you, I was happy to have the opportunity to do you a favor.

"When I rang the bell, you told me over the intercom that I should let myself in. So I did. I walked in, and the first thing I saw was your table, already completely set for Shabbos. There was a beautiful, bright, white tablecloth on the table and the challahs were already there, covered with a velvet cloth. I couldn't help imaging at that moment what my own house probably looked like. Our table was never set before Shabbos. Sometimes it wasn't set at all.

"Then I saw you, still busy in the kitchen with some chores. And next to you stood your husband. He was washing some dishes, and the two of you were talking to each other. You said something and he laughed. Then he said something and you smiled. There was such kindness and friendship between you. When I looked at the two of you together, it seemed as if there was a glow around you. My eyes filled with tears, and I said to Hashem, 'This is what I really want, and I am going to have it.'

"That was the turning point in my life. I decided then and there that I was going to finish high school and go to seminary, and then, with the help of Hashem, I would find a husband who would learn in *Kollel*, just like your husband. What I saw in your house, a husband and wife talking to each other with respect, each hearing and enjoying what the other had to say, that represented to me a true Torah home."

Rebbetzin Heiman listened to the young woman's simple story. There had been no thunder and lightning, no awe-inspiring miracle or life-altering crisis. There had been just a husband and wife enjoying each other's company as they prepared for Shabbos together. Chava had grabbed onto that scene like a drowning woman grabbing for a lifeline, and had used it to pull herself out of turmoil and onto safe and solid ground.

Now Chava reached into her small leather purse and pulled out a photograph.

"I want you to have this," she said to Rebbetzin Heiman as she handed her the photo. Within the borders of the 4x6 print was the visual proof of Chava's remarkable story. The picture showed Chava's husband, a young man dressed in the garb of a *ben Torah*, smiling as he sat surrounded by his wife and five children. The boys had *payos* and the little girls were dressed with the same modest, refined taste as their mother. Rebbetzin Heiman studied the photo carefully, and then handed it back to Chava.

"Oh, no," said Chava. "This is for you to keep. It's really yours, because it's all thanks to you and your husband. May your home be a source of inspiration and *berachah* to all who enter it."

Chava's words were like a comforting embrace that soothed the Rebbetzin's bereft heart. Her husband was gone, but his deeds, even the smallest, most routine moments of his daily life, were still bearing beautiful fruit in the world.

We never know how a few words or simple actions can affect others. Understanding that our actions have the power to change people's lives, we should strive, at all times and in all places, to act in a way that sanctifies Hashem's Name.

Glossary

aleph-beis — the twenty-two letters of the Hebrew alphabet

aliyah — being called to the Torah

arba minim — the four species used on Succos

aron kodesh — holy ark in the synagogue, where the Torah scrolls are kept

aveirah — transgression

avodas Hashem — the service of G-d

baal teshuvah — a penitent returnee to Jewish life

baalei tefillah — those who lead the prayer services

bashert — "predestined", often refers to one's predestined spouse

becher — ceremonial cup

bein hazmanim — intersession

beis medrash — study hall

bentch — say a blessing

bentching — saying Grace After Meals

berachah — blessing

bimah — table in synagogue from which the Torah is read

Bircas HaMazon — Grace After Meals

bochur (pl. *bochurim*) — young man

bris — circumcision

chacham — wise man

chasunah — wedding

chavrusa — study partner

Chazal — the Sages of the Mishnah and Talmud

chazzan — leader of prayer services

cheder — elementary school

chesed — kindness; acts of beneficence

chevrah kaddisha — burial society

chinuch — education

chizzuk — encouragement

Chumash — Five Books of Moses

chuppah — canopy under which the marriage ceremony takes place

d'var Torah (pl. *divrei Torah*) — a Torah thought

daf — page (of Talmud)

Daf Yomi — worldwide Torah study project in which all Jews study the same folio page of Talmud every day

daven(ing) — pray(ing)

farher — to give a test; a test

gabbai — synagogue sexton; attendant of a Rebbe

gadol (pl. *gedolei*) *hador* — Torah giant of the generation

gadol b'Torah — one who is great in Torah

Gan Eden — The Garden of Eden

gaon — genius

gedolim — Torah leaders

Gemara — loosely, a synonym for the Talmud as a whole

haghbah — lifting the open Torah for all to see, depending on custom, this is done immediately preceding or following the Torah reading

Hakafos — the dancing around the *bimah* in the synagogue on Simchas Torah

halachah — Jewish law

hashgachah pratis — Divine providence

Havdalah — ceremony marking the end of Shabbos and festivals

Kabbalas Shabbos — Shabbos eve prayers

Kaddish — prayer sanctifying G-d's Name, often recited by mourners

kallah — bride

kapparos — ritual performed on Erev Yom Kippur

kedushah — holiness

kesubah — marriage contract

Kiddush — blessing recited over wine expressing the sanctity of Sabbath and festivals

kiruv rechokim — teaching non-observant Jews about Judaism

Klal Yisrael — Jewish people in general

Kol Nidrei — prayer which begins the Yom Kippur service

kollel — academy of higher Jewish learning, whose students are mostly married men

levayah — funeral

lulav — palm frond taken as part of the four species on Succos

malachim — angels

mekubal (pl. *mekubalim*) — mystic; one who is well-versed in Kabbalah

melamed (pl. *melamdim*) — teacher

melaveh malkah — meal eaten Saturday night in honor of the departed Sabbath

menachem aveil — to comfort a mourner

menahel — principal

mesader kiddushin — person officiating at a wedding

mesechta — tractate

mesiras nefesh — self-sacrifice

minhag — custom

minyan — quorum of ten men for prayer service

moshav — settlement

Motza'ei Shabbos — Saturday night

perek — chapter

rabbanim — rabbis

refuah sheleimah — a full recovery

Ribbono Shel Olam — Master of the World, i.e. G-d

s'chach — "roof" of a succah, usually bamboo, branches, or reeds

seder — period of learning in a yeshivah

sefer (pl. *sefarim*) — book

Sefer Torah — Torah scroll

shalom aleichem — lit. "Peace unto you;" a traditional greeting; the opening words of a liturgical song sung at the Friday night meal

shalom zachor — a celebration held the first Friday night after a baby boy is born

shammash — sexton; the candle on the menorah used to light the others

shul — synagogue

simchah — joy; celebration

Shemoneh Esrei — the 18 blessings recited three times a day

shidduch — marriage match

shiur (pl. *shiurim*) — lecture; lesson

shivah — seven-day period of mourning

siddur — prayer book

siyata d'Shmaya — Heavenly assistance

tallis — prayer shawl

talmid (pl. *talmidim*) — student

talmid chacham — Torah scholar

tefillah (pl. *tefillos*) — prayer

tefillin — phylacteries

tehillim — Psalms

teshuvah — repentance

tzaddik — righteous person

tzedakah — charity

Yahrtzeit — the anniversary of a person's passing

yarmulka — skullcap